Pro .NET 2.0 Code and Design Standards in C#

Mark Horner

Apress®

Pro .NET 2.0 Code and Design Standards in C#

Copyright © 2006 by Torville Pty Ltd

ISBN (pbk): 1-59059-560-2

9 8 7 6 5 4 3 2 1

Lead Editor: Ewan Buckingham
Technical Reviewer: Jon Reid
Editorial Board: Steve Anglin, Dan Appleman, Ewan Buckingham, Gary Cornell, Tony Davis,
    Jason Gilmore, Jonathan Hassell, Chris Mills, Dominic Shakeshaft, Jim Sumser
Associate Publisher: Grace Wong
Project Manager: Beckie Brand
Copy Edit Manager: Nicole LeClerc
Copy Editors: Freelance Editorial Services and Ami Knox
Assistant Production Director: Kari Brooks-Copony
Production Editor: Ellie Fountain
Compositor: Molly Sharp
Proofreader: Linda Seifert
Indexer: Toma Mulligan
Artist: Kinetic Publishing Services, LLC
Interior Designer: Van Winkle Design Group
Cover Designer: Kurt Krames
Manufacturing Director: Tom Debolski

Distributed to the book trade worldwide by Springer-Verlag New York, Inc., 233 Spring Street, 6th Floor, New York, NY 10013. Phone 1-800-SPRINGER, fax 201-348-4505, e-mail orders-ny@springer-sbm.com, or visit http://www.springeronline.com.

For information on translations, please contact Apress directly at 2560 Ninth Street, Suite 219, Berkeley, CA 94710. Phone 510-549-5930, fax 510-549-5939, e-mail info@apress.com, or visit http://www.apress.com.

The source code for this book is available to readers at http://www.apress.com in the Source Code section.

Contents at a Glance

Contents

PART 1 ■■■ Code Policy Standards

PART 2 ▪▪▪ Design Policy Standards

PART 3 ■ ■ ■ **Pattern Standards**

PART 4 ■ ■ ■ References

About the Author

MARK HORNER is Principal Enterprise Architect and .NET Application consultant with Torville Software. He is a 25-year veteran of the industry and has worked with a host of blue-chip organizations, including Citibank, NRMA Insurance, ANZ Banking Group, Unilever, Hewlett-Packard, British Aerospace, and CPA Australia. You can contact him at markhorner@hotmail.com.

About the Technical Reviewer

**JON REID** is the Vice-President of Engineering for Indigo Biosystems (www.indigobio.com), an independent software vendor providing data management solutions for the life sciences, where he writes tools using C#, Java, and XML. Jon was editor of the Object Query Language and C++ Working Groups of the Object Data Management Group (ODMG) and has coauthored many books on .NET and C#, including *Beginning C# Databases: From Novice to Professional* (Apress, 2004) and *Pro Visual Studio .NET* (Apress, 2004). Jon would like to thank his family, his colleagues, and the great group at Apress for supporting his writing efforts.

Acknowledgments

This book is a composite of teamwork, and there are so many contributions to acknowledge. The book started off as a simple idea: I thought that the C# community needed "A catalog of standard practices." The idea quickly got the backing of Gary Cornell, Kylie Johnston, Ewan Buckingham, and Dominic Shakeshaft; and veteran author Donald Xie shared his views in the preliminary stages. The book was guided through the twists and turns of development by the forever-alert "Becks" (Beckie Brand). Ewan Buckingham, as lead editor, expertly nurtured the content of the book. The experience of fellow Apress author Jon Reid, in the role of technical reviewer, was invaluable, while Angela Buckley of Freelance Editorial Services and Ami Knox smoothed many of the rough edges. Thanks also to the rest of the team, including Grace Wong, Nicole LeClerc, Kari Brooks-Copony, Ellie Fountain, Molly Sharp, Linda Seifert, Toma Mulligan, Kinetic Publishing, Van Winkle Design Group, Kurt Krames, Tom Debolski, and Matthew Mason for the photograph. Finally, a special thanks to the design team at Microsoft for the C# language: Anders Hejlsberg, Scott Wiltamuth, Peter Golde, Peter Sollich, Eric Gunnerson, Peter Hallam, Shon Katzenberger, Todd Proebsting, Anson Horton, Don Syme, and Andrew Kennedy.

Introduction

This is *not* a book that tells you what you should or shouldn't do! So, in the immortal words of Douglas Adams (www.douglasadams.com): "Don't Panic!" Yes, it is a book on standards, but the standards are not presented as a set of rules; rather, they are presented and explained as a catalog of *standard* practices that are commonplace in the development community. My job is to bring them to your attention, and it's your choice whether you use them.

Generally, there are two categories of standards: *internal* and *external*. Internal standards are those standards that are in-house standards, whereas external standards are standards that are used between organizations to standardize a selection of industry practices (e.g., IEEE-1016 documentation for software design or IEEE-830 software requirements standard).

There are two leading organizations that develop external standards relevant to architects and developers: IEEE and W3C. Whereas IEEE focuses on standards for a wide range of industries, including information technology, W3C has a sharper focus on Internet technology.

Note IEEE-SA is an acronym for Institute of Electrical and Electronics Engineers Standards Association. The association is the leading developer of international standards for a wide range of industries: information technology, telecommunication, biomedical and health care, and power and energy, for example. It offers a subscription service to access the standards; you can check out their website at www.ieee.org. W3C is an acronym for the World Wide Web Consortium, which develops products and standards on Internet technology (e.g., HTML, XML, and Encryption). It offers a nonsubscription service to access the standards; you can check out their website at www.w3c.org.

This book is about internal standards only. Its role is to present to you a catalog of standards that are understood to be in the public domain and free to use and specialize for your situation. Standards have been categorized as code, design, and patterns. Code standards discuss policy, structure, development, and documentation of code. Design standards discuss code design from a policy, structure, development, and documentation perspective. Finally, pattern standards discuss a subset of the design patterns catalogued by Drs. Gamma, Helm, Johnson, and Vlissides (known as the "Gang of Four," or "GoF"). It also acknowledges the contribution to the pattern community by Professor Alexander, Professor Reenskaug, and GoF.

The Motivation: Why Do We Need Standards?

There are three key reasons to use standards: *success, uniformity,* and *transparency.* First, in an industry as volatile as information technology, if a given code or design practice lasts for a few seasons, then it tends to do so because it is *successful.* However, that success does not mean that the given practice is the only way to do a given task; often, there are successful alternatives. By and large, the community tends to make standards out of practices that they know are effective, efficient, and intuitive, and, in the main, disregard practices that may be the ideal but that are complex or unintuitive. Second, by using a standard, an organization can design and develop with *uniformity.* Conforming to a uniform way of designing and coding applications minimizes risks and problems associated with application architects and developers switching projects, for example. Third, standards offer *transparency:* that assists governance by making clear how design and code are developed in an organization.

The Choice of Standards

A common problem with wanting to follow standards is trying to find them! Although there are organizations that offer standards and there are also a few books that discuss best practices, they tend to specialize or generalize or theorize or in the case of an organization take years to formally approve a standard—which is cool, when that is what you want. However, if you are time-poor and need to put together an in-house standard for C# development, then you would experience problems. So, this book does the work for you by cataloging a set of standards that are common to the C# community and broad in scope: code, design, and design pattern standards. Code and design standards are presented from two perspectives: pure (policy) and applied (structure and development). The pure and applied perspectives of code and design merge in the presentation of design patterns. I am conscious that for you to adopt any standard, you will want to be convinced of its merit. So, rather than state the standard and give a quick example, I have prepared the standards in a common format that makes it easy for you to see if it is what you want, for your situation.

The Format of the Standards

The standards are presented using an intuitive format that has four sections: *What, Where, Why,* and *How.* The *What* section identifies what the standard is; the *Where* section identifies where to use it; the *Why* section identifies the motivation for using it; and the *How* section identifies how to use it.

How to Use the Standards

The standards may be used in several ways, principally in the following manner: (1) as in-house team standards; (2) as a template to develop in-house team standards; (3) by professionals wanting to reference community standards; and (4) by students wanting to adopt community standards in preparation for a career as a developer or application architect.

In addition to the introduction of each standard, there is a short statement that acknowledges its use in the community—for example: "*The standard acknowledges . . .*" Note that the statement does not begin with "*The standard recommends . . .*" It is not the intention of this book to make recommendations; as previously mentioned, the book is simply a catalog of standards. Determining the appropriate standard for your situation is for you to judge; you know your circumstance. The choice is yours! However, only standards that are understood to be accepted and in common use have been included. Although the catalog is not exhaustive,

I have endeavored to collect a good base set of standards, in this first edition of the book, and the catalog will grow in subsequent editions. Where a new feature has been introduced in version 2.0 of the C# language, that fact is indicated by the use of square brackets after the name of the standard. For example, *Partial Types* was introduced in C# 2.0, and its standard is indicated as follows:

Partial Types [Introduced C# 2.0]

Otherwise, all standards were introduced in versions 1.0, or 1.1 of the language and do not show square brackets. I shall now briefly introduce the chapters in the book.

Introducing the Chapters

The book is divided into four parts: code, design, patterns, and references. The code part of the book discusses code policy, structure, development, and documentation. The design part of the book discusses code from a design-policy, structure, development, and documentation perspective. In the patterns part of the book, design patterns are introduced and then discussed within the traditional category of creational, structural, and behavioral design patterns. The reference part of the book includes an appendix, a standards index, and a glossary. Throughout the book, the code examples are based on the fictitious Model T domain: a car manufacturing plant that makes Model T cars.

Chapter 1: Code Policy

This chapter notes that successful code is written through code management and not by chance. It introduces code style, which includes a discussion on code notation—for example, what are Pascal, Camel, and Hungarian notation, and where they may be used.

Chapter 2: Code Structure

The discussion progresses to how code is structured strategically to maximize its visibility, extensibility, and reusability. In so doing, this chapter examines program structure, namespaces, and the types that are commonly used to hold code, such as classes, interface types, and the new partial type.

Chapter 3: Code Development

In this chapter, the focus is on the lexical features of the C# language, which includes a discussion of code fundamentals that are categorized as class accessibility; class fundamentals; inheritance; expression and statement; flow control; and iteration.

Chapter 4: Code Documentation

Code documentation is the first of a pair of chapters on documentation (the other is design documentation). This chapter introduces documentation policy and identifies common ways that code is documented.

Chapter 5: Design Policy

The discussion on code now finished, three chapters on design follow. This chapter examines design objective and design style, and in so doing, it also discusses the architecture framework, target architecture, architecture roadmap, and many of the architectures that are in common use, including enterprise, application, and data architectures.

Chapter 6: Design Structure

In this chapter we start to apply the concepts that were discussed in the design policy by using structural design. Architectures are mapped to layers or tiers that are commonly used to develop enterprise functionality. The discussion includes the popular three- and five-tier application designs.

Chapter 7: Design Development

The chapter on design development discusses the common ways that applications are developed and in so doing identifies a number of dilemmas, expressed as dichotomies, associated with developing design. For example: when should we use an interface type rather than an abstract class or prefer interface inheritance over class inheritance?

Chapter 8: Design Documentation

This is the second chapter on documentation, and here we examine how through a documentation policy, design is documented. In so doing, we discuss application, application architecture, and enterprise framework documentation.

Chapter 9: Patterns

Design patterns have a checkered history: they are extremely useful but are often difficult to understand. This chapter introduces patterns and pattern language and explains the simplified approach that is used to demystifying design patterns. To commence the examination of design patterns, we first look at the Model–View–Controller (MVC) pattern, which is arguably the mother of all design patterns, before examining the patterns catalogued by GoF, in the subsequent three chapters.

Chapter 10: Creational Patterns

Creational patterns are about strategically manipulating the instantiation of classes. In this chapter and all the subsequent pattern chapters, the code is kept to a bare minimum, so that we can strip the patterns of their mystery and focus on the bare basics of how they work. In this chapter we examine the Abstract Factory, Factory Method, and Singleton patterns.

Chapter 11: Structural Patterns

This chapter examines structural patterns. Classes can be manipulated into a structure to overcome design problems, and the most notable example is the Adapter pattern, which uses an interposed class as a "go-between" to map two incompatible class interfaces. In addition to the Abstract pattern, we discuss two versions of the Proxy pattern (Surrogate and Remote-Proxy), Composite and Facade patterns.

Chapter 12: Behavioral Patterns

This final chapter discusses behavioral patterns, which can be manipulated to leverage communication, responsibility, and algorithms to help enhance behavior or overcome problems. The patterns that are discussed are Chain of Responsibility, Observer, Strategy, and Template Method.

Appendix A: Environment Variables and Remote Proxy Example

In structural patterns we simplified the Remote-Proxy pattern by developing the example outside of the comfort of the Visual Studio IDE. We did that so that we can work directly with the C# compiler, to fully understand all aspects of the Remote-Proxy pattern and observe the role of the compiler. To assist with that exercise, Appendix A includes an overview of environment variables and details on how to use the command line to access the C# compiler directly and code the example.

List of Standards

In the list of standards, we have listed all of the standards for your reference.

Glossary

The glossary includes an assortment of code, design, and general definitions that are included in the book or are common day-to-day terms.

Reading the Book

The book has been prepared so that it may be read from start to finish or at random. I do, however, suggest for the code part (Chapters 1 to 4) and the design part (Chapters 5 to 8) that on first reading you read the respective chapters in sequence, to appreciate the effect that policy has on code and design implementation.

Errors in the Book

The editorial team at Apress pride themselves on catching authors' errors, and they do an excellent job! But sometimes, even the best-trained eyes miss errors. Missing an error is not good at the best of times, and it is quite embarrassing in a book about standards. So, if any errors get through the safety net, we apologize in advance. We would greatly appreciate it if you find one to forward details to the Apress team via the support address (support@apress.com). Please note that Visual Studio .NET 2005 Beta 2 and RC were used in the writing of this book and not all of its functionality was in place at that time. It was necessary to use Visual Studio 2003 for the XML Comment Tool example in the Code Documentation chapter. That example also includes a reference to a freeware XML Documentator tool.

■**Note** To contact us with a correction, please email us at support@apress.com. Or if you prefer, you can email the author directly: markhorner@hotmail.com.

Suggest a Standard

We intend to release a new edition of this book in line with future editions of Microsoft's C# language, so we very much see the book as a living set of standards. If in the interim, you know of a standard that has been omitted from this catalog, and it is commonplace in the C# community, then please email the author (markhorner@hotmail.com) with the details. If it is included in the next edition of the book, we will gratefully acknowledge your observation in a *community contributors list* in the next edition. We very much want this book and subsequent editions to be an accurate reflection of the current standards used in our community.

PART 1

■ ■ ■

Code Policy Standards

This part of the book discusses code policy standards by looking at code style, management, structure, development, and documentation.

CHAPTER 1

■ ■ ■

Code Policy

A code policy encourages the development of successful and low-risk code. It does that through a collection of policy statements that regulate the way code is developed. This chapter discusses what a code policy is and presents an outline of its main features.

What

A code policy is an in-house plan that identifies important aspects of code development. Its scope is limited to making definitive statements on those areas of development that impact code quality, reliability, and viability. A code policy is regularly reviewed and updated (e.g., quarterly).

Where

The policy is applied to all code development across an enterprise. It may also extend to stakeholder development.

Why

A code policy is an effective and efficient way to successfully manage code development, by coordinating development across the enterprise.

How

A code policy doesn't have a definitive structure; it is developed around what are considered to be the key aspects of code development, such as (1) a code management policy, (2) a code development methodology, and (3) code notation and formatting guidelines. Figure 1-1 illustrates a code policy that is a collection of in-house standards:

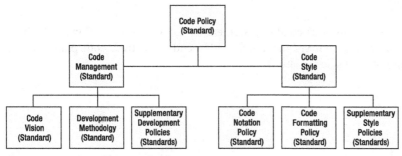

Figure 1-1. *Code policy standards structure*

3

The Standard: Code Policy

The standard acknowledges that a code policy is an effective and efficient way to successfully manage code development by coordinating development across the enterprise.

Code Management

Code, like any other valuable resource, benefits from being managed using successful management practices.

What

Code management refers to the way that code development is regulated. All major aspects of development are managed through a code policy.

Where

Code is managed across the enterprise throughout its development and life cycle.

Why

Successful code is not written by chance; it is the result of managing a volatile creative process.

How

Generally, a code policy will identify (1) a vision statement (e.g., "To become a 100% .NET environment"), (2) a best practice development methodology (e.g., eXtreme Programming or Rational Unified Process), and (3) a set of supplementary policies.

The Standard: Code Management

The standard acknowledges that code is a valuable resource that benefits from management throughout its development and life cycle.

Code Vision

A code policy uses a code vision to articulate a statement that identifies a direction in which code should be developed. The code vision is supported by code objectives, code plan, and a code strategy; these will be discussed shortly.

What

A code vision is a bit like a mission statement but articulates the direction of code development. For example, in recent years many organizations have adopted a ".NET vision" and are using that vision to direct code development that progressively migrates and develops code into .NET. They are re-positioning themselves by moving from a legacy state to a .NET state.

Where

A code vision forms part of the code policy.

Why

A code vision unites a development team and gives them a technical direction. Without a shared vision, there is the risk that development may fragment or suffer from inertia.

How

A code vision or a set of code visions may be developed as statements. For example, a code vision could read as follows: "We are committed to Microsoft technology and ensuring that all functionality across the enterprise will be .NET technology or .NET compliant by June 2007."

The Standard: Code Vision

The standard acknowledges that a code vision creates a sense of direction that unites a development team to work toward a shared technical goal.

Code Objectives

Once a code vision(s) has been expressed, it needs to be implemented across all development through a set of code objectives.

What

The code objectives identify what is necessary to achieve the code vision.

Where

A set of code objectives forms part of the code policy.

Why

Code objectives are important because they express in concrete terms what needs to be done to realize the code vision. Or to paraphrase Jessie Liberty, "from clouds to code."

■**Tip** Jessie Liberty is one of the preeminent authors in the C# community. His first C# book (*Programming C#*, by O'Reilly & Associates) was published in July 2001, and since then it has moved on to its fourth edition. You can check out Jessie's website at www.libertyassociates.com.

How

A gap analysis is used to determine what is required to move from one state (e.g., code that is a mix of legacy and .NET) to the vision state (e.g., code that is 100% .NET or .NET compliant). The issues identified in the gap analysis are then expressed as objectives. For example: Objective 1: Rewrite HTML/Javascript Web pages as ASP.NET/C# Web pages.

The Standard: Code Objective

> *The standard acknowledges that code objectives are an essential part of the development process because they identify what aspects of the enterprise need to change to realize a code vision.*

Code Plan

Once a set of code objectives has been prepared, then a code plan is developed.

What

A code plan identifies a way to move the state of the code from its present one (e.g., a mix of legacy and .NET) to that specified in the code vision (e.g., 100% .NET or .NET compliant).

Where

A code plan forms part of the code policy.

Why

It is necessary to identify how the objectives are to be achieved, by expressing them clearly and concisely in a language that assists application architects and developers.

How

A code plan is developed as a project plan: it identifies the tasks that are necessary to achieve each code objective and allocates resources.

The Standard: Code Plan

> *The standard acknowledges the use of a code plan to identify tasks and allocate resources to progress code from its current state to its future state.*

Code Strategy

Once a code plan has been prepared, then it is up to the technical team to determine how the plan is to be implemented.

What

The strategy is the *how* statement: "This is how we are going to undertake the tasks in the code plan."

Where

A code strategy forms part of the code policy.

Why

It is not obvious how objectives are best achieved, from a technical perspective, so a strategy is prepared to guide the development team. Often it is necessary to iterate a code strategy, as early feedback may indicate problems implementing a given aspect of a code strategy. For example, wrapping a given COM file as .NET may result in an unacceptable performance hit and thus require that part of the file to be migrated into a C# code file.

How

A code strategy is developed by a technical team having examined the technical and functional implications of the code plan and objectives. For example: A strategy to migrate HTML/Javascript Web pages into ASP.NET/C# Web pages may involve abstracting common legacy functionality into an enterprise services layer.

The Standard: Code Strategy

> *The standard acknowledges that a code strategy can be used to determine the best way to implement a code plan and achieve a set of code objectives.*

Development Methodology

A best-of-breed code development methodology is used to maximize the likelihood of developing successful code and to minimize risk.

What

A code development methodology is a structured set of guidelines that control the way code is developed. Popular methodologies include eXtreme Programming (XP) and Rational Unified Process (RUP).

■**Note** You can find out more about XP and RUP by visiting their websites: XP (www.extremeprogramming.org) and RUP (http://www-306.ibm.com/software/rational/).

Where

A code development methodology is used across the enterprise.

Why

There is too much that can go wrong when developing code, and a best-of-breed development methodology standardizes development across applications and minimizes or prevents problems from occurring.

How

An organization evaluates a development methodology and then adopts it as part of its code policy. A brief overview of RUP and XP methodologies now follows:

XP

eXtreme Programming articulates a programming process that is built around four core best practices: planning, designing, coding, and testing. Some of the features of the best practices include:

- Planning

  - User stories.

  - Release planning.

  - Small release.

  - Measuring project velocity.

  - Iteration planning.

  - Rotating team.

  - A quick (stand-up) meeting at the start of each day.

  - Fixing any XP methodology problems as they occur.

- Designing

    - Simplicity.

    - Creating spike solutions to reduce risk.

    - Refactoring mercilessly (XP defines this as removing redundancy, eliminating unused functionality, and rejuvenating obsolete designs throughout the whole project life cycle).

- Coding

    - The customer is always available.

    - Writing code to agreed standards.

    - Pair programming production code.

    - Having only one pair integrate code at a time.

    - Coding the unit test first.

    - Integrating frequently.

    - Collective ownership (XP defines this as allowing any developer to change any line of code—there is no personal ownership of code).

    - No overtime (developing code when in a tired state significantly increases the risk of error).

- Testing

    - All code is unit tested.

    - All code must pass a unit test prior to release.

    - When there are bugs, create a test.

    - Acceptance tests are run frequently and the results are published, for all to see.

RUP

Rational Unified Process articulates a framework of iterative software design that is built around core best practices, including the following:

- Develop software in iterations.

- Manage requirements.

- Favor component-based architecture.

- Model software visually.

- Verify the quality of software.

- Control changes to software.

The preceding methodologies are favored choices among the community and share the common theme of managing the development of low-risk code through a formal, structured, and transparent methodology.

The Standard: Code Development Methodology

The standard acknowledges the use of code development methodologies such as XP and RUP, which are used to maximize the likelihood of developing successful code.

Supplementary Development Policies

A code development methodology is not exhaustive, and it may rely on supplementary development policies to ensure dependencies are in place (e.g., unit testing). Or there may be additional development practices that need to be expressed in a supplementary policy: conveniently, a set of in-house standards may be referenced as supplementary policies. We discuss six standards that are generally included as supplementary development policies.

Peer Review

A common practice is to subject the code written by each developer to a peer review.

What

A peer review is an examination or review of the code that a team member has written, by his or her peers (fellow team members or members from another team). The team studies the code to identify strengths, weaknesses, opportunities, and inconsistencies with the code policy.

Where

A peer review is employed across all code development (e.g., application development; refactoring; maintenance; integration and reengineering).

Why

There are at least four key reasons why peer review is popular: (1) it improves the quality of code development by improving the skills of the developer; (2) it is an effective way to share knowledge; (3) it assists in ensuring that code policies are being implemented correctly; and (4) it builds team cohesion.

How

A peer review can follow a continuous or periodic process. In a continuous peer review, a developer codes with a partner and each partner continuously reviews the other's code (refer to XP "pair programming"). Or a periodic review may be undertaken at the end of an iteration, for example.

■Note XP's practice of "pair programming" is in effect a continuous peer review that happens while the code is written.

The Standard: Peer Review

The standard acknowledges the benefits of peer review: (1) improvement of the quality of code by improving the skills of the developer, (2) knowledge sharing, (3) compliance with code policies, and (4) building team cohesion.

Unit Testing

It is high-risk not to unit test functionality when it is developed or released into production.

What

A unit test is a test of the functionality of a class: it passes data to its methods and verifies the get and set functionality. If you adhere to an XP methodology, for example, then you develop the unit tests before you develop the code and run tests during the development process.

Where

A unit test is performed against all class development and maintenance.

Why

If the actual functionality of an object differs from what is expected, then that may adversely affect object collaboration, which in turn may affect stability and reliability of an application.

How

Unit tests are written within a test framework, and the framework is used to test class functionality.

■Tip Most versions of Visual Studio 2005 come with a unit test framework that is accessible from the main menu (i.e., Test menu). Otherwise, a unit test framework is available from Nunit (www.nunit.org)—it is written in C#.

The Standard: Unit Testing

The standard acknowledges the importance of unit testing, which is used to examine the reliability of calling the methods of an object.

Refactoring

During the life cycle of an application, there is always code that needs tweaking to accommodate change or improve its quality.

What

Refactoring is a technique to transform code by altering its internal behavior without affecting its external behavior.

Where

Refactoring is used where there is a need to make adjustments to code to accommodate change or to improve the quality of code.

Why

Generally, code is refactored because it is cheaper and quicker to transform code that way, rather than redesign it.

How

Code is progressively transformed, in small increments, to reduce the risk of affecting its external behavior.

Tip Martin Fowler is a leading authority on refactoring and manages a website dedicated to it: www.refactoring.com.

The Standard: Refactoring

The standard acknowledges that refactoring is a useful tool to transform the internal workings of an application without affecting its external workings.

Development Imperative

Generally, there are two ways to develop code: from an enterprise perspective or from a domain perspective. Commonly, a supplementary policy is prepared to clarify when code is to be written as enterprise or domain code. The decision is often not obvious and presents a dilemma that may be settled by issuing a policy statement based on a general code rule such as, "If it is assessed that code has a reasonable likelihood of being used in three or more situations, then it is developed as enterprise code and consumed by domain applications as an enterprise service." The enterprise–domain dilemma is discussed further as the "Enterprise–Domain Dichotomy" in Chapter 6.

Enterprise Imperative

An enterprise imperative recognizes that many applications have similar functionality and that resources may be more efficiently used by abstracting that functionality into a shared or enterprise service.

What

Developing code with an enterprise imperative refers to the practice of identifying code that has the potential for reuse and then developing it generically into class libraries to be published as an enterprise service.

Where

An enterprise imperative may be used in developing any functionality, except where it is obvious that functionality is unlikely to be reused.

Why

Code developed from an enterprise perspective minimizes duplication and maintenance. In theory, once there is a rich set of enterprise services, then domain applications may be developed rapidly, because the amount of marginal development is minimal, as the domain application leverages a repository of enterprise services.

How

The general approach is to identify what is enterprise functionality and develop it into a services layer from where applications reference it. Candidates for enterprise functionality include data access, business logic, user interfaces, controls, and integration functionality.

The Standard: Enterprise Imperative

> *The standard acknowledges that developing code with an enterprise imperative improves efficiency by minimizing code duplication and maintenance.*

Domain Imperative

Although it is great to leverage the benefits of enterprise code, it is not always practical or politically acceptable to incur the upfront overhead costs of developing generic code and then specializing it in a domain application.

What

Developing code with a domain imperative refers to developing code that is coupled to a domain implementation.

Where

A domain imperative is used where there is a domain requirement that is not common to the enterprise, or where it is impractical or politically unacceptable to develop reusable code from an enterprise perspective.

Why

The code is domain specific or there is insufficient opportunity or incentive to develop code from an enterprise perspective. Commonly, much functionality is coupled to a domain requirement and there is no advantage in developing it generically.

How

Code is developed solely to meet the requirements of the domain.

The Standard: Domain Imperative

The standard acknowledges that a domain imperative is used where a requirement is tightly coupled to a domain or there is insufficient opportunity or incentive to develop it otherwise.

Source-Code Control

A critical aspect of code development is making sure that the source code is protected by a source-code control system.

What

Source-code control manages code that is developed by teams. It is a system that protects source code from being accidentally overwritten or lost; backups code; and tracks changes.

Tip If you don't have access to Microsoft Visual SourceSafe (www.microsoft.com), then you may want to review an open standard alternative: CVS (www.nongnu.org/cvs/).

Where

A source-code control system is used across the enterprise on all code development projects.

Why

A source-code control system protects code by reducing the risks associated with team development (e.g., the risk of one developer's code being overwritten by another developer's code).

How

Developers check out a piece of code (e.g., a class) from a central repository into an allocated folder (private workspace) where they make changes. While they are working on the code, other developers are unaffected. When they have finished, they then check in the code to the central repository.

The Standard: Source Code Control

> *The standard acknowledges that a source code security control reduces the risks associated with team development.*

Code Obsolescence

Warning developers that functionality is flagged for depreciation saves a lot of problems—which can easily be done by using the Obsolete attribute.

What

An Obsolete attribute is an attribute that signifies a type or members of a type are flagged for depreciation.

Where

An Obsolete attribute is used in situations where it is known that functionality is scheduled to be depreciated.

Why

It is bad practice to fail to give adequate warning that functionality has been scheduled for obsolescence. Timely notification minimizes the risks associated with obsolescence.

How

Obsolescence may be signified with a special attribute: ObsoleteAttribute. The attribute may be used with class, struct, enum, interface, delegate, method, constructor, property, field, and event. For example:

```
...
[Obsolete("Obsolete - use XYZ() method")]
public void ABC()
{...}
...
```

Tip It is considered that a notice period of one major version is a minimum period in which to notify that functionality is to be depreciated. Apart from using the Obsolete attribute, in addition, consideration may also be given to communicating planned depreciation through a developer's blog and/or by email.

The Standard: Obsolescence

The standard acknowledges the benefits of early warning of obsolescence. Notice should be given in a timely manner: it is considered that a notice period of one major version is a minimum.

Code Style

In this section we turn our attention to another aspect of code development that is controlled by code policy: code style.

What

A code style is a set of guidelines that regulate the way developers write code. Code styles can be simple or comprehensive; generally, simple code styles are more successful because they tend to be more intuitive and easy to remember.

Where

A code style is used across all code development.

Why

A code style is adopted because it encourages uniformity or consistency in code development—which improves understandability of code and makes it relatively easy to rotate developers from project to project or from team to team.

How

The first thing to do is decide what is in scope. Then, once that is determined, a style guide or manual is prepared and distributed to the development team; Visual Studio 2005 has significantly simplified the process of controlling code style by including a wide range of formatting styles that can be configured directly into the IDE. The IDE also includes a wide range of code snippets that can be used to standardize style.

The Standard: Code Style

The standard acknowledges the use of a code style to encourage uniformity or consistency in the way that code is written. It improves understandability of code and makes it relatively easy to rotate developers from project to project or from team to team.

Code Notation

There are three common types of code notation: Pascal, Camel, and Hungarian. In recent years there has been wide variation in the use of these notations, and this has led to a state of uncertainty in the community. After much research I could not find a definitive and comprehensive statement on how to notate C# code; I found it to be fragmented or specialized. (If you know better, then please email me: markhorner@hotmail.com). What I have been able to piece together is that there is a mix of Pascal and Camel, and that although Hungarian notation is "politically incorrect," it is still commonly used with variables to identify Web and Windows control types. It is the use of Hungarian notation for controls that seems to cause the greatest debate. One side of the argument is that Hungarian shouldn't be used because the name of a variable should indicate its semantics and not its type, and if you need to know the type of the control, then you can hover the mouse over the variable (which presumes that you are not reading from a hardcopy code listing, for example). On the other side of the argument is the view that using Hungarian notation to identify the type of a control is ubiquitous and very convenient. My research of websites, weblogs, and computer books shows that there is substantial support, in the C# community, for using Hungarian notation to identify the type of a Web/Windows control. Acknowledging the respective arguments, I have put together two code notation standards:

Camel–Hungarian–Pascal Notation Standard

1. Instance member variables/fields and parameters: Use Camel notation (e.g., `myVariable`).

2. Web/Windows control variables: Use Hungarian notation (e.g., `btnSubmit`).

3. All other identifiers: Use Pascal (e.g., `MyClass`).

Camel–Pascal Notation Standard

1. Instance member variables/fields and parameters: Use Camel notation (e.g., `myVariable`).

2. Web/Windows controls variables: Use Camel notation (e.g., `submit`).

3. All other identifiers: Use Pascal (e.g., `MyClass`).

■**Note** Where case sensitivity is not relied on to distinguish a variable from its type, then the variable may commonly be prefaced with an underscore (`_myVariable`)—refer to the section Supplementary Style Policy, later in this chapter. The use of (`_Variable`) as a variable name would contravene Camel notation, whereas the use of (`_variable`) complies with Camel notation and a policy that discourages differentiation of a variable name and its type by relying on case sensitivity—however, using an underscore does look a bit odd when selecting the variable in IntelliSense.

Pascal Notation

Pascal notation is a code notation used to name identifiers.

What

In Pascal notation, the first letter of the identifier starts in uppercase, then drops to lowercase until the start of the second word, if there is one, when it rises to uppercase for the first letter of the second word and then drops down to lowercase for the remainder of the word, and so on.

Where

Pascal notation is used to identify class, constant, delegate, enum type, enum value, event, event handler, exception, static member variable, interface, method, namespace, and property. Table 1- lists the identifiers that use Pascal notation.

Table 1-1. *Identifiers—Pascal Notation*

Identifier	Notation	Example
Class	Pascal	Car
Constant	Pascal	MaximumValue
Delegate	Pascal	ChangeInformation
Enum Type	Pascal	ColorChoice
Enum Value	Pascal	OnlyBlack
Event (Delegate)	Pascal	ChangeDirection
Event Handler	Pascal	OnChangeDirection
Exception	Pascal	OutOfOrderException
Static Member Variable	Pascal	ThisValue
Interface	Pascal	IEngine
Method	Pascal	StopEngine()
Namespace	Pascal	Enterprise.BusinessRules
Property	Pascal	RadiatorCap

Why

Pascal notation represents identifiers that are significant, whereas Camel notation is used to represent identifiers that are less significant and accessed through a method (e.g., instance member variables and parameters).

How

Pascal notation is written as: "ThisIsPascal" (multiword) or "Pascal" (single word).

The Standard: Pascal Notation

The standard acknowledges the use of Pascal notation for class, constant, delegate, enum type, enum value, event, event handler, exception, static member variable, interface, method, namespace, and property.

Camel Notation

Camel notation is a code notation used to name identifiers.

What

In Camel notation, the first *word* of the identifier is lowercase, the first letter of the second word of the identifier—if there is one—is uppercase, and the remainder of the word is lowercase. The pattern used in the second word repeats for subsequent words.

Where

Camel is used to identify instance member variables and parameters.

Why

Camel notation represents identifiers that are less significant or accessed through a method.

How

Camel notation is written as "thisIsCamel" (multiword) or "camel" (single word). Table 1-2 lists the identifiers that use Camel notation.

Table 1-2. *Identifiers—Camel Notation*

Identifier	Notation	Example
Instance Member Variable	Camel	carTire
Parameter	Camel	valueIn

The Standard: Camel Notation

The standard acknowledges the use of Camel notation for instance member variables and parameters.

Hungarian Notation

Hungarian notation is a code notation used to name identifiers.

What

In Hungarian notation, the first word or acronym (which may be a single letter, although none are shown in the following table) of the identifier is lowercase and represents the Web/Windows visual or user interface control type. In subsequent words of the identifier, the first letter is uppercase and the remainder of the word in lowercase.

Where

Hungarian notation is used with variable identifiers that hold Web/Windows controls. Historically, it was common practice to use Hungarian notation to identify the types of *all* variables (e.g., iAge or strName); however, that practice is no longer in vogue. There is still debate as to whether Hungarian notation should be used at all, but, as previously mentioned, it has been steadfastly supported for variable identifiers that hold Web/Windows visual or user interface controls types.

Why

Hungarian notation is used because it is a longstanding convention and it is useful to identify Web/Windows visual control types when reading code.

How

Hungarian notation is written as `cmbEmployees` or `lstEmployees`. Table 1-3 lists Web/Windows visual controls that use Hungarian notation.

Table 1-3. *Identifiers—Hungarian Notation*

Control #	Control Category	Control Type	Prefix	Example
1A	ASP.NET	AdRotator	ar	arName
2A	ASP.NET	Button	btn	btnName
3A	ASP.NET	Calendar	clr	clrName
4A	ASP.NET	CheckBox	cb	cbName
5A	ASP.NET	CheckedListBox	clb	clbName
6A	ASP.NET	CompareValidator	cv	cvName
7A	ASP.NET	CrystalReportViewer	crv	crvName
8A	ASP.NET	DataGrid	dg	dgName
9A	ASP.NET	DataGridColumn	dgc	dgcName
10A	ASP.NET	DataGridItem	dgi	dgiName
11A	ASP.NET	DataList	dl	dlName
12A	ASP.NET	DropDownList	ddl	ddlName
13A	ASP.NET	HyperLink	hl	hlName

Control #	Control Category	Control Type	Prefix	Example
14A	ASP.NET	Image	img	imgName
15A	ASP.NET	ImageButton	ib	ibName
16A	ASP.NET	Label	lbl	lblName
17A	ASP.NET	LinkButton	lbn	lbnName
18A	ASP.NET	ListBox	lbx	lbxName
19A	ASP.NET	Literal	ltl	ltlName
20A	ASP.NET	MultiPage	mp	mpName
21A	ASP.NET	Panel	pnl	pnlName
22A	ASP.NET	PlaceHolder	ph	phName
23A	ASP.NET	RadioButton	rb	rbName
24A	ASP.NET	RadioButtonList	rbl	rblName
25A	ASP.NET	RangeValidator	rv	rvName
26A	ASP.NET	RegularExpressionValidator	rev	revName
27A	ASP.NET	Repeater	rpr	rprName
28A	ASP.NET	RepeaterItem	rpi	rpiName
29A	ASP.NET	RequiredValidator	rv	rvName
30A	ASP.NET	Table	tbl	tblName
31A	ASP.NET	TableCell	tbc	tbcName
32A	ASP.NET	TableRow	tbr	tbrName
33A	ASP.NET	TabStrip	ts	tsName
34A	ASP.NET	TextBox	tb	tbName
35A	ASP.NET	Toolbar	tbr	tbrName
36A	ASP.NET	TreeView	tv	tvName
37A	ASP.NET	ValidatorSummary	vs	vsName
38A	ASP.NET	Xml	xml	xmlName
1H	HTML	Button	btn	btnName
2H	HTML	CheckBox	cb	cbName
3H	HTML	DropDownList	ddl	ddlName
4H	HTML	FileField	ff	ffName
5H	HTML	FlowLayoutPanel	flp	flpName
6H	HTML	GridLayoutPanel	glp	glpName
7H	HTML	Hidden	hdn	hdnName
8H	HTML	HorizontalRule	hr	hrName
9H	HTML	Image	img	imgName
10H	HTML	Label	lbl	lblName
11H	HTML	ListBox	lb	lbName
12H	HTML	PasswordField	pwf	pwfName
13H	HTML	RadioButton	rdb	rdbName

Continued

Table 1-3. *Continued*

Control #	Control Category	Control Type	Prefix	Example
14H	HTML	ResetButton	rsb	rsbName
15H	HTML	SubmitButton	sbb	sbbName
16H	HTML	Table	tbl	tblName
17H	HTML	TextBox	tb	tbName
18H	HTML	TextArea	ta	taName
1W	WINDOWS	Binding	bdg	bdgName
2W	WINDOWS	Bitmap	bmp	bmpName
3W	WINDOWS	Brush	brh	brhName
4W	WINDOWS	Button	btn	btnName
5W	WINDOWS	CheckBox	cb	cbName
6W	WINDOWS	CheckedBoxList	cbl	cblName
7W	WINDOWS	Color	clr	clrName
8W	WINDOWS	ColorPalette	clrp	clrpName
9W	WINDOWS	ComboBox	cb	cbName
10W	WINDOWS	ContextMenu	ctm	ctmName
11W	WINDOWS	CrystalReportViewer	crv	crvName
12W	WINDOWS	Cursor	csr	csrName
13W	WINDOWS	DataGrid	dg	dgName
14W	WINDOWS	DataGridColumn	dgc	dgcName
15W	WINDOWS	DateTimePicker	dtp	dtpName
16W	WINDOWS	DialogControl	dc	dcName
17W	WINDOWS	DirectoryEntry	de	deName
18W	WINDOWS	DirectorySearcher	ds	dsName
19W	WINDOWS	DomainDropDown	ddd	dddName
20W	WINDOWS	ErrorProvider	ep	epName
21W	WINDOWS	EventLog	el	elName
22W	WINDOWS	FileSystemWatcher	fsw	fswName
23W	WINDOWS	Font	fnt	fntName
24W	WINDOWS	Form	frm	frmName
25W	WINDOWS	Graphics	gps	gpsName
26W	WINDOWS	GraphicsPath	gp	gpName
27W	WINDOWS	GroupBox	gb	gbName
28W	WINDOWS	HelpProvider	hp	hpName
29W	WINDOWS	HorizontalScrollBar	hsr	hsrName
30W	WINDOWS	Icon	ico	icoName
31W	WINDOWS	Image	img	imgName
32W	WINDOWS	ImageList	imgl	imglName

Control #	Control Category	Control Type	Prefix	Example
33W	WINDOWS	Label	lbl	lblName
34W	WINDOWS	LinkLabel	lnkl	lnklName
35W	WINDOWS	ListBox	lb	lbName
36W	WINDOWS	ListView	lv	lvName
37W	WINDOWS	ListViewItem	lvi	lviName
38W	WINDOWS	MainMenu	mmnu	mmnuName
39W	WINDOWS	MenuItem	mnui	mnuiName
40W	WINDOWS	MaskEditBox	meb	mebName
41W	WINDOWS	MessageQueue	msq	msqName
42W	WINDOWS	MetaFile	mf	mfName
43W	WINDOWS	MonthCalendar	mclr	mclrName
44W	WINDOWS	NotifyIcon	nico	nicoName
45W	WINDOWS	NumericUpDown	nud	nudName
46W	WINDOWS	PageSettings	pstg	pstgName
47W	WINDOWS	Panel	pnl	pnlName
48W	WINDOWS	Pen	pen	penName
49W	WINDOWS	PeformanceCounter	pfmc	pfmcName
50W	WINDOWS	PictureBox	picb	picbName
51W	WINDOWS	Point	pnt	pntName
52W	WINDOWS	PrintController	prtc	prtcName
53W	WINDOWS	PrintDocument	prtd	prtdName
54W	WINDOWS	PrinterSettings	prts	prtsName
55W	WINDOWS	Process	pcs	pcsName
56W	WINDOWS	Rectangle	rec	recName
57W	WINDOWS	Region	rgn	rgnName
58W	WINDOWS	ReportDocument	rptd	rptdName
59W	WINDOWS	ServiceController	srvc	srvcName
60W	WINDOWS	Size	sze	szeName
61W	WINDOWS	Timer	tmr	tmrName

The Standard: Hungarian Notation

The standard acknowledges the debate about the use of Hungarian notation with Web/Windows visual controls and notes it has steadfast and wide community support, thus making its use, for a variable assigned a visual control, optional.

Code Formatting

Visual Studio 2005 has introduced a comprehensive list of code formatting options that are configurable within the IDE, as are code snippets. These features effectively eliminate the need to manually prepare a set of formatting standards. The formatting options are listed in the following sections, and all that remains for a development team is to agree the options, configure the respective IDEs, and note them as in-house standards. Then those standards may be referenced in a policy statement.

Visual Studio Formatting Options

Tabs

- Indenting
    - None
    - Block
    - Smart
    - Tab
    - Tab size
    - Indent size
    - Insert spaces
    - Keep tabs

Indentation

- Indent block contents
    - Indent open and close braces
    - Indent case contents
    - Indent case labels
- Label indentation
    - Place goto labels in leftmost column
    - Place goto labels one indent less than current
    - Indent labels normally

New Lines

- Braces
    - Place open brace on new line for types
    - Place open brace on new line for methods
    - Place open brace on new lines for anonymous methods
    - Place open brace on new lines for control blocks
- Keywords
    - Place "else" on new line
    - Place "catch" on new line
    - Place "finally" on new line

Spacing

- Method declarations
    - Insert space between method name and its opening parenthesis
    - Insert space within argument list parentheses
    - Insert space within empty argument list parentheses
- Method calls
    - Insert space between method name and its opening parenthesis
    - Insert space within argument list parenthesis
    - Insert space within empty argument list parenthesis
- Set spacing for other
    - Insert space after control flow keywords
    - Insert space within parentheses of expressions
    - Insert space within parentheses of type casts
    - Insert space within flow control construct parentheses
    - Insert space after cast
- Spacing for brackets
    - Insert space before open square bracket
    - Insert space within empty square brackets
    - Insert spaces within square brackets

- Spacing for delimiters
  - Insert space after colon for base or interface in type declaration
  - Insert space after comma
  - Insert space after dot
  - Insert space after semicolon in "for" statement
  - Insert space before colon for base or interface in type declaration
  - Insert space before comma
  - Insert space before dot
  - Insert space before semicolon in for statement
- Spacing for operators
  - Insert space before and after binary operators
  - Ignore spaces around binary operators
  - Remove white space before and after binary operators

Wrapping

- Leave block on single line
- Leave statements and member declarations on the same line

Supplementary Style Policy

Case sensitivity is not a standard that fits within code notation or formatting policy, but it is inserted into code policy as a supplementary style policy—as are other standards that are appropriate.

Case Sensitivity

.NET comes with two types of development languages, case sensitive (e.g., C#) and case insensitive (e.g., Visual Basic). This presents a bit of a problem for teams that support both language types, and so there is always an option to accept a .NET standard, which rules against using case sensitivity (e.g., in C# language).

What

Case sensitivity refers to a language that recognizes that code syntax can be differentiated on case.

Where

Alpha characters are case sensitive in the C# language and are not in Visual Basic language.

Why

Case sensitivity is leveraged by developers for convenience and readability.

How

A variable name is differentiated by case; for example, in C# language the following variable (car) is differentiated, by the compiler, from its type (Car):

```
Car car; (C#)
```

However, in Visual Basic the equivalent syntax would result in a compile error:

```
Dim car as Car (VB)
```

To maintain a consistent variable naming style across the languages, a common practice is to (1) rule against the use of case sensitivity in C# code; or (2) prefix a variable with an underscore in both languages, as in the following example:

```
Car _car; (C#)
```

```
Dim _car as Car (VB)
```

The Standard: Case Sensitivity

> *The standard acknowledges that where C# and Visual Basic are supported, for consistency in naming variables, a choice is made between (1) ruling against the use of case sensitivity in C# code; or (2) prefixing variables—in C# and VB code—with an underscore.*

CHAPTER 2

Code Structure

In this chapter I discuss structuring code and note that .NET has three levels of code structure: assembly; namespace, and complex types. We can choose an assembly to structure specialist functionality (e.g., security code) or structure functionality within a hierarchy of nested namespaces or structure functionality in an interface; struct; class; partial class; or generic type. The choices that we make impact not only accessibility to our code, but they also impact the flexibility and maintainability of the code; and the larger the application, the greater the impact!

Assembly

An assembly is used to control the way functionality is accessed and distributed.

What

An assembly is a repository that is used to store related functionality. There are two types of assemblies: an executable (EXE) and a dynamic link library (DLL).

Where

An assembly is used where there is a need to partition or encapsulate functionality into a logical unit.

Why

An assembly can be used to control the way that code is made accessible or distributed to a client. For example, code distributed in an EXE assembly is accessible indirectly through its functionality, whereas code that is in a DLL assembly is accessible directly through its interface.

How

If we use our copy of Visual Studio 2005 as an example, we can see how an assembly is leveraged to structure functionality. In the object browser we see that the core library functionality (mscorlib.dll) is structured in a DLL assembly, as is the security functionality (System.Security.dll). However, Visual Studio 2005 itself is structured in an EXE assembly (devenv.exe), which illustrates how the code designers have used respective code structures to prepare code for different roles. As we know, assemblies are generally created as a Visual Studio project type, although they may be created on the command line.

The Standard: Assembly

The standard acknowledges that an assembly may be used to partition specialized functionality and to control distribution and accessibility to that functionality. The choices made to structure code impact not only accessibility to code but also the flexibility and maintainability of the code.

Namespace

A namespace resides in an assembly, and it is used as a tool to structure code.

What

A namespace is a compilation unit in which code can be structured. Implicitly, the visibility of a namespace is public and its access modifier cannot be changed. An assembly may include multiple namespaces where namespaces are commonly embedded in a hierarchy to enable granular or strategic referencing of code.

Where

A namespace is used where there is a requirement to structure functionality within logical units.

Why

Code is more manageable when it is categorized into units of logically related functionality. Namespaces may also be used to avoid conflict between classes or variables with the same names (e.g., ThisNamespace.Class1 and ThatNamespace.Class1).

How

Namespaces are coded by using the namespace keyword followed by a block consisting of opening and closing braces. Namespaces may be nested; the following example illustrates the nesting of the EngineParts namespace within the Inventory namespace. The Piston class may be referenced as Inventory.EngineParts.Piston.—it is accessible or visible within the EngineParts namespace and not immediately within the Inventory namespace:

```
namespace Inventory
{
  namespace EngineParts
  {
    class Piston
    { ...}
  }
}
```

The Standard: Namespace

The standard acknowledges the use of namespaces and embedded namespaces to strategically structure code and to avoid naming conflicts.

Interface Type

An interface type offers flexibility in the way that code can be structured because of its support of multiple inheritance, it can be implemented at any level in a class hierarchy or in another interface hierarchy.

What

An interface type is a complex reference type that may contain properties, methods, events, and indexers. It exposes an interface without committing the derived type to an implementation. It supports multiple inheritance (implementation inheritance), unlike a class (in .NET) that supports single class inheritance. It may be inherited by a class, a struct, or by another interface type: Its role is structural and polymorphic—not code reuse.

Where

An interface type is used to enhance the interface of a class or struct—it is commonly used to signify that a class or struct performs a given role, which is usually indicated in the name of the interface, such as IDisposable or IBinarySerialize. As it can be inherited anywhere in a class hierarchy, it can be used to enhance a design when it is most appropriate or convenient.

Why

In complex domains, the interface type overcomes the limitations of single class inheritance and offers the opportunity to treat classes that are not part of the same class hierarchy as if they were, by using polymorphism. A class designer may use an interface type to avoid having to reengineer a base class or to enhance its interface through interface inheritance, particularly when features of the interface are optional. For example, the concepts of sedan and tourer can be treated as an embellishment to the car base class, rather than as an attribute of car. The use of an interface type adds flexibility; for example, when new car concepts are introduced (e.g., station wagon or convertible), they can be simply implemented where convenient rather than having to disturb the base class or class hierarchy.

How

An interface type is defined as follows:

```
namespace ModelT.Interfaces
{
  interface ISedan
  {
    int Doors {get; set;}
```

```
    void DoSomething();
  }

  interface ITourer
  {
    int Doors {get; set;}
    void DoSomethingElse();
  }
}
```

By using an interface type, we can keep the definition of car generic and inherit the appropriate functionality using interface inheritance, as in the following example:

```
using System;
using ModelT.Interfaces; //reference namespace

namespace ModelTInterfaceExample
{
  class Car: ISedan //inherit Sedan functionality
  {
    int _door;

    //implement property
    public int Door
    {
      get {return _door;}
      set {_door = value;}
    }

    //implement method
    public void DoSomething() {;}
  }
}
```

From the previous code snippet, we can see the definition of interface types and the subsequent use of them by a car type to embellish its interface with the interface of a sedan. Class objects instantiated from this class may now be treated polymorphically as Car or Sedan type. Although an interface type requires that its interface is implemented, by an inheriting class or struct, this may be inconvenient; where only part of the interface type is required by a class or struct, the unwanted part of the interface may be implemented as a stub. For example, an inheriting class may implement a method without functionality, as shown here:

```
public void DoSomething()
{
  ; //code stub
}
```

The Standard: Interface Type

The standard acknowledges that an interface type may be used to add flexibility to the way that code is structured. It is commonly used to signify that a class or struct performs a given role or to leverage its ability to support multiple inheritance.

struct Type

A struct is a lightweight alternative to a class and can be used to structure functionality without incurring the overhead penalty of a reference type.

What

A struct is a complex value type that may contain constructors, fields, properties, methods, nested types, operators, and indexers. A struct does not support inheritance itself (unlike a class or interface type), but it may inherit from an interface type.

Where

A struct is used where there is a requirement for a lightweight complex type that isn't required to support class-inheritance or reference or instantiation semantics. For example, we could use a struct type as a base type for a Car and specialize functionality through interface inheritance. That would be useful in a situation where memory resource allocation is critical (i.e., a program that has to run on a mobile device)—each active instance of a Car would consume less memory if it was built as a struct rather than as a class type. Why? Because the struct is a value type, it is more efficient because it resides on the stack and requires less memory than a class, which is a complex type and resides on the heap.

How

The following code snippet illustrates the definition of a struct type, which inherits the ISedan interface type.

```
struct myCar: ISedan
{
  int _door;

  //implement property
  public int Door
  {
    get {return _door;}
    set {_door = value;}
  }

  //implement method
  public void DoSomething() {;}
}
```

If we compare the code structure of a sedan car defined by using the `class` and `struct` types, we see that they are identical. However, the sedan car built with the `struct` type is more resource efficient: it doesn't have to be instantiated, and it doesn't have the overhead of a reference type. It is a worthwhile alternative to a class when class inheritance is not required.

The Standard: struct Type

The standard acknowledges a `struct` type may be used as a lightweight alternative to a class to structure code and leverage interface inheritance in situations where memory allocation is scarce or class-inheritance and referencing are not required.

Class Type

A `class` is the most sophisticated type used to structure functionality; it supports class inheritance and can be coded as an abstraction or as an implementation.

What

A `class`, which is a complex reference type, is the definition of an object. Once instantiated, the class is known as a concrete class or object. It may be modified as `abstract`, which prevents it from being instantiated, or it may be modified as `sealed`, preventing it from being extended (i.e., inherited). It supports single class inheritance and multiple interface inheritance.

Where

A `class` is used where there is a requirement to support class-inheritance or instantiation semantics, and the overhead of a reference type is not an issue. For example, we use a `class` type as a base type where the benefits of inheriting functionality outweigh the additional memory cost of supporting a reference type.

Why

A `class` is the richest data type in .NET through which all aspects of object-oriented design and development are accessible (abstraction, encapsulation, inheritance, and polymorphism).

How

A `class` is defined, and then it may be instantiated into an object. However, it need not be instantiated to access functionality if a member is modified as `static`. It may be extended through class or interface inheritance. The following is an example of a class structure:

```
class myCar: ISedan
{
  int _door;

  //implement property
  public int Door
```

```
{
  get {return _door;}
  set {_door = value;}
}

//implement method
public void DoSomething() {;}

//class constructor
public myCar () {;}
}
```

The Standard: Class Type

The standard acknowledges the use of a class type where there is a requirement to support class-inheritance or reference semantics and the overhead of a reference type is not an issue.

Partial Type (Introduced C# 2.0)

What

A partial type is a type that is permitted to use the partial modifier. There are three types that may use the partial modifier: class, struct, and interface. Note that the partial modifier is not permitted on the delegate class, however.

Where

A partial type is used where there is a requirement to split a type over multiple files. A consequence of modifying a type as partial is that once the type is compiled, it cannot be extended.

Why

A partial type enables simultaneous development of different aspects of a type in different files. Splitting development is convenient when team members have special skills; for example, one developer may develop the properties that map a user interface, in one file, while another developer may develop complex functionality in methods that reside in another file. Or method development may be split between developers and files.

How

The type is modified with the partial modifier, and all parts must be declared with the partial modifier and reside in the same namespace. Note that a partial type may be nested. The following trivial example illustrates the concept of a partial type. Functionality for MyCar class is developed in different code files by different developers. The two files reside in the same name-space, and when the files are compiled, the functionality is combined by the compiler.

File1.cs

```
namespace ModelT
{
  //part 1
  public partial class MyCar
  {
    public void StartEngine() {;}
  }
} //end namespace
```

File2.cs

```
namespace ModelT
{
  //part 2
  public partial class MyCar
  {
    public void StopEngine() {;}
  }
} //end namespace
```

The Standard: Partial Type

> *The standard acknowledges the use of partial type where there is a requirement to split a type over multiple files but cautions that once the type is compiled, it cannot be extended.*

Generic Type (Introduced C# 2.0)

Generics introduce a flexibility that combines type safety with the ability to avoid committing to a type at design time.

What

Generics enable class, delegate, interface, and struct types, and methods to be created with type parameters that are placeholder types, which can be substituted when the type is known.

Where

Generics are commonly used in data structures—for example, collections and arrays, or in passing method parameters.

Why

Generics overcome the overhead issues of casting and boxing between types, which adversely affects performance.

How

Generics are specified within a pair of delimiters ("<" and ">") placed after the respective type or method name. When the type is known, it is substituted for the generic placeholder, as the following code snippet illustrates. Note that the method GenericMethod is declared as generic, as is its parameter. In the Main function, we vary the types of the method.

```
using System;
using System.Collections.Generic;
using System.Text;

namespace ModelT
{
  public class ModelTGenerics
  {
    public static void GenericMethod<T>(T arg)
    {
      Console.WriteLine("Calling Model T generic method, " + arg.GetType());
    }

    public static void Main()
    {
      //Call the generic method passing different types:
      GenericMethod<string>("Hallo Generics");
      GenericMethod<double>(16.75);
    }
  }
}
```

The Standard: Generic Type

> *The standard acknowledges the use of generics to reduce overhead and increase type flexibility while retaining the protection of type safety.*

CHAPTER 3

■ ■ ■

Code Development

The previous chapter focused on how code can be structured into assembly, namespace, and complex types. This chapter builds on that knowledge by focusing on how to develop the code that will use those structures. The discussion will cover development perspectives, application development methods, application architecture, class development, building a class interface, accessibility, and class fundamentals.

Development Perspectives

There are two ways of looking at application code development: developing an application or developing an enterprise. Generally, the immediate thought lies with developing an application and its functionality. However, to stop there would result in an overly narrow view, because an application is not an island: it is part of an enterprise that may host 50 or 5,000 applications, for example. The application may consume common functionality, or it may contribute functionality that is published through an integration or services layer, which in turn is consumed by other applications. So, to get the full picture of developing an application, we need to look at it not from one but from two perspectives: application and enterprise. Figure 3-1 illustrates a nonexhaustive set of issues we need to consider, and as you can see, there is a lot to consider. It should be noted that perspectives are interdependent: what can and can't be done from an application perspective impacts what is possible from an enterprise perspective, and, alternatively, what can and can't be done from an enterprise perspective impacts what is possible from an application perspective.

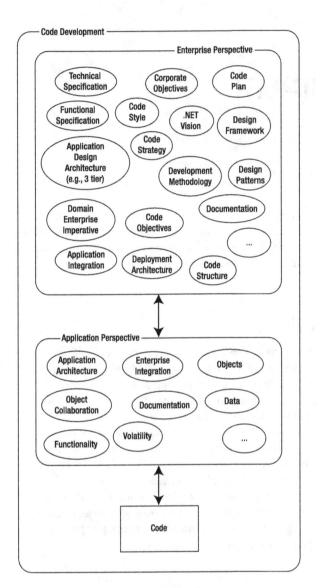

Figure 3-1. *Perspectives of code development*

We now continue our code discussion by examining two commonly used application development methods: *top-down* and *bottom-up*.

Application Development Methods

There are two methods for developing application code: top-down and bottom-up. Each method offers a different development perspective, and determining which is most appropriate is a case-by-case or application-by-application decision. It may be easier to develop a particular application one way but develop another application with a different method.

Essentially, the difference between the two methods is that the top-down method iterates development by starting with the big picture of the domain (the top) and works downward by *decomposing* the domain into assemblies, namespaces, and classes (the bottom). In contrast, a bottom-up method, which is also an iterative process, starts at the class level (the bottom) and works upward to the top, by *composing* classes, namespaces, and assemblies. Historically, object-oriented design and development theorists have advocated decomposing a complex domain into manageable units, which is a top-down method. However, many pragmatists have since recognized that there are times when starting with a vague abstraction is counter-productive and a more tangible approach (i.e., starting by developing classes) is preferred.

Tip Two books that are most useful in understanding object-oriented development are (1) *Object-Oriented Analysis and Design with Applications*, by Grady Booch (Addison-Wesley, 1994), which gives excellent coverage of the theory of object-oriented analysis and design, and (2) *Expert C# Business Objects*, by Rockford Lhotka (Apress 2003), which gives comprehensive and clear coverage of the applied aspects of object-oriented design and development.

Top-Down Method

A top-down development method is one of two commonly used approaches to develop an application (the other is the bottom-up method).

What

An application is developed as an iterative *decomposition* of the domain. The process starts with a high-level abstraction (clouds) and works downward to implementation (code).

Where

A top-down method is used in developing domain or enterprise applications.

Why

The top-down approach is commonly used because it follows a traditional object-oriented design, which advocates that complexity is best understood by starting with an abstraction and decomposing it into smaller units. However, although that approach usually works, there are times when working with an abstraction is problematic and it is more productive to start with the basics and work upward (bottom-up method).

How

The domain is viewed from the big picture, and application development is commenced by developing an architecture, then working through assemblies and namespaces to develop classes. The architecture is prepared before code is developed, and it may be tweaked as code development progresses.

The Standard: Top-Down Method

The standard acknowledges the use of the top-down development method to develop a solution by developing an application by decomposing a domain problem.

Bottom-Up Method

A bottom-up development method is one of two commonly used approaches to developing an application (the other is the top-down method).

What

An application is developed as an iterative *composition* of the domain.

Where

A bottom-up method is used in developing domain or enterprise applications.

Why

The bottom-up approach is used because it starts off more tangibly by developing small units of functionality (classes) and incrementally composes the complexity from class level to assembly level.

How

The domain is viewed from a detailed picture, and application development is commenced by developing classes and working upward to develop the structure (e.g., namespaces and assemblies). The architecture is prepared as part of code development; it evolves as a consequence of assembling the solution.

The Standard: Bottom-Up Method

The standard acknowledges the use of the bottom-up development method to develop an application by composing a domain solution.

Application Architecture

Whether a top-down or bottom-up development method is used, an application is developed with an architecture: it may be prepared before code development (top-down) or it may evolve during development (bottom-up).

What

An application architecture is a design or structural framework in which to organize application functionality. An application may reuse an application framework or template for its architecture (see the section Application Framework Solution in Chapter 7, *Design Development*) or develop it from scratch.

Where

An application architecture is used for all nontrivial application development. It is commonly used where there is a need to structure development across layers or tiers of functionality (e.g., a three-tier application architecture).

Why

By using an application architecture, the application is more able to accommodate volatility within the domain and the enterprise.

How

Regardless of which development method is used, an application architecture has to be pieced together. Figure 3-2 illustrates a nonexhaustive list of elements that are considered as part of an application architecture.

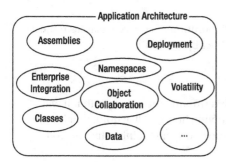

Figure 3-2. *Application architecture*

There is no definitive process for assembling an application architecture; however, the following is a guide.

- *Structure*: Decompose the domain through assemblies, then namespaces and classes.

- *Object Collaboration*: Determine how objects are expected to collaborate within the architecture. An application functions through object collaboration, so objects that need to collaborate are more efficient if they are in the same namespace or assembly.

- *Data*: Consider the most efficient way to organize an object's access to data. What is at first logical from an application perspective may have to be modified to be acceptable from an enterprise perspective (e.g., to optimize a data load–balancing algorithm).

- *Enterprise Integration*: Determine how objects will interrelate with the enterprise— determine whether they will consume and/or publish services through application and enterprise integration layer.

- *Deployment*: Consider the most appropriate deployment architecture of assemblies, to maximize efficiency, visibility, and maintainability.

- *Volatility*: Identify the likely sources of change, and design the architecture to minimize the impact of volatility—for example, by separating that volatility from nonvolatile functionality.

The previous guide is not exhaustive, and each item is not considered in isolation: often when one item (for example, data) is considered, other, related items (e.g., classes, object collaboration, and deployment) are considered in concert as the architecture is tweaked.

The Standard: Application Architecture

The standard acknowledges the use of application architecture, observing that an application developed using architecture is more likely to be efficient and maintainable, as well as better equipped to accommodate volatility within the domain and the enterprise, than is an application that is not developed using architecture.

Class Development

The functionality in an application comes from the collaboration of concrete classes (objects), so class development plays a key role in the success of the application.

What

Class development includes identifying a class's role; determining the interface that it will expose to collaborate with other concrete classes; identifying how it will acquire that interface (internal functionality or through an association—composition and/or inheritance); and building functionality using algorithms and so forth.

Where

Class development occurs within the application architecture and throughout the life cycle of the application.

Why

The class *is* the application—so class development is fundamental to the success of the application.

How

There is no standard way to develop classes. However, Figure 3-3 illustrates a number of the aspects that need to be considered.

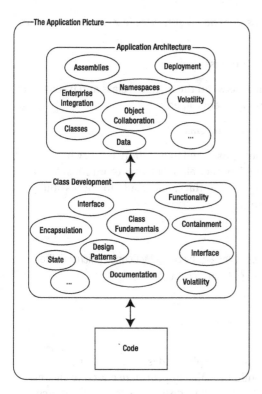

Figure 3-3. *Developing Application classes*

The classes are developed within namespaces within the application framework. There are many elements that need to be considered when developing classes, including the following:

- *Build a Class as a Collaborative Object*: Although a class is a template of an object, it is not until the class is instantiated and collaborating with other objects that the effectiveness and efficiency of the class is determined.

- *Design Patterns*: Consider whether design patterns will be of assistance in developing creational, structural, or behavioral collaborative ability.

- *Build an Interface*: Determine what functionality each class will expose for other classes to call—in other words, what collaborative role will a given concrete class play in the application?

- *Inheritance*: Consider the role of class and interface inheritance in evolving an interface and functionality of a class.

- *Composition/Containment*: Consider the role of composition or containment in evolving an interface and functionality of a class.

- *Encapsulation/Accessibility*: Consider the most appropriate way to encapsulate accessibility to functionality through modifiers.

- *State*: Identify how classes will manage state.

- *Functionality*: Code the functionality—consider code techniques (e.g., encapsulate and abstract volatility out of critical classes).

- *Unit Test*: Test the functionality exposed by the class.

- *Collaboration Testing*: Test the collaboration between the instance class and its collaborators to identify if the relationship is working as envisaged.

- *Iteration*: Iterate the design and construction of the class.

These elements are not exhaustive and are not considered in isolation; often, when one element—for example, functionality—is considered, other, related elements are considered in concert as the class is designed and developed (e.g., interface, encapsulation accessibility, design patterns, and inheritance and containment).

■**Tip** To advance your development skills, consider *Code Complete*, by Steve McConnell (Microsoft Press, 2004). It is widely acclaimed as the best book on practical software construction.

The Standard: Class Development

The standard acknowledges that class development is complex and is an iterative process in which many elements have to be considered to build the most appropriate concrete classes, including interface, encapsulation, accessibility, functionality, design patterns, inheritance, containment, and state.

Composition

Although class inheritance is powerful, it comes at a cost: it is relatively inflexible compared with composition, which offers flexibility at minimal cost.

What

Composition or *containment* refers to the practice of a concrete class acquiring functionality from internal instances of other classes; in other words, an object is composed of other objects and leverages their functionality rather than implementing or inheriting it.

Where

Composition is used where an object requires given functionality and that functionality (in part or in full) is available in another object(s).

Why

Composition is cheap! It is easy to reuse existing functionality and relatively easy to alter the functionality of a class by altering the composition of objects. Composition does, however, rely on stability of the implementation and interface of the contained objects. It is favored over inheritance because of its flexibility and because its functionality can be readily modified by varying the composition of objects—there is no hierarchy or base class to consider.

How

Composition may be specified as follows (note that the functionality is internalized and that there may be methods or properties which wrap the functionality and expose it through its interface—e.g., public methods and properties).

```
public class Automobile
{

    private eng Engine;
    private rad Radiator;

}
```

The Standard: Composition

> *The standard acknowledges the flexibility of composition in building a class interface and that it is favored over inheritance.*

Inheritance Fundamentals

We now consider the fundamentals of class and interface inheritance. A class and an interface are reference types and offer different types of inheritance.

Class Inheritance

Class inheritance is the ability to strategically and progressively structure functionality, from a root of abstraction through to a specialization or implementation.

What

.NET supports single class inheritance (that is to say, a class may inherit directly from only one other class). The C# language is not alone in adopting single class inheritance; it follows Objective-C and Java languages, for example. Class inheritance is transitive—in other words, a third-generation class may inherit the class members directly from the second (its base class) and indirectly from the first generation (note: a class may not inherit instance and static constructors, nor destructors). Although all class members are inheritable, except for the aforementioned exceptions, declared accessibility in a base class may prevent a subclass from accessing an inherited member (e.g., private variables).

A class may extend its parent class by overriding or overloading existing functionality (discussed shortly), or by adding new functionality. A class is nonvirtual by default, which means that for a subclass to override inherited functionality (indexers, methods, or properties), the base class must modify the members as virtual.

Where

To participate in class inheritance, a subclass must reside in the same compilation space as a parent class. Note, however, that if a class is modified as a `partial` type, once compiled it cannot be extended (see the section Partial Types in Chapter 2).

Why

Class inheritance offers the opportunity to strategically and progressively extend and reuse proven design and functionality.

How

Class inheritance may be specified as follows:

```
public class Car: Automobile
{;}
```

where class `Car` is the subclass (specialization) and `Automobile` is the base class (generalization or abstraction). Note that commonly, the base class (root) is defined as an `abstract` class or an `interface` type, both of which are pure abstractions. With a single class inheritance language, care must be taken in the choice of root type: a common cause of reengineering is an inappropriate selection of a base type.

The Standard: Class Inheritance

The standard acknowledges the use of class inheritance and notes that it is used to strategically and progressively extend and reuse design and functionality. It cautions that inappropriate base type selection is a common cause of reengineering.

Interface Inheritance

Interface inheritance offers the ability to define an interface that may be implemented at any level in an inheritance hierarchy (e.g., `class` or `interface` hierarchy).

What

Interface inheritance offers multiple inheritance of an interface (public members), but unlike a class, it does not offer implementation—or looked at from another perspective, it does not impose an implementation. An implementing entity must implement every member of an `interface` type, unless the inheriting entity is another `interface` type.

Why

Interface inheritance offers the opportunity to extend and reuse design by publishing a `class`, `interface`, or `struct` with a given interface. It is commonly used to signify that a type which implements it performs a role, and it may be attached at any level of a `class` or `interface` hierarchy.

Where

To participate in interface inheritance, an implementing type must reside in the same compilation space as the interface type.

How

Interface inheritance may be specified as follows:

```
//Convertible interface - note 'I' prefix
interface IConvertible
{
   void OpenRoof();
}

//Car class inherits IConvertible interface
public class Car: IConvertible
{
   //implementing OpenRoof()
   void OpenRoof()
   {//implement functionality}
}
```

The Standard: Interface Inheritance

The standard acknowledges the use of interface inheritance as a versatile means to strategically implement an interface through using multiple interface inheritance, as required.

Overriding

Overriding is the ability of a subclass to superimpose its own functionality over a virtual method.

What

Overriding is a process in which a virtual method, in a base class, has its functionality superimposed or overridden by a method, in a subclass, which has the same name and signature. A method signature comprises the method name and the number, modifiers, and types of its parameters—it does not include the return type of the method.

Why

Base or parent functionality should be generic or generalized by default; overriding is used to specialize the functionality in a given class implementation.

Where

Overriding is set up in the base class where a method is modified with the virtual keyword and is effected in a subclass, where a method is modified with the override keyword.

How

Overriding may be specified as follows:

```
//code in the base-class
abstract class Automobile
{
    //virtual or overridden member
    virtual void Start()
    {//generic start functionality for automobiles}
}

//code in the subclass
public class Car: Automobile
{
    //overriding member
    override void Start()
    {//specialized start functionality for a car}
}
```

Note The designer of the Automobile class intentionally gave the designers of derived classes (e.g., Car) a choice of whether to inherit generic Automobile start functionality or to override base functionality, by specializing the Start() method.

The Standard: Overriding

The standard acknowledges the use of overriding to specialize generic functionality.

Overloading

Overloading is the ability to include more than one method, in the same class, with the same name.

What

An overloaded method has the same name as another method, in the same class, but it has a different method signature. A method signature comprises the method name and the number, modifiers and types of its parameters—it does not include the return type of the method.

Why

Overloading gives the class developer flexibility regarding how to implement functionality and offers a low-risk way to vary or extend functionality, in an established class, without having to reengineer existing functionality or compromise the interface of a class.

Where

Overloading may occur in a base class, subclass, or interface type. It is used where the overloaded methods implement flavors of similar functionality by using different types and numbers of parameters.

How

Overloading may be specified as follows:

```
public class Car: Automobile
{
    public void Start()
    {;}

    //this method overloads Start() method
    public void Start(bool isColdStart)
    {;}
}
```

The Standard: Overloading

The standard acknowledges the use of overloading as a low-risk way to vary or extend functionality, where the overloaded methods implement similar functionality using different types and numbers of parameters.

abstract

A class or method may be modified as `abstract`, which defers implementation to a subclass.

What

The `abstract` modifier, when used on a class, signifies that the class cannot be instantiated, and when used on a method, it signifies that the method must be implemented in a subclass. A class that is not modified as `abstract` is by default abstract if it contains a method that is modified as `abstract`.

Why

A class is commonly modified as `abstract` because it represents a concept or serves as a container that holds common functionality, which may or may not be specialized by subclasses. A method is commonly modified as `abstract` because there is some logical reason to defer implementation to a subclass.

Where

The abstract modifier is used at class level or within a class at method level.

How

An abstract modifier may be specified as follows:

```
//an abstract class
abstract class Automobile
{
    //an abstract method
    abstract void Stop();

    //note: an abstract class may contain a non-abstract method
    override void Start()
    {;}
}
```

The Standard: Abstract

> *The standard acknowledges that the role of an* abstract *class is to contain generalized functionality or an interface and that the* abstract *method is used to defer implementation to a subclass.*

sealed

The keyword sealed is used to indicate that a class cannot be inherited.

What

A sealed modifier signifies that a given class cannot be derived from or inherited.

Where

The sealed modifier is placed in the type declaration.

Why

A sealed modifier is used when it is necessary to indicate that it is not logical or not permissible to extend a class, in a given domain.

How

The sealed modifier may be specified as follows:

```
sealed class RubberTube {;}
```

The Standard: sealed Modifier

The standard acknowledges the use of sealed *to indicate that it is not logical or permissible to extend a class.*

new

The keyword new is both an operator and a modifier. In the role of an operator it is used to instantiate a class; however, in the role of modifier, which is what we are interested in, it hides a derived class method or delegate.

What

A new modifier signifies that a given method or delegate hides an inherited method or delegate declared, respectively, with the same signature as a method or delegate in a base class.

Where

The new modifier is placed in the method or delegate declaration.

Why

Hiding part of an interface enables a type to evolve with its own specialization.

How

The new modifier may be specified as follows:

```
//class example
public class Car()
{ public Start(); }

public class ModelT : Car
{ new public Start(); }

//delegate example
public class Car()
{ protected delegate void DelegateX (int i); }

public class ModelT : Car
{ new delegate void DelegateX (double d); }
```

The Standard: new Modifier

The standard acknowledges the use of new *modifier to hide a derived method or delegate.*

Accessibility

In Chapter 2, we saw how accessibility may be controlled physically or logically through the use of assemblies, namespaces, and complex types; class accessibility takes that a step further. A problem that application architects and developers face in developing an object-oriented program is how to control object collaboration given that, natively, client code can call the constructor of a class and access its functionality. However, to regulate a domain, accessibility to class functionality needs to be controlled, so responsibility is used and encapsulated at assembly, class, and class member levels.

Access modifiers are used to encapsulate that responsibility, and they have an additional role: they also control the level of coupling. If client code were to become privy to the internal workings of a program or a class, then such tight coupling and lack of modularity would impact the level of flexibility of a program to accommodate change. For example, a minor change in a domain requirement may require major reengineering or refactoring of code. Access to a class and its members is controlled through declared accessibility. There are five accessibility declarations: private, protected, internal, protected internal, and public.

private

The keyword private is an accessibility declaration used to modify visibility of a type.

What

A private modifier signifies that accessibility is limited to the containing type (class). A class field, for example, is modified private, and its value is accessed indirectly through a class property.

Where

The private modifier is placed in the type declaration.

Why

A private modifier limits visibility or access to class level. It is used to comply with the encapsulation requirement of object-oriented programming, which requires that the internal workings of a class be hidden.

How

The private modifier may be specified as follows:

```
public class Car
{
    //private modifier
    private string carColor;
}
```

The Standard: private Modifier

The standard acknowledges the use of the private *modifier where there is a requirement to limit accessibility within a given class. Note that a class field should be modified* private *and its value accessed through a class property, to comply with encapsulation.*

protected

The keyword protected is an accessibility declaration used to modify visibility of a type.

What

A protected modifier signifies that accessibility is limited to the given class and to any class derived from that class.

Where

The protected modifier is placed in the type declaration.

Why

A protected modifier extends accessibility to the level of class hierarchy.

How

The protected type modifier may be specified as follows:

```
public class Car
{
   //protected modifier
   protected string somePart;
}
```

The Standard: protected Modifier

The standard acknowledges the use of the protected *modifier where there is a requirement to limit accessibility to a class hierarchy.*

internal

The keyword internal is an accessibility declaration used to modify visibility of a type.

What

An internal modifier signifies that accessibility is limited to objects within the program. Thus functionality cannot be accessed by client code outside of the assembly.

Where

The `internal` modifier is placed in the type declaration.

Why

An `internal` modifier extends accessibility to assembly or program level.

How

The `internal` type modifier may be specified as follows:

```
public class Car
{
    //internal modifier
    internal DoSomething()
    {;}
}
```

The Standard: internal Modifier

> *The standard acknowledges the use of the* `internal` *modifier where there is a require-*
> *ment to limit accessibility to other classes in the same program or assembly.*

protected internal

The keyword `protected internal` is an accessibility declaration used to modify visibility of a type.

What

A `protected internal` modifier signifies that accessibility is limited to a member(s) within a given class, a class(es) derived from that class, and a nonderived class(es) in the same assembly. The `protected internal` modifier yields `protected` *or* `internal` accessibility.

Where

The `protected internal` modifier is placed in the type declaration.

Why

A `protected internal` modifier offers a little more flexibility than `protected` by enabling objects that are not part of the class hierarchy but are resident in the same assembly or program to access functionality. It is commonly used to enable access within the given assembly yet allow functionality to appear abstract to another assembly or program.

How

The `protected internal` modifier may be specified as follows:

```
public class Car
{
    //protected internal modifier
    protected internal DoSomething()
    {;}
}
```

The Standard: protected internal Modifier

> *The standard acknowledges the use of the* `protected internal` *modifier where there is a requirement to limit accessibility to a class, a class(es) derived from that class, or other classes in the same assembly.*

public

The keyword `public` is an accessibility declaration used to declare that there is no limit to accessibility or visibility of a type.

What

A `public` modifier signifies that there is no limit to accessibility.

Where

The `public` modifier is placed in the type declaration.

Why

A `public` modifier is used when there is no need to limit access to a class. It is commonly used to define and publish the interface of the concrete class (object), which signifies how client code can collaborate with it.

How

The `public` type modifier may be specified as follows:

```
public class Car
{
    //public modifier
    public DoSomething()
    {;}
}
```

The Standard: public Modifier

The standard acknowledges the use of the public *modifier where there is a requirement not to limit accessibility to functionality by defining and publishing an interface against which client code can collaborate.*

static

The keyword static is a type modifier that is used to associate a type with a class.

What

A static type modifier signifies that a given type is a member of the class and not an instance member.

Where

The static type modifier is placed in the type declaration.

Why

A static type modifier is used when it is necessary that a class has a member that may be called independently of instantiation. A static member may be called from a class, without the class having been instantiated. Although the most obvious example is the Main() method, utility classes commonly are used to gain access to static functionality, saving the overhead of instantiating classes (refer to the technique as used in the .NET Framework, for example: System.Math).

How

The static type modifier may be specified as follows:

```
public class Client
{
    //static type modifier
    static void Main()
    {;}
}
```

The Standard: static Modifier

The standard acknowledges the use of static *to differentiate a class member from an object member and also to leverage the ability to access class functionality without the overhead of instantiation.*

Accessibility Summary

Table 3-1 summarizes .NET accessibility.

Table 3-1. *.NET Accessibility*

Item	Modifier
Class	abstract, internal, sealed, protected, private, and public.
Class members	new, private, protected, internal, protected internal, and public.
Enumeration members	Implicitly public (no access modifiers allowed on member declaration).
Interface members	Implicitly public (no access modifiers allowed on member declaration).
Namespace	Implicitly public (no access modifiers allowed on namespace declaration).
Structure members	Default is private, internal, and public (implicitly sealed).
Types	Default is internal, public (applies to types declared in namespaces or compilation units).

■**Tip** A class may contain an inner class, which may be modified as private or protected.

Class Fundamentals

We now consider the following class fundamentals: sealed and static modifiers, attribute class, class header, and class members (field, constant, delegate, enumeration, event, constructor, property, and method).

Attribute

The Attribute holds metadata that may be accessed programmatically, at runtime, to interrogate entities within an assembly.

What

An Attribute is a class that derives from class System.Attribute. It holds metadata or declarative information that is accessible, through reflection. An Attribute may be inherited; if, however, that is not desirable, then it may be modified as sealed. There are two types of attributes: intrinsic and custom. Intrinsic attributes are part of the CLR (Common Language Runtime)—for example, [serializable] or [assembly: AssemblyTitle("")]. Custom attributes are roll-your-own attributes.

Where

An `Attribute` may be applied to assembly, class, delegate, enum, event, field/member variable, interface, method, module, parameter, property, return value, or struct.

Why

An `Attribute` is an adornment that is used to add information about an element which may be accessed programmatically, at runtime.

How

Intrinsic attributes are the most commonly used attribute type, and they are specified as follows:

```
[serializable]
class Car {;}
```

However, where there may be ambiguity, such as in the case of a method (method—default value) or return value (return—default value), a default value is used with the attribute to indicate which element the attribute references, as in the following example:

```
//declare a method with an attribute using the 'method' default attribute.
[method: ThatAttribute] int MethodTwo(int i)

//declare a return value with an attribute using the 'return' default attribute.
[return: OtherAttribute] int MethodThree(int i)
```

The Standard: Attribute

> *The standard acknowledges the use of* `Attribute`, *which may be used to enrich an entity with metadata that may be accessed programmatically, at runtime.*

Class Header

The class header is used to define the high-level domain features of the entity, for which it is an abstraction.

What

A class header identifies the class: it contains the class modifier (e.g., `public`); the keyword `class`; and the name of the class.

Where

The class header is placed at the top of the class block.

Why

A class header is used to specify the visibility of the class through its modifier (public); that it is a class type; and that an object instance may be referenced explicitly by its custom type name (e.g., Car).

How

The class header may be specified as follows:

```
public class Car
{;}
```

The Standard: Class Header

The standard acknowledges the use of class header, which comprises the keyword class, modifier, and class name. It is noted that consideration may be given to using a short and generic class name that is appropriate to the domain.

const

The constant (const) is a class variable whose value is constant, and it is commonly used in simple situations.

What

A const is a static modifier, which is a value type and used on local variables or member fields; once its value is assigned, it can't be changed at runtime. A const can be used with bool, byte, char, decimal, double, enum, float, int, long, short, string, or a reference type.

Where

The const keyword is placed as the modifier in the type declaration.

Why

A const is a quick solution compared with an enum. It is commonly used in simple situations where there are one or two constants. It may also be used in situations where the underlying value of the constant needs to be a string type—an enum does not offer that functionality. In more complex situations, where there are many constants that are related (e.g., colors), an enum is commonly used.

How

A constant may be specified as follows:

```
const int wheels = 4;
```

The Standard: Constant

The standard acknowledges the use of const *in simple situations or where the underlying value has to be a* string *type.*

delegate

The delegate is a convenient way to avoid explicitly committing code to call functionality from a named object. It adds the flexibly to call methods with the same signature in different objects, by delegating the collaboration to a delegate object.

What

A delegate is a class that is a reference to a method that has a given signature (parameter list and return type) and wraps a method.

Where

The delegate keyword is placed after the modifier in the type declaration.

Why

A delegate offers an efficient way to access the functionality of another object. A given delegate may be used, by a containing object to reference different methods from different class types, as long as the signature of the methods is identical to the signature of the delegate. It is commonly used to support events, which are based on a publisher-subscribe model.

How

The delegate may be specified as follows:

```
public delegate void Change (object sender, EventArgs e);
```

The Standard: Delegate

The standard acknowledges the use of delegate *for programmatic efficiency and flexibility.*

enum

The enum (enumeration) is a convenient way to store, extend, and use related constant values.

What

An enum is a distinct value type that contains an enumerator list (a set of named numeric constants). It supports the following underlying types: byte, sbyte, short, ushort, int, uint, long, and ulong. By default its underlying type is int (Int32).

Where

The enum is commonly used in complex situations where there are many constants that are related (e.g., colors), or where there isn't a requirement for the underlying value to be a string type (in which case, use a const). It may be placed in the class file or in a separate code file, within the same namespace or referenced.

Why

An enum is an intuitive and convenient way to manage and give context to constant values. (It may also be used to harness the benefit of IntelliSense, in the Visual Studio IDE).

How

The enum may be specified as follows:

```
enum Radiator
{
    Briscoe,
    Detroit,
    McCord
}
```

■**Note** Each constant value is ended with a comma, except for the last constant value.

The Standard: Enumeration

The standard acknowledges the use of enum *in situations that are complex or where a* string *type is not required as the underlying type of each constant value (otherwise, a* const *may be used).*

event

.NET adheres to an event model based on a publisher-subscriber architecture.

What

The event is a methodology by which a class may raise a notification. It is declared as a delegate class and published by an object against which other objects subscribe by attaching or registering an event handler of the same signature (parameter list and return type) as the delegate type of the event.

Where

An event keyword is placed after the modifier in the type declaration.

Why

The event is a way by which objects may collaborate. Note: subscribers to an event may register or deregister, at runtime.

How

An event may be specified as follows:

```
//declare a delegate
public delegate void Alarm (string location);

//declare event of type delegate
public event Alarm OnOverHeating (string location);
```

The Standard: Event

The standard acknowledges the use of event *as a way for objects to collaborate.*

Field

The *field* is a variable that has a type or class level association.

What

A field is associated with a class type or with an instance of a class (i.e., object). A field modified as static is a *class* field; otherwise, it is an *instance* field.

Where

The field is commonly placed immediately below the class header, in the body of the class. It is used to hold the state of a property.

Why

Generally, a member field serves three purposes: it stores the underlying value of an object's property, in which case it is declared private; it is declared as static to hold a value for the class; or it is used as a utility variable to service requirements of the class.

How

A member field may be specified as follows:

```
public class
{
    int count;
}
```

The Standard: Field

The standard acknowledges that a field is associated with a class and is commonly used to store the underlying value of a property of an object, or if modified as static *to store a value for the class.*

Indexer

In the C# language, an *indexer* is analogous to a default property.

What

The indexer is a special kind of property that enables an object to be indexed. This enables a collection contained within the object to be accessed on the name of the object, using the this keyword.

Where

An indexer is placed in the body of a class, as a special property.

Why

The indexer offers the efficiency of a default property.

How

An indexer may be specified as follows:

```
public class Car
{
    private int[] myArray;

    //specify indexer - note the use of this operator.
    public int this[int index]
    {
        get{return myArray[index];}
        set{myArray[index] = value;}
    }
}
```

The Standard: Indexer

The standard acknowledges the use of indexer as a default property.

Method

The *method* is an object-oriented way for objects to collaborate, by sending messages (calling methods) to access functionality of another object.

What

A method is a construct that encapsulates discrete functionality of the class or object. A class may not have two methods with the same signature (method name; the number of parameters; the modifiers of the parameters; and the types of the parameters). For efficiency, methods are functional-specific and developed to minimize the overhead of chatty communication between objects.

Where

The method is commonly placed immediately below the list of properties, within the body of a class.

Why

A method represents functionality that can be accessed through the class or object. It is part of a default interface that enables an object to perform a role in an object collaboration.

How

The method may be specified as follows:

1. Singleline, where the block commences and completes on the same line as the property header.

```
public int Display (string a)  {return Console.Write ("Display " + a);}
```

2. Sameline, where the block commences on the same line as the property header and finishes on a line under the property header.

```
public int Display (string a){
        return Console.Write ("Display " + a);
}
```

3. Underline, where the block commences and completes on lines under the property header.

```
public string Display
{
   return "Display " + a;
}
```

■Tip Visual Studio 2005 introduces functionality within the Tools menu to format blocks and heaps of other stuff —refer to Visual Studio or the section Visual Studio Formatting Options in Chapter 1.

The Standard: Method

The standard acknowledges the use of a method to support collaboration between objects and notes for efficiency, methods are functional-specific and developed to minimize the overhead of chatty communication between objects.

Property

The *property* is an object-oriented way to set and get the underlying state of an object.

What

A property is a construct that acts as a facade through which client code may access the underlying value or state, which is stored in a `private` member field. In the development community, there is debate about whether a property may be substituted for a member field that is modified with `public` visibility. The two sides to the debate are:

1. The "pro public member field" argument:

    - Properties are useful only when they include functionality other than merely set and get the underlying value stored in the `private` member field (to which the property is mapped).

    - In cases where the role of the property is identical to a `public` member field, coding a property is inefficient use of a developer's time.

2. The "anti public member field" argument:

    - Using a public member field is contrary to encapsulation.

    - If, at a latter stage, domain requirements change and value checking is required, for example, then reengineering of the class is required—which may impact its interface and affect client code.

Where

The property is placed immediately below the list of events, in the body of a class.

Why

A property implements the object-oriented pillar of encapsulation, which states that the internal workings of a class are to be hidden to external code; and it offers an opportunity to add functionality (e.g., value checking). It is used where a class has state.

How

The `property` may be specified as follows, where _name is a `private` field of the class:

1. Singleline, where the block commences and completes on the same line as the property header.

```
public int Name {get { return _name; } set { _name = value; }}
```

2. Sameline, where the block commences on the same line as the property header and finishes on a line under the property header.

```
public int Name {
    get
    {
        return _name;
    }

    set
    {
        _name = value;
    }
}
```

3. Underline, where the block commences and completes on lines under the property header.

```
public int Name
{
    get {return _name;}
    set {_name = value;}
}
```

Tip Visual Studio 2005 introduces functionality within the Tools menu to format blocks and many other things—refer to Visual Studio or the section Visual Studio Formatting Options in Chapter 1.

The Standard: Property

The standard acknowledges the preferred use of property over the use of a `public` *member field, in line with the object-oriented requirement to keep the internal workings of a class or object hidden from client code.*

Variable

The *variable* is a variable that has an association at procedure level.

What

A variable is associated with a procedure. It may be categorized as a local variable in a procedure (e.g., method); an element of an array; or an input parameter (as a reference or value type) or an output parameter.

Where

A variable is placed according to its category; for example, a local variable is placed immediately below the procedure header, and an input parameter is placed within the parentheses of a procedure, as an argument.

Why

The variable is required as a utility to hold a value or reference where there is an association at procedure level.

How

A variable may be specified as follows:

```
//local variable
public Car()
{
   int wheels;
}

//variable as an element in an array
int [] x = {2,4,7};

//variable as an input parameter
public Car (int wheels) {;}

//variable as an output parameter
static void DoThis(string firstName, string secondName, out string fullName)
{
   fullName = firstName + "  " + secondName;
}
```

The Standard: Variable

The standard acknowledges the definition of variable as a variable that has a procedure-level association, as distinct from a member field, which is a variable that has a type-level association. A variable may be categorized as a local variable in a procedure (e.g., method); as an element of an array; or as an input or output parameter.

Flow Control

How objects collaborate and perform functionality is controlled by managing the flow of execution of the program. The C# language offers a standard set of tools to manage flow control, including if, if-else, nested if, switch and case, break, default, continue, goto, throw, try-catch, try-finally, and try-catch-finally.

if

The if statement is a flow control statement that contains a single condition.

What

An if statement is a conditional branching statement that redirects the flow of control only if the condition is true.

Where

The if statement may be used in a code block—for example, within a method or Main function. It is used for simple branching.

Why

An if statement permits the conditional execution of functionality, which is a common requirement of many domains.

How

The if statement may be specified as follows:

```
if (a == b)
{//do something}
```

The Standard: if

> *The standard acknowledges the use of* if *statement for simple branching.*

if-else

The if-else statement is a flow control statement that contains a single condition which explicitly identifies an alternative else statement.

What

An if-else statement is a conditional branching statement that redirects the flow of control only if the condition is true and offers an option when the condition is false.

Where

The if-else statement may be used in a code block—for example, within a method or Main function.

Why

An if-else statement permits the conditional execution of functionality that is a common requirement of many domains and offers an option when the condition is false.

How

The if-else statement may be specified as follows:

```
if (a == b)
    {//do something}
else
    {//do something different}
```

The Standard: if-else

> *The standard acknowledges the use of* if-else *statement where there is a requirement to have a single condition that explicitly identifies an alternative.*

Nested if

The nested if statement is a flow control statement that nests or contains more than one if statement.

What

A nested if statement is the nesting of a series of if or if-else statements. If used excessively it degrades readability and increases risk of logical errors—there is a preference to use a switch statement.

Where

The nested if statement may be used in a code block—for example, within a method or Main function.

Why

A nested if statement permits the layering of conditions of execution of functionality, which is a common requirement of many domains, and coupled with an nested if-else statement, it offers an option when a condition is false.

How

The nested if statement may be specified as follows:

```
if (a <10)
   {//do something
   if (a>=5)
      {//do something extra}
   }
```

The Standard: Nested if

The standard acknowledges the nested if *statement. However, it is mindful of the adverse effect that deep nesting has on readability and productivity. Where a nesting exceeds two layers, consideration may be given to using a* switch *statement or encapsulating the logic in a method.*

switch and case

The switch and case statements are a partnership of flow control statements that elegantly encapsulate a set of logical options. For efficiency, consider placing case statements in a logical hierarchy where the case statement most likely to execute is placed closest to the switch statement (although with modern compilers, the efficiency gain may be negligible). The valid types for the switch parameter are byte, char, enum-type, int, long, sbyte, short, string, uint, ulong, and ushort.

What

A switch and a case statement are paired as an alternative to nesting of if statements, and it is easily extensible without adding complexity or degrading readability. If a case statement matches the parameter passed to the switch statement, then execution is transferred to that block of code, within the case statement.

Where

The switch statement may be used in a code block—for example, within a method or Main function—and it is partnered by a set of case statements.

Why

A switch and case statement offers flexibility to build granular layers of conditions, of execution of functionality, without loss of simplicity and readability.

How

The switch-case statement may be specified as follows:

```
switch (noOfCars)
{
    case 0:
       //do something;
       break;
    case 1:
       //do something else;
       break;
    default:
       //if none of the above, then do this;
}
```

Note The use of a break statement is to explicitly terminate execution within the case block, and the use of the default label explicitly catches any condition that is not met.

The Standard: switch and case

The standard acknowledges the use of the switch *and* case *statement as a conditional execution statement in any scenario where there are two or more options or conditions.*

break

The break statement is a flow control statement that stops execution in the current block, starting from where execution moves to the next executable statement. It may be used in flow control and in iteration statements.

What

A break statement is a jump statement that causes the flow of the program to exit from the immediate code block.

Where

The break statement may be enclosed within switch, do, for, foreach, or while statements.

Why

A break statement transfers control of the program to the target of the statement (the next element in a switch statement, for example).

How

The break statement may be specified as follows:

```
if (a == b) break;
```

or

```
try{
    //do this
    break;
}
```

The Standard: break

> *The standard acknowledges the use of a* break *statement in a* switch *block as an explicit way to alter the flow of execution.*

default

The default label is a flow control statement that partners a switch and case statement to offer a default execution option.

What

A default label is a statement that offers an option of last resort in a switch block.

Where

The default label is placed as the last label in a switch block.

Why

The C# language does not permit "fall-through"; in other words, if there is no default label and control of execution falls through to the end point of a switch block, a compile error will result. Anyway, requiring a default statement makes the logic more readable.

How

A switch-case statement that shows the use of the default label may be specified as follows:

```
switch (noOfCars)
{
    case 0:
        //do something;
        break;
    case 1:
        //do something else;
```

```
        break;
    default:
        //if none of the above then do this;
}
```

The Standard: default

The standard acknowledges the use of default *label in a* switch *block to explicitly offer an option of last resort and as a way to prevent fall-through—which would result in a compile error.*

continue

The continue statement is a flow control statement that stops execution in the current block, starting from where execution moves to the next executable statement.

What

A continue statement is a jump statement that transfers the program flow to commence a new iteration of the closest do, for, foreach, or while statement.

Where

The continue statement can be found enclosed within a do, for, foreach, or while statement.

Why

A continue statement is used when it is required to recommence a loop and avoid executing the statements after the continue statement.

How

The continue statement may be specified as follows:

```
if (a == b)
{
  Console.WriteLine("At: continue");
    continue;
}
```

The Standard: continue

The standard acknowledges the use of continue *statement to commence a new iteration at the closest iteration statement.*

goto

The goto statement is a legendary redirection statement—it is not for the fainthearted!

What

A goto statement redirects the flow of control to another statement, which is marked with a label within the current code block: it transfers the control out of nested scope.

Where

The goto statement may be used in a code block—for example, within a switch statement.

Why

There are two situations in which having the ability to redirect the flow of control to a target is accepted practice: redirecting the flow of control to a case statement or to a default label.

How

A goto statement may be specified as follows:

```
switch(a)
{
    case 1:
        //do something
        break;
    case 2:
        //do something else
        goto case 1;
    case 3:
        goto default;
    default:
        //do something different
    break;
}
```

The Standard: goto

> The standard acknowledges the reluctance to use the goto statement and notes two accepted practices: using it within a switch statement to redirect the flow of control to a case statement or to a default label.

throw Statement

The throw statement is used to raise an exception, and unconditionally the control flows to the first catch clause in a try-catch block.

What

A `throw` statement is a way to signify that there is an abnormal condition, or an exception, in the program. Upon encountering the condition, the Common Language Runtime (CLR) pauses execution of the program while it seeks an exception handler. If there is no exception handler, then the CLR terminates the program.

Where

The `throw` statement is commonly found within a `try` statement, although it may be found in a method.

Why

When a program encounters an abnormal condition or exception, it should be handled. The `throw` statement is an opportunity to programmatically raise and handle exceptions in a program.

How

A `throw` statement may be specified as follows:

```
try
{
    //do something
    throw new System.Exception();
}
```

The Standard: throw

> *The standard acknowledges the use of the* `throw` *statement to programmatically raise an exception to be handled.*

try-catch

The `try-catch` statement or block is used to handle an `exception` that has been thrown.

What

The `try-catch` statement or block is a simple exception handler in which executable code may be tried and an exception(s) may be specified and subsequently handled, if applicable. Where there are several `catch` statements, for efficiency, it is preferred to arrange them in a descending hierarchy of likelihood (i.e., most likely `catch` statement is placed closest to the `try` statement).

Where

A `try-catch` statement is located in a class code block—for example, in a method.

Why

When there is the likelihood of an abnormal condition, for example, a connection to a database server may be temporarily unavailable, and then an appropriate exception may be thrown and subsequently handled (e.g., switch to another database server). To handle different types of abnormalities or exceptions, the action (e.g., connection to server) is wrapped in a try statement, and then code to handle specific types of exceptions may be placed in the catch statement.

How

The try-catch statement or block may be specified as follows:

```
try
{
    //do something

    catch (Type1Exception e)
    {//code to handle exception}

    catch (Type2Exception e)
    {//code to handle exception}

    catch (Type3Exception e)
    {//code to handle exception}

}
```

The Standard: try-catch

The standard acknowledges the use of the try-catch *statement or block where there is not a requirement for the guarantee of a* finally *statement. It is mindful of the extra resources necessary to support the* catch *statement and the benefit of arranging them in descending likelihood of occurrence.*

try-finally

The try-finally statement or block is a way to ensure that a block of code that is located in a finally block is run when execution leaves the try block.

What

A try-finally statement or block is a mechanism in which an action may be tried, without a specific catch statement, when code is placed in a finally statement that is guaranteed, by the CLR, to run, irrespective of whether an exception is thrown or not.

Where

The try-finally statement is found in a class code block—for example, in a method.

Why

Given the context, it may not be appropriate to code a catch statement and the try-finally statement or block may be sufficient. The try-finally statement or block is suitable in situations where executable code is wrapped in a try statement and it is necessary to run code, in the finally statement, regardless of whether or not an exception is thrown.

How

A try-finally statement or block may be specified as follows:

```
try
   {//do something}
finally
   {//run some code}
```

The Standard: try-finally

> *The standard acknowledges the use of the* try-finally *statement as a mechanism where it is necessary to attempt to execute a block of code (in the* try *block) and, regardless of the outcome, execute a subsequent code block (in the* finally *block).*

try-catch-finally

The try-catch-finally statement or block is a comprehensive way to handle an exception that has been thrown.

What

A try-catch-finally statement or block is a rich exception handler that facilities the wrapping of executable code in a try statement; the catching of a specific exception, in a catch statement, against which specific handler code may be written; and a finally statement in which code must run even in the event that there is no exception thrown. Where there are several catch statements, for efficiency, it is preferred to arrange them in a descending hierarchy of likelihood (i.e., most likely the catch statement is placed closest to the try statement).

Where

The try-catch-finally statement or block is located in a code block—for example, in a method.

Why

A try-catch-finally statement or block is used where there is the requirement to handle exceptions in a comprehensive manner, when a try-catch or a try-finally are inadequate.

How

The `try-catch-finally` statement or block may be specified as follows:

```
try
{
   //do something

   catch (Type1Exception e)
   {//code to handle exception}

   catch (Type2Exception e)
   {//code to handle exception}

   catch (Type3Exception e)
   {//code to handle exception}

   finally
   {//run some code}

}
```

The Standard: try-catch-finally

> *The standard acknowledges the use of* try-catch-finally *statement or block where a comprehensive exception handling methodology is a requirement. It is mindful of the extra resources necessary to support* catch *statements and the benefit of arranging them descending in likelihood of occurrence.*

Iteration

One of the ways that functionality is managed is through iteration of a given block of code or a set of controls. There is a short list of tools we can use to iterate code and controls: do-while, while, for, and foreach.

do-while

The do-while statement is a pair of iteration statements that combine to iterate a block of code at least once.

What

A do-while iterative statement manages the conditional looping or execution of an embedded statement(s) until the loop evaluates to false.

Where

The do-while statement is placed in a code block, with the do statement placed at the head of the iteration block, and the while statement placed at the tail of the iteration block.

Why

A do-while statement is used when there is a need to restrict the flow of code to iterate a set of statements at least once, until a given condition is met.

How

The do statement may be specified as follows:

```
int i = 0;

do
{
    //do something
    i++;
}

while (i < 3);
{
    //do something else
}
```

The Standard: do-while

The standard acknowledges the use of the do-while *statement where there is a requirement to iterate an iteration block at least once.*

while

The while statement is an iteration statement that iterates zero or more times.

What

A while iterative statement loops through an embedded statement. It may be used on its own or paired with a do statement.

Where

The while iterative statement is placed in a code block at the head or tail of an iteration block. A while iterative statement is used where there is a need to restrict the flow of code to iterate a set of statements until a given condition is met.

Why

If the while statement is placed at the top of an iteration block, it will iterate zero or more times; however, if it is put at the tail of an iteration block (e.g., when a do is placed at the head of the iteration block), it will run at least once.

How

The while statement may be specified as follows:

```
int i = 0;

while (i < 3) //while at head of iteration block
{
    //do something
    i++;
}
```

or refer to the do statement, discussed previously, for an example of while at the tail of an iteration block.

The Standard: while

> *The standard acknowledges the use of* while *statement where there is a requirement for iterative flexibility: to iterate zero or more times (place* while *at the head of an iteration block) or at least once (place a* while *statement at the tail of an iteration block and a* do *statement at the head of the iteration block).*

for

The for statement is an iteration statement that evaluates a set of initialization expressions and then may iterate an iteration block.

What

A for iteration statement tests for a value before entering into a loop and iterates until a condition is no longer true.

Where

The for statement is placed in a code block, with the for statement placed at the head of an iteration block.

Why

A for statement is used when there is a requirement to test a value before deciding whether or not to commence an iteration, and it uses a variable to record the number of iterations within the block.

How

The for statement may be specified as follows:

```
for (int i=0; i<10; i++)
{
    //do something
}
```

The Standard: for

> *The standard acknowledges the use of the* for *statement where there is a requirement to test a condition, by using the value in the index variable, before entering an embedded code block.*

foreach

The foreach statement is an iteration statement that enumerates a collection.

What

A foreach iterative statement enumerates each element in a collection and executes the embedded statement for each of the elements.

Where

The foreach statement is placed in a code block at the head of an iteration block.

Why

A foreach statement is useful when there is a requirement to loop through a collection of items (e.g., objects or controls).

How

The foreach statement may be specified as follows:

```
foreach (Tire t in Car)
{
    AirPump.StartPumping();
}
```

The Standard: foreach

> *The standard acknowledges the use of the* foreach *statement where there is a requirement to iterate a collection—for example, objects or controls.*

■ ■ ■

CHAPTER 4

Code Documentation

This chapter is one of a pair of chapters that look at documentation: this chapter focuses on standards for documenting code, and Chapter 8 is about documenting application design. Code documentation is managed through a documentation policy; the policy seeks to ensure that procedures are in place to assist code stakeholders (e.g., architects and developers) and to protect the organization's investment in software assets. The major risk that documentation seeks to minimize is knowledge degradation: (1) knowledge goes with the developers when they leave the team, and (2) over time, we forget the details about code that we wrote two, three, or four projects ago!

Documentation Policy

A documentation policy is a statement that contains a set of guidelines or rules to manage the documentation of code.

What

The policy seeks to coordinate and standardize code documentation across all development by requiring developers to follow a set of common guidelines or rules. Devising an implementable policy can be a difficult task because the policy has to balance two countervailing issues: the time demands on developers to develop code, against the time demands on them to document that development. However, to some degree the two tasks need not be mutually exclusive if documentation is performed as an integral part of designing and developing code, rather than as a discrete after-the-fact task. The following is a template of issues that may be considered as part of a documentation policy:

Documentation Policy Template

- Agree the scope and nature of the documentation.

- Develop a uniform documentation policy for all development.

- Review the policy regularly (e.g., every six months).

- Develop and distribute a documentation manual (online and/or hardcopy).

- Engage the whole team in developing the documentation policy.

- Require all developers to be trained in documentation.

- Consider incorporating documentation as part of the design and development phases of a project.

- Sign off on documentation and subject it to peer group and or an independent technical review (e.g., by an external IT auditor).

- Categorize documentation as code design and code development documentation. (Note that development includes code maintenance.)

- Consider housing the documentation where it is accessible to application architects and developers (e.g., Visual Studio solution) and stored safely (e.g., Visual SourceSafe).

Tip Write a policy as a set of pragmatic statements rather than as a lengthy dialog.

Where

A code documentation policy is used by all of the development teams.

Why

A documentation policy minimizes the risk of knowledge degradation.

How

A policy is the result of a consultation process among stakeholders (project managers, application architects, and developers). Once agreed on, it may be distributed as part of a documentation manual (online and/or manual).

The Standard: Development Documentation Policy

The standard acknowledges the importance of knowledge retention and that a documentation policy may be used to minimize the risk of knowledge degradation.

Documentation of Code

When documenting, code is separated into two categories: (1) code design and (2) code development. The separation recognizes the inadequacy of relying solely on code comments; although they do document code development, however, they do not document the underlying code design strategy, rationale, and structure.

Code Design Documentation

Documenting code design refers to identifying how and why the code has been designed the way that it has been.

What

Documentation of code design discusses code from a design perspective. It briefly explains the underlying strategy, rationale, and structure used in developing the code and highlights critical aspects of the design. What items are documented is a matter of site policy—for example, critical aspects only; identify design patterns used; identify important classes and their respective roles; explain design choices; identify critical dependencies; identify code fragility; and list key assumptions, and so forth. What is best documented will evolve over time, and in that regard, the adequacy of documentation may be discussed regularly in team meetings (including a discussion of a program to verify the adequacy of respective documentation).

Where

Code design documentation should be readily accessible for developers and application architects.

Why

Code design documentation enables a team to retain and share critical design knowledge that identifies and explains the underlying intention of the developers and application architects.

How

Design documentation may be written in a log file (see the section Code Design Log, later in this chapter), which may be a txt, html, or xml file and stored in a Visual Studio solution, for example. To ensure format consistency, the log may be copied from a template.

The Standard: Code Design Documentation

The standard acknowledges the importance of documenting code design so that it readily identifies and explains key aspects of the underlying code design strategy, rationale, and structure.

Code Design Log

A code design log is a simple form of documentation that is readily accessible to be referenced and updated.

What

A design log is a register in which key design information is stored. It contains documentation about modification history, assumptions, fragility, and a profile of key classes and types, for example. It may be used at solution level or folder level (e.g., UI Class folder and Utility Class folder would each contain a code design log, which documents the classes within each respective folder).

Where

A design log resides in each Visual Studio solution and/or folder that stores code.

Why

A design log is an intuitive and quick method to document design; it supports a note format that minimizes the time demands on developers and application architects. It puts the documentation where it is most convenient for application architects and developers to reference.

How

A template is prepared as a txt, xml, or html file and copied to each Visual Studio folder in which code is written. The following is a template of the contents of a code design log; it may be modified to suit the requirements of a development team (subject to policy):

```
---------------------
Code Design Log
---------------------


----------------
Log Header
----------------
Log Filename: AlgorithmAssembly
VS Solution: ModelT.Enterprise
Log Purpose: List major issues
Note: Item format: Number, [Date of Entry; Author's email address], Comment.
---------------------------
Modification History
---------------------------
1. [01/10/05; petern@modelt.com] Code classes: A,B,C,D,E.
2. ...
-------------
Overview
-------------
[01/10/05; stevek@modelt.com] All algorithms are coded in "algorithm" classes, which
 are subsequently contained in client classes.
2. ...


------------------
 Assumptions
------------------
1. [01/10/05; andrewb@modelt.com] Monetary precision is to the nearest dollar.
2. ...
```

```
----------------------------------------
```
Type Roles and Relationships
```
----------------------------------------
```
1. [01/10/05; billb@modelt.com] EngineAssemblyAlgorithm has seven classes which
participate in this algorithm (A,B,C,D,E,F,G). Class C is the controller
class, while class A and B ...
2. ...

```
--------------------
```
Design Patterns
```
--------------------
```
1. [01/10/05; sammyc@modelt.com] Strategy Pattern (Classes A,B,C..F);
(Class A, B, C, D, E);
2. ...

```
----------
```
Types
```
----------
```

```
----------
```
Classes
```
----------
```
1. [01/10/05; sammyc@modelt.com] Class 'AC' is an abstract controller class (MVC). A
 controller
class is used to manage algorithm worker classes and view and data requirements.
2. ...

```
----------
```
Structs
```
----------
```
1. [01/10/05; sammyc@modelt.com] Struct 'B' represents the attributes which comprise
 an
engine. An abstract class has not been used in this instance because...
2. ...

```
-----------
```
 Interface
```
-----------
```
1. [01/10/05; billb@modelt.com] IAccessory represents the base interface for the
hierarchy
of accessory types.
2. ...

```
----
```
...
```
----
```

The Standard: Code Design Log

The standard acknowledges the use of a code design log as an intuitive and quick method to document code design. It may be prepared as a txt, xml, or html template and stored inside a folder within a Visual Studio solution, for example.

Documentation of Code Development

There are four types of documentation of code development commonly used: line comments, block comments, XML comments, and object browser comments.

Line Comment

A line comment uses a delimiter (e.g., "//") to signify that the line of code is a comment line and is not part of the compilation.

What

The line comment is a comment that takes up all or part of a single line in a code module (e.g., class or code file). Where a comment requires more than one line, several line comments may be stacked line after line, as an alternative to a block comment.

Where

A line comment is placed above a line of code with *no* line space between the comment and the code, and one or no spaces between the delimiter and the start of the comment. A line comment may also be placed at the end of a line of code.

Why

The line comment is a convenient way for a developer to document or signify something that is noteworthy about a line or block of code.

How

A line comment may be placed above a line of code, specified as:

```
// Note: integer is used and not double.
int noTires;
```

or a line comment may continue over multiple lines:

```
// Note: integer is used and not double -- car has five tires,
// which includes the spare tire. Write Property setter code to limit
// the number of tires to five, per car.
int noTires;
```

or a line comment may be placed at the end of the line of code:

```
int noTires = 0; // always assign a default value
```

The Standard: Line Comment

> *The standard acknowledges the use of the line comment, which may be used as a single line comment, a multiline comment, or an end-of-line comment.*

Block Comment

A block comment uses an opening and closing delimiter to identify a block of comments.

What

The block comment is a multiline comment used for large comments running over multiple consecutive lines.

Where

A block comment is placed above the block of code with *no* line spacing between the last line of the comment block and the first line of the code.

Why

The block comment is a convenient way for a developer to document or signify something that is noteworthy about a block of code.

How

A block comment uses opening ("/*") and closing ("*/") delimiters, which may be specified as:

```
/*
The following block of code manages data access to a SQL Server database. The
code, below, is wiring which leverages the data access classes, which are
referenced from the ModelT.Enterprise.DataManager DLL. Note that data access
classes rely on the file ConnectionString.XML which resides in the 'Data' folder.
If you need to modify the connection string, then do so using that file.
*/
DataSet ds = new ModelT.Enterprise.DataManager.Open("DS", "spSalesHistory");
...
```

The Standard: Block Comment

> *The standard acknowledges the use of the block comment where documentation is extensive. However, it notes that Visual Studio's line comment tool may be a more convenient method to comment blocks.*

XML Comment

An XML comment is a supplement to the line and block code comments. Using an add-in tool (e.g., Visual Studio XML Documentator), XML comments can be published to an HTML page and object browser.

Caution Visual Studio 2005 Beta 2 and RC were used in preparing this book. At that time the XML Documentator tool was not available. The discussion and following example use the tool in an earlier version of Visual Studio. It is noted, however, that a freeware XML Documentator tool is available at http://ndoc.sourceforge.net.

What

The XML comment is a single line or block of XML comments, visible within or external to a code module—unlike a line or block comment, which is not visible outside of the code module.

Where

An XML comment is placed above a line or block of code with *no* line spacing between the XML comment and the first line of code.

Why

The XML comment is a convenient way for a developer to publish documentation externally. Note, however, that XML comments can be verbose.

How

An XML comment uses a comment delimiter, which may be specified as:

```
/// <summary>
/// Note: integer is used and not double -- car has 4 tires.
/// </summary>
int noTires;
```

or a line comment to carry a comment over more than one line:

```
/// <summary>
/// Note: integer is used and not double -- car has five tires,
/// which includes the spare tire. Write Property setter code to limit
/// the number of tires to five, per car.
/// </summary>
int noTires;
```

Note Visual Studio automatically inserts "<summary>" and "</summary>" tags, when you key in the xml delimiter ("///").

The Standard: XML Comments

The standard acknowledges the use of XML comments as a form of internal and external code documentation.

Object Browser Comments

An object browser comment is a comment that resides in Visual Studio's object browser window (refer to Figure 4-5 for a screenshot of object browser comments).

What

The object browser comments is a type of documentation that Visual Studio automatically publishes in object browser as part of the process of using the XML Documentator tool.

Where

An XML comment is placed immediately above the signature of a type or a member of a complex type.

Why

An object browser comment is a valuable form of type documentation because it publishes the documentation in the IDE, which makes it readily accessible for developers and application architects.

How

An XML comment is placed immediately above the signature of a type or a member of a complex type definition. An object browser comment uses an XML delimiter, which may be specified as:

```
/// <summary>
/// Note: integer is used and not double -- car has 5 tires.
/// </summary>
int noTires;
```

or over more than one line:

```
/// <summary>
/// Note: integer is used and not double -- car has five tires,
/// which includes the spare tire. Write Property setter code to limit
/// the number of tires to five, per car.
/// </summary>
int noTires;
```

The Standard: Object Browser Comments

The standard acknowledges the use of object browser comments as a form of internal and external type documentation, and notes that it conveniently publishes the documentation in the Visual Studio IDE, which makes it readily accessible for developers and application architects.

XML and Line/Block Comments

Should XML comments replace line/block comments? Although XML comments have great advantages (e.g., they are easy to publish to object browser or HTML pages), they do have a minor downside: they can be verbose—which may or may not be okay—and they cannot be tagged onto the end of a code line. So, there will be situations where you may want to use all three comment tools rather than put everything in an XML comment.

What

XML and line/block comments are documentation methods that serve different purposes (discussed earlier). When used in a partnership, they offer the developer a rich choice of tools.

Where

XML comments may be used whenever documentation needs to be published externally; otherwise line/block comments may be more convenient.

Why

Because XML comments tend to be verbose, there are times when line/block comments are a more appropriate choice for a small comment (e.g., at the end of a code line).

How

XML and line/block comments may be combined to document code development, as in the following example:

```
namespace ModelT.Enterprise.Vehicle
{
    /*********************************************
    In this code file is the definition of
    enumerators,
    Car and Radiator.
    *********************************************/
    // Enumerators - leave a blank line else the XML comment
    // is ignored by Visual Studio

    /// <summary>
    /// Note: that there is only one color
    /// on offer.
    /// </summary>
```

```csharp
enum CarColor
{
  Black
}

/// <summary>
/// Car class is used to instantiate a Model T
/// car, regardless of model type.
/// </summary>
public class Car
{
  // Private fields
  int _wheels;

}

public class Radiator
{
  // Private fields
  private double radiatorCapacity;


  // Methods

  /// <summary>
  /// Call FitRadiatorCap() to
  /// fit the radiator cap to the
  /// radiator.
  /// </summary>
  public void FitRadiatorCap()
  {
    ;
  }

  // Properties

  /// <summary>
  /// Radiator capacity, represents
  /// maximum number of pints of water.
  /// </summary>
  public double RadiatorCapacity
  {
    get {return radiatorCapacity;}
    set {radiatorCapacity = value;}
  }

}
}//end namespace
```

Code Comment Template

Consider copying a code documentation template (shown next) into a class or code file template, and then when the class or code file template is reused, the outline of the documentation is automatically available to the developer.

```
namespace ModelT.Enterprise.Vehicle
{

    /*********************************************
     * namespace header section
     * -------------------------------------------
     *
     * place comments here
     *********************************************/


    /*********************************************
     *  interface section
     * -------------------------------------------
     *
     * place comments here
     *********************************************/



    /*********************************************
     *  struct section
     * -------------------------------------------
     *
     * place comments here
     *********************************************/
    /// <summary>
    /// struct comments go here
    /// </summary>
    struct Engine
    {
      // private fields
      private int _piston;
      private int _valve;

      //properties
      /// <summary>
      /// Piston comments go here
      /// </summary>]
      public int Piston
      {
        get{ return  _piston; }
```

```
    set{ _piston = value; }

  }

  /// <summary>
  /// Valve comments go here
  /// </summary>
  public int Valve
  {
    get{return _valve; }
    set{ _valve = value; }

  }

}

/********************************************
 *  class section
 *  -----------------------------------------
 *
 * place comments here
 ********************************************/


/* ******************************************
 *  ...
 *  -----------------------------------------
 *
 * place comments here
 ********************************************/

}//end namespace ModelT.Enterprise.Vehicle
```

The Standard: XML and Line/Block Comments

The standard acknowledges the partnership of XML and line/block comments in documenting code.

Visual Studio XML Comment Tool

Publishing XML comments as HTML pages and as type descriptions in object browser is done using Visual Studio. If you do not have a version of Visual Studio with the XML Comment Tool (Build Comment Web Pages), which is accessed via the Tools menu, then you may want to download a freeware tool (http://ndoc.sourceforge.net/).

The following screenshots walk you through the process of using the in-built functionality of Visual Studio, to develop HTML files that can be used outside of Visual Studio (perhaps in a developer portal) and documentation that is automatically added to the object browser.

Note Visual Studio 2005 Beta 2 and RC were used in preparing this book. At that time the XML Documentor tool was not available. The following example uses Visual Studio 2003. (Obviously, this anticipates that the XML Comment tool will be included in the final release—fingers crossed. If not, then consider the freeware tool mentioned previously.) Also note that the following example is an illustration and is not included with the code download for the book. To experiment with the XML Documentor tool, develop a simple test application and use it.

---

1. Select "Build Comment Web Pages" from the Tools menu (see Figure 4-1).

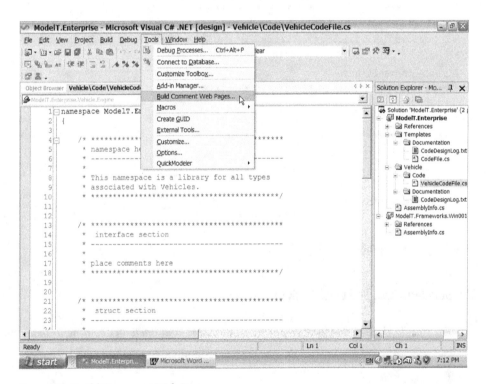

Figure 4-1. *Build Comment Web Pages*

2. Accept the default "Build for entire Solution" option. Selecting this option will create a set of external HTML files at your default location, or if you prefer you can create a documentation folder on your C drive or at a server location (I have chosen to create a folder on the C drive, for illustrative purposes). Note that the HTML file will open up automatically, in Visual Studio, once you have finished Step 2 (see Figure 4-2).

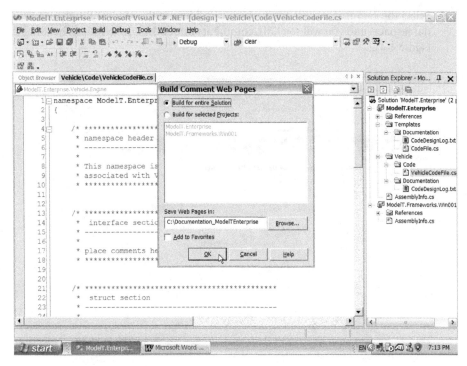

Figure 4-2. *Build for entire Solution*

3. On the HTML page, click the ModelT.Enterprise.Vehicle project hyperlink (see Figure 4-3).

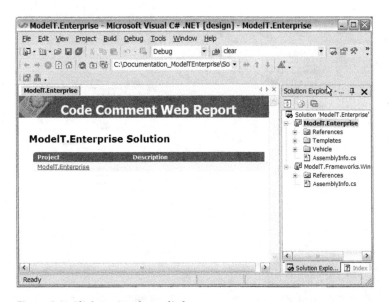

Figure 4-3. *Click Project hyperlink*

4. Select the `Radiator struct` type, which is resident in the ModelT.Enterprise.Vehicle namespace, and you will see XML comments under the "Description" heading (see Figure 4-4).

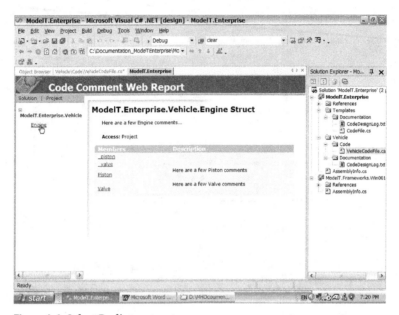

Figure 4-4. *Select Radiator structure*

5. Notice that the XML comments have been published to the "Summary" section, in the Object Browser window (see Figure 4-5).

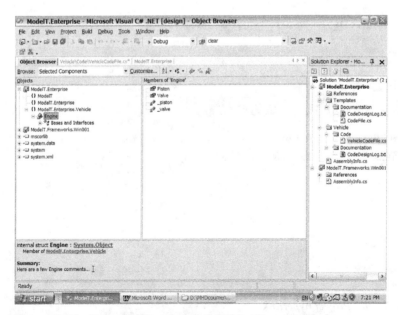

Figure 4-5. *The "Summary" section in the Object Browser window*

■ ■ ■

Design Policy Standards

This part of the book discusses design policy standards by looking at design style, code management, structure, development, and documentation.

CHAPTER 5

■ ■ ■

Design Policy

Chapter 1 contained a discussion of code policy, which is used to manage the important aspects of *code*. This chapter examines policy as it relates to *design* and identifies how *architecture* is used to manage the enterprise.

What

A design policy is a plan that is used to identify and manage the important aspects of architecture—it expresses how an enterprise will be configured to support the technical and functional objectives implicit in an organization's business strategy.

Where

A design policy is applied across the enterprise, and it may extend to stakeholders.

Why

A policy is an effective and efficient way to coordinate the management of a range of interrelated architectures (e.g., enterprise, application, data, and network architectures), each with different dynamics.

How

A design policy, like a code policy, doesn't have a definitive structure; it is developed around how best to coordinate the enterprise, which will vary on a case-by-case basis. A structure may be developed around a set of design objectives and use a design style to implement them. Figure 5-1 illustrates a design policy that licenses the open-source architecture framework (TOGAF) standard and uses a set of in-house standards that complement the architecture framework.

Note TOGAF is a methodology that uses an architectural framework to manage a set of architectures across an enterprise. TOGAF is open-source technology that is available from The Open Group (www.opengroup.org) through a public licensing arrangement. Members of The Open Group include IBM, HP, SAP, Intel, OMG, Apple Computer, Oracle, Computer Associates International, Sun Microsystems, NASA, the U.S. Department of Defense, and Citigroup.

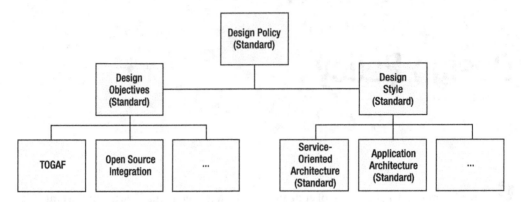

Figure 5-1. *Design policy structure*

The Standard: Design Policy

The standard acknowledges that a design policy is an effective and efficient way to coordinate the management of a range of interrelated architectures that have different dynamics.

Design Objectives

A design policy relies on a set of objectives to express how it is implemented across the enterprise.

What

Design objectives identify what is necessary to satisfy the requirements of the design policy.

Where

Design objectives form part of the design policy.

Why

Objectives are important because they express how a policy statement will be realized in concrete terms.

How

Each policy statement is considered in terms of architecture—what needs to be done to fulfill a given policy statement. For example, a policy statement might say: "The enterprise is to be designed to maximize loose coupling." From that statement one considers the implications and prepares a set of objectives, such as the following:

- Objective # 020: Implement a service-oriented architecture (enterprise services)

- Objective # 030: Integrate applications through an application integration layer

- Objective # . . .: etc.

The Standard: Design Objectives

The standard acknowledges that design objectives are an essential part of managing the design of an enterprise because they identify in concrete terms what needs to be done.

Design Style

This section discusses *design style*, which refers to the arrangement of architecture.

What

A design style describes the use of an architecture framework and architectures (e.g., data and network architectures) to style an enterprise.

Where

A design style is used across the enterprise, and it may extend to stakeholders.

Why

A design style coordinates architecture decision making, across all architectures, to ensure that the enterprise is and remains structured in a way that complements an organization's (dynamic) business strategy.

How

Developing a design style involves several key steps: (1) choose an architecture framework (e.g., TOGAF)—a methodology to manage a set of architectures; (2) identify a target architecture—how the enterprise will look in 12 to 24 months; (3) prepare a gap analysis—what needs to be done to get from the present situation to the target or destination architecture; (4) develop a roadmap; (5) develop a migration plan; and (6) implement the roadmap.

The Standard: Design Style

The standard acknowledges the use of design style, which seeks to ensure that the enterprise is and remains structured in a way that complements an organization's (dynamic) business strategy.

Architecture Framework

An enterprise is managed through architecture. An architecture framework orchestrates a set of architectures that manage the specialist technical areas of an enterprise (e.g., software, data, or network development).

What

An architecture framework is a tool that defines and strategically aligns specialist architectures (e.g., network, application, integration, and data architectures). A small set of architecture framework tools are recognized as international standards, including Zachman, C4ISR/DoDAF, FEAF, and TOGAF.

Where

An architecture framework sits across the enterprise.

Why

An enterprise needs to be strategically managed, in line with a business strategy, and an architecture framework is a tool that can be used to regulate the enterprise consistent with the technical and functional requirements implicit in a business strategy.

How

An architecture framework is selected from a set of recognized international standards and implemented. Implementation includes defining a target architecture, undertaking a gap analysis, preparing an architecture roadmap, and applying an architecture development methodology.

The Standard: Architecture Framework

The standard acknowledges the use of an architecture framework to strategically use architecture to manage an enterprise.

Target Architecture

The framework manages architectural change through the definition of its target architecture, which expresses the future structure of the enterprise.

What

A target architecture is the architecture that an organization wants to have at a future point in time, to support a business strategy.

Where

A target architecture is part of the architecture framework.

Why

A design policy has to accommodate the changes in a business strategy that impact functional and technical objectives, and this often means that an architecture needs to adapt. The target architecture encapsulates and coordinates change as a version or iteration of the enterprise and avoids the high risk associated with implementing structural change in an impulsive or ad hoc manner.

How

The architecture framework defines the target architecture and manages the impact of technical and functional change across an enterprise.

The Standard: Target Architecture

> *The standard acknowledges that the target architecture encapsulates and coordinates change as a version or iteration of the enterprise and avoids the high risk associated with implementing structural change in an impulsive or ad hoc manner.*

Architecture Roadmap

To move an existing architecture to a target architecture, the technical team follows an architectural roadmap.

What

An architectural roadmap identifies the *when, what,* and *how* of an existing architecture being migrated to a target architecture.

Where

An architecture roadmap is part of the architecture framework.

Why

A roadmap acts as a guide by which tasks can be readily identified and sequenced.

How

An enterprise architecture or team of architects, in consultation with technical staff (e.g., application developers and network and data administrators), defines a roadmap in which tasks are identified, sequenced to be progressively iterated, as milestones, to eventually arrive at the target architecture.

The Standard: Architecture Roadmap

> *The standard acknowledges the use of an architecture roadmap as a guide to migrating an existing architecture to a target architecture.*

Architecture

An architecture is a structure that organizes artifacts into a cohesive system.

What

An architecture is defined as "the fundamental organization of a system, embodied in its components, their relationships to each other and the environment, and the principles governing its design and evolution" (ANSI/IEEE Std 1471–2000).

Where

An architecture resides within an architecture framework. Common types of architectures presented as standards are as follows:

- Enterprise architecture—defines the technology structure that represents the organization; it may cross stakeholder domains.

- Network architecture—defines the structure of a network of servers within an enterprise.

- Technical architecture—defines middleware software.

- Application architecture—defines application design, development, and integration.

- Data architecture—defines the structure of physical and logical data; how it is stored, accessed, and distributed within the enterprise.

- Deployment architecture—defines the deployment of applications on network nodes within the enterprise, or it may cross stakeholder domains (e.g., remoting).

- Integration architecture—describes how applications that are internal and external of the enterprise share functionality and data.

- Service-oriented architecture—defines a type of integration architecture premised on loose coupling, which distributes functionality and data as published services.

- Business architecture—defines business and technical objectives, and IT governance and business processes.

Why

An architecture is an efficient and effective way to manage the artifacts of an enterprise, as it wraps complexity by presenting a simple interface through which activity may be coordinated.

How

An architecture is prepared in the context of its role (e.g., a service-oriented architecture has an integration-services role) within an architecture framework, which is determined by the technical and functional objectives of a business strategy.

The Standard: Architecture

The standard acknowledges the use of architecture to manage enterprise artifacts in line with technical and functional objectives.

Enterprise Architecture

Defines the structure that represents the enterprise, which may cross stakeholder domains.

What

An enterprise architecture is an architecture that coordinates technology, across the enterprise, in line with a given business strategy.

Where

An enterprise architecture resides within an architecture framework and spans an organization or across organizations.

Why

Technology is complex, particularly when it expands not only an organization's domain but across stakeholder domains. An enterprise architecture is an efficient and effective way to manage technology in line with a business strategy.

How

An enterprise architecture is prepared in the context of its role within an architecture framework, which is determined by the technical and functional objectives of a business strategy.

The Standard: Enterprise Architecture

The standard acknowledges the use of enterprise architecture as an efficient and effective way to manage technology, across an enterprise, in line with a business strategy.

Network Architecture

A network architecture is an artifact of an enterprise architecture.

What

Network architecture defines the structure of a network of servers within an enterprise.

Where

A network architecture resides within an architecture framework and spans an organization or across organizations.

Why

A network of servers needs to be structured and managed in a manner that supports the software, technology, data, and deployment architecture, and this can be done through architecture.

How

A network architecture is designed and maintained on the basis of the support requirements of software, technology, data, and deployment architectures.

The Standard: Network Architecture

> *The standard acknowledges the use of network architecture as a tool to support the strategic requirements of software, technology, data, and deployment architectures, within the context of an architecture framework.*

Technical Architecture

A technical architecture is an artifact of an enterprise architecture.

What

A technical architecture comprises middleware software, which is software that performs the role of an intermediary between two discrete artifacts. Commonly the Model–View–Controller (MVC) design pattern is used as an *architecture design pattern* to implement decoupling between architectures. MVC is discussed in Chapter 9.

Where

A technical architecture resides within an architecture framework and spans an organization or across organizations.

Why

The use of middleware promotes loose coupling and minimizes the risk of duplicating functionality, by abstracting the functionality into a central service to which artifacts may subscribe.

How

Functionality is published as a service and not duplicated and coupled to an application's implementation. For example: rather than write similar data functionality in many Web pages that couple the pages directly to the interface of a database, the functionality is abstracted to data service middleware, which acts as an intermediary between the pages and the data source. In the event of change to the interface of the database, the maintenance is confined to the relationship between the middleware and the database, leaving the interface exposed by the middleware to its clients (the Web pages) unchanged. Generally, it costs less to maintain middleware than multiple clients.

The Standard: Technical Architecture

The standard acknowledges the use of technical architecture as an efficient and effective way to maximize decoupling and minimize duplication, within the context of an architecture framework.

Application Architecture

A software or application architecture is an artifact of an enterprise architecture.

What

An application architecture is a blueprint for application design, development, and integration.

Where

An application architecture resides within an architecture framework and spans an enterprise.

Why

An application architecture ensures applications are designed, developed, and integrated consistently, which minimizes the risk of nonconformity and exposure to additional costs of maintenance and reengineering.

How

Application architectures are commonly designed as application frameworks or templates from which applications are developed as implementations of the framework or template. The framework contains prebuilt common enterprise functionality, which reduces development to adding specific application functionality and specializing enterprise functionality, as required.

The Standard: Software or Application Architecture

The standard acknowledges the use of application architecture as an efficient and effective way to manage application design and development within the context of an architecture framework.

Data Architecture

Data architecture is an artifact of an enterprise architecture.

What

Data architecture defines the structure of physical and logical data and how it is stored, accessed, and distributed within and across domains (e.g., nontransactional data is denormalized and stored in a warehouse [OLAP], and it may be published as Web services).

Where

A data architecture resides within an architecture framework and spans an enterprise or across enterprises.

Why

A data architecture is an efficient and effective way to manage and protect the investment in data and information.

How

Data is modeled physically and logically and stored in repositories (e.g., database and warehouse), from where it is distributed in a timely and efficient manner to clients.

The Standard: Data Architecture

The standard acknowledges the use of data architecture as an efficient and effective way to support information requirements within the context of an architecture framework.

Deployment Architecture

A deployment architecture is an artifact of an enterprise architecture.

What

Deployment architecture defines the deployment of applications or functionality and data on network nodes. For example, although it may be logical to deploy functionality and data to a given server, owing to high transaction volumes it may be more efficient (e.g., responsive) to replicate or split functionality and data across multiple servers to better balance peak workloads.

Where

A deployment architecture resides within an architecture framework; it spans a domain network or may cross stakeholder domains.

Why

A deployment architecture plays an important role in defining distribution and accessibility to enterprise functionality and data.

How

A deployment architecture is designed to complement the requirements of an enterprise architecture by deploying functionality in an optimal manner that promotes efficiency, reliability, and security.

The Standard: Deployment Architecture

The standard acknowledges the use of deployment architecture as an efficient and effective way to deploy functionality and data throughout an enterprise within the context of an architecture framework.

Integration Architecture

Integration architecture is a methodology by which artifacts within a domain or across domains are integrated.

What

Integration architecture describes how applications share functionality and data. Commonly, there are two types of integration architecture: synchronous and asynchronous. Hub-n-spoke (including Web services) is synchronous, and integration is tightly coupled to an interface. A message bus is an example of asynchronous integration that is loosely coupled (the consumer of the service does not know the source of the functionality—it only has to know the message protocol and which queue to send the message to).

Where

An integration architecture resides within an architecture framework; it spans a domain network or may cross stakeholder domains.

Why

Integration architecture is critical because it defines how application functionality and data are moved within and across domains. The choice of integration architecture (synchronous and asynchronous) may significantly impact the efficiency and effectiveness of an enterprise to meet the requirements of a business strategy.

How

Asynchronous integration acts through an interim layer or middleware that decouples the client from the provider. By contrast, with hub-n-spoke integration the client integrates directly with the provider. Commonly the Model–View–Controller (MVC) design pattern is used as an *architecture design pattern* to implement decoupling between architectures. MVC is discussed in Chapter 9.

The Standard: Integration Architecture

The standard acknowledges the use of integration architecture as an efficient and effective way to manage the integration of functionality and data throughout an enterprise within the context of an architecture framework.

Service-Oriented Architecture

Service-oriented architecture (SOA) is premised on providing or publishing functionality or data as a service against which clients subscribe.

What

SOA is synonymous with Enterprise Application Integration (EAI) and is a type of integration architecture that is loosely coupled and through middleware supports asynchronous and synchronous communication between publisher and subscriber.

Where

SOA resides within an architecture framework; it spans a domain network or may cross stakeholder domains.

Why

SOA offers an enterprise the opportunity to integrate using either asynchronous or synchronous communication. In domains where there are large transaction volumes or complex transactions, SOA's ability to support asynchronous communication has a lower risk profile than synchronous transaction support.

How

SOA may be designed as follows: hub-n-spoke, Web service, or message bus. The hub-n-spoke model (Figure 5-2) is the traditional synchronous model used to share functionality, where the hub is a server and the entities are client applications. Although functionality is reused, access is limited to a LAN/WAN architecture. The entities (clients) are coupled to the interface of the server (hub); using a hub in peak times may impact performance.

A Web service model (Figure 5-3) is a variation of the hub-n-spoke model, as it, too, is a synchronous model; however, it is not restrained by LAN/WAN, as it leverages Internet technology to distribute services. The entities (clients) are coupled to the interface of the Web service.

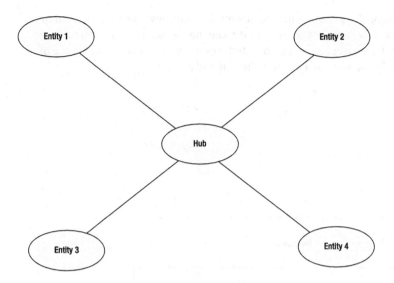

Figure 5-2. *Hub-n-spoke*

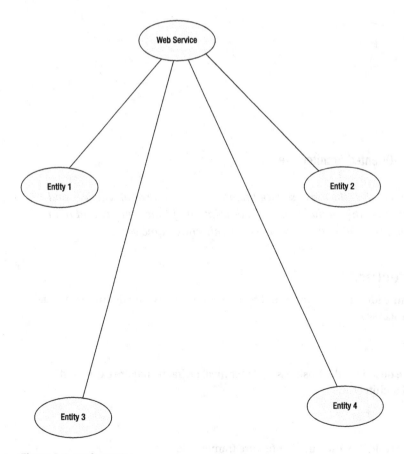

Figure 5-3. *Web service*

The message bus (Figure 5-4) is an asynchronous model which leverages queues and messages, where functionality is accessed by sending and receiving messages via a given message queue. The entities (clients) are not coupled to an interface—they do not know the source of the functionality, they only know about a message format and a queue.

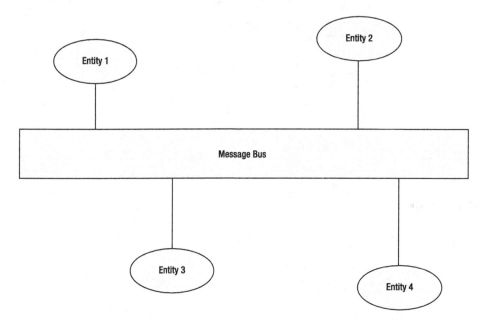

Figure 5-4. *Message bus*

The Standard: Service-Oriented Architecture

> *The standard acknowledges the use of service-oriented architecture as an efficient and effective way to manage the publication and subscription of functionality and data throughout an enterprise within the context of an architecture framework.*

Business Architecture

The business architecture identifies business and technical objectives, and defines IT governance and business processes.

What

A business architecture describes the business and technical artifacts that are expressed through a hierarchy of architectures.

Where

A business architecture resides within an architecture framework.

Why

A business architecture identifies the strategic purpose that unites and coordinates the set of architectures used to manage and safeguard the enterprise.

How

A business architecture is developed by a software development committee, an architecture committee, and an IT governance committee. The software development and architecture committees are responsible for supervising the implementation and management of the business architecture; however, they are accountable to the IT governance committee for its performance.

The Standard: Business Architecture

The standard acknowledges the use of business architecture to identify a strategic purpose to unite and coordinate a set of architectures to manage and safeguard the enterprise.

CHAPTER 6

Design Structure

The previous chapter introduced the concept of managing design *strategically* using a policy that seeks to coordinate design across an enterprise to marshal resources in line with the business strategy of the organization. We now look at how strategy is applied in the way we structure design across an enterprise. That is done by discussing structural design and the underlying concepts, such as the Enterprise-Domain design dichotomy, modularity, coupling, and layers. Design is given a context and structure with a framework.

Structural Design

Structural design is concerned with managing the design of a large structure that is a composite of smaller structures, which themselves may be composite structures. Given that an enterprise can be very large and complex, we use structure to decompose the complexity into units or modules of specialty, which are orchestrated towards a shared objective. We are familiar with the concept of structural design, but in a smaller way, in user interface development. When we design a page class as a container of other classes (e.g., text boxes and buttons), we structurally design for a specific role: for example, we use structural design when we design a page class as a container to hold other classes specific to a login page of a website. However, in the matter before us, the container is instead an enterprise architecture, which is an abstraction of the enterprise, and the controls are smaller architectures, which are represented by layers or tiers that contain artifacts, such as applications and servers.

What

Structural design is a methodology that is used to design a container structure and its constituent substructures.

Where

In situations where there is complexity, structure is used to decompose that complexity by encapsulating related functionality (e.g., applications or network servers) into containers or layers, for example.

Why

Structures are organized or designed as a system of orchestrated structures, so that they may achieve a given objective in an efficient and effective manner.

How

Structural design is guided by a design policy, which encourages coordinating the design of a set of structures within a context using a framework.

The Standard: Structural Design

> *The standard acknowledges the design and management of an enterprise through the use of a structural design methodology.*

The Enterprise-Domain Dichotomy

An everyday question is when is functionality better designed and exposed as an enterprise service or encapsulated as domain functionality? For example, is it better to access data from a database by developing generic enterprise functionality and then permit variability by over-riding that functionality in an application, or should each application manage the whole data access process itself?

What

The enterprise-domain dichotomy recognizes the design dilemma that architects and developers grapple with: What functionality is better defined as enterprise or domain functionality?

Where

The dichotomy is present throughout the enterprise wherever the same or similar functionality is required by multiple applications, or similar functionality is required within a given application.

Why

It is not always obvious when functionality has an enterprise implication. Often, with hindsight, it may have been better to design an application not as a domain application, but as abstract functionality in the enterprise services layer or platform. However, using an enterprise or services option consumes more design and development resources, and the last thing that we want to do is waste resources by cluttering enterprise services with functionality that turns out not to be sufficiently enterprise in nature. On the other hand, while "domain" functionality that turns out to have an "enterprise" role may be migrated from the domain to the enterprise services layer, which is a common practice, that may be expensive and disruptive.

How

The ways that the dichotomy is handled may be classified using the following terminology: *proactive code review*, *reactive code review*, and *passive code review*. A *proactive* code review requires that all proposed functionality is reviewed to determine whether there is an enterprise implication, as a preliminary to design and development. Often, an "in-house" cutoff rule may be used as a measure to determine whether functionality is a candidate for an enterprise service; for example, if there is a reasonable likelihood that given functionality may be used three or more times (in one or multiple applications), then it qualifies to be designed and developed as enterprise functionality. A *reactive* code review requires that if functionality fails the proactive review (i.e., it was considered that it would be used once or twice), then it is developed as domain code, where maximum use is made of variable or discretionary coupling (see the section "Coupling" later in this chapter) and maximum use is made of generalization (i.e., programming against abstract classes and interface types). Then, if subsequently it emerges that the functionality has been used three times, consider migrating the functionality into the services layer and referencing it by the domain application. Finally, a *passive* code review is the extreme high-risk option: don't review code from an enterprise perspective (in other words, ignore the dichotomy). That option exposes the organization to the cost of duplication, likelihood of application lock-ins, and reengineering or application replacement in the future. The terminology is summarized as follows:

- Proactive code review: Prior to development, review all new functionality and apply a cutoff reuse rule: for example, where functionality is likely to be used three or more times, then develop it as an enterprise service (e.g., develop a regex enterprise class).

- Reactive code review: Subsequent to a proactive code review, if code is duplicated three times, then review code and consider reengineering the functionality as an enterprise service (e.g., develop a regex domain class and subsequently reengineer or refactor it as regex enterprise functionality).

- Passive code review: Exclude code from a proactive or reactive review (e.g., develop similar or duplicate regex classes) with domain coupling and without generalization.

The Standard: Design Dichotomy

The standard acknowledges that consideration may be given to determine whether functionality has an enterprise or a limited domain role. The earlier the consideration is made, the better.

Modularity

Implicit in an information technology structure is the componentization of software and hardware, which is encapsulated within layers and coordinated into a seamless system of functionality.

What

Modularity refers to the ability to encapsulate functionality into a unit, which exposes an interface against which other modules may connect. A module may be independent or rely on a dependency. The Unified Modeling Language (UML) notation has a module (e.g., class) shared in two types of *dependencies* or *associations* (e.g., *aggregation* and *composition*) with other modules of functionality.

■**Note** An *aggregation association* is one where two modules may exist independently; however, they may form a relationship to make up a whole. For example, a garage may be used independently, as may a car; however, they may form an association that enables the car to be parked in the garage. A *composition association*, which is a form of an aggregation association, is one where there is an independent and a dependent party. For example, a car tire is independent of a car—it may be used on a trailer; however, the car is dependent on a tire (or several of them), because a car is composed of tires (and other components).

Where

Modularity is used across the enterprise framework, from an architecture layer to a class module.

Why

Modularity is premised on cohesion and self-responsibility, which are attributes essential to designing, developing, and maintaining composite structures (e.g., software and hardware structures). The importance of modularity to structural design further underscores the value of development using a first class object-oriented development tool, such as C#.

How

There are many implementations of modularity, for example, class module, namespace, assembly, layer, and architecture. To encapsulate modularity, the unit must also expose an interface through which it may participate in an association with other modules, in order to form a composite or super structure. To minimize maintenance and maximize longevity, the interface should be sufficiently abstract, loosely coupled, and appropriately deployed.

The Standard: Modularity

The standard acknowledges the use of modularity as a method to design, build, and maintain complex structures.

Coupling

A tenet of good design is that artifacts are loosely coupled, yet coupling is ambivalent: it represents an association and detachment.

What

Coupling represents the association between two or more artifacts; for example, a business object is coupled to the schema of a database table. Or an application is coupled to an operating system. There are two aspects to coupling: it has fixed and variable attributes. *Fixed coupling* refers to that part of the association over which, within a given context, there is no discretion. For example, if a business object represents an employee and all employee data is held in tblEmployee table, then the business object has a fixed coupling with the table. *Variable or discretionary coupling* refers to how a fixed coupling is implemented. A business object, for example, may access employee data indirectly through an interposed data-controller object, or it may access the data directly. If the object was to directly access the data from tblEmployee, then it would be a tightly coupled association; however, if it accessed the data through an interposed object, then it would be loosely coupled, relative to tblEmployee. It is only through recognizing a fixed and a variable attribute that we are able to explain the ambivalence of coupling.

Where

Coupling is present throughout the enterprise framework; it is unavoidable where there are associations.

Why

Coupling is a necessary part of associations or collaborations. It recognizes that artifacts have specialized roles and that to compose functionality, artifacts have to be able to associate or collaborate directly to indirectly with other artifacts.

How

The key to coupling is to manage it appropriately. The strategy is to exercise discretion where the consequence of fixed coupling, which is tight coupling, is problematic. For example, when an employee object is tightly coupled to tblEmployee, then if there is change in the schema of tblEmployee, the use of the object is impacted and it will need to be reengineered. However, if the interface of the object is loosely coupled to the tblEmployee through middleware, then change may have no effect on the object, because the change may be accommodated within the middleware, leaving the interface between the employee object and the middleware unchanged. In this case, the coupling is loosened by exercising discretion and designing an association with an interposed party (e.g., middleware). The rationale for using an interposed party is that it is preferable to form a direct association or coupling with a party that is less demanding when circumstances change. The point is illustrated when comparing a three-tier and a five-tier application design (refer to the section "Application Design Architectures" later in this chapter). The five-tier design differs from the three-tier design, because the business layer is interposed by UI and data integration layers, which directly manage the relationship between the presentation and data source tiers, respectively. The loose coupling shelters the business layer from those underlying layers. The interposed integration layers may fully or substantially accommodate a change in circumstances (e.g., supplementing a Web interface with a Windows interface or changing a data schema). The consequences may be absorbed in the interposed layers, leaving the business layer unaffected or having to accommodate minimal change. The endpoint of decoupling is that the cost associated with change can be more efficiently managed, thereby lowering cost of ownership and safeguarding longevity of an application.

The Standard: Coupling

The standard acknowledges the appropriate management of coupling and the value of decoupling where the exercise of discretion effects a net positive return on investment.

Layers

Layers are tiers, which are a convenient way to encapsulate, decompose complexity, and marshal specialty while recognizing the value of a sphere of responsibility.

What

A layer is an abstract or concrete composition of modularity, for example, a business object layer or a network services layer.

Where

Throughout an enterprise architecture, there are layers of functionality. Layering may be used to structure functionality within an application framework (e.g., UI, BO, and DB layers) or to represent architectures within an enterprise framework.

Why

An efficient and effective way to design, develop, maintain, and manage complex and large structures is to decompose them into smaller units that exhibit a defining characteristic (e.g., integration or security layer). Layers encourage the development of specialized skills, which in turn encourages the development of expertise.

How

Defining a layer is situation dependent: a large site has more options than a small site, or what works in theory may not work in practice in a given situation. Unfortunately, layering is not easily reversed, and to do so may require expensive reengineering or replacement. However, as organizations are dynamic, a key to defining layers is to design them cohesively and flexibly, and do it early. Layering is a two-edged sword: on one hand, it is extremely useful in decomposing and managing complexity; yet on the other hand, each layer is an overhead that the network and the budget have to support. The art is in striking the right balance for the situation: in other words, how layers are implemented, in a given situation, is a matter of considered judgment. Often, the structure of layers tends to follow industry lines, where common business objectives are deterministic.

The Standard: Layers

The standard acknowledges the use of layers as an efficient and effective way to design, develop, maintain, and manage complex and large structures.

Design Context

The role of the design context is to give the design policy a context in which it is applied.

What

The design context defines the workspace or domain in which the design policy is to be implemented. For example, certain enterprise functionality may be excluded from an enterprise design context because it is legacy and flagged for depreciation, or domain functionality may be excluded because it is managed by a functional department (e.g., Microsoft Access applications and spreadsheets in the marketing department).

Where

A design context is used, for example, by an enterprise architecture framework as the conceptual foundation (or land) on which the framework is to be built. A design context may be limited to a given layer or architecture, however.

Why

The workspace has to be identified so that appropriate resources may be organized. In practice, not all of the functionality of an enterprise may be included within an enterprise context, for example. Commonly, organizations are iterating architecture towards a target architecture and may include or exclude functionality flagged for redundancy from the context of a structural design.

How

The design context is defined as the workspace to be structured. In Figure 6-1, the design context is defined as the enterprise architecture workspace, as identified within the design policy.

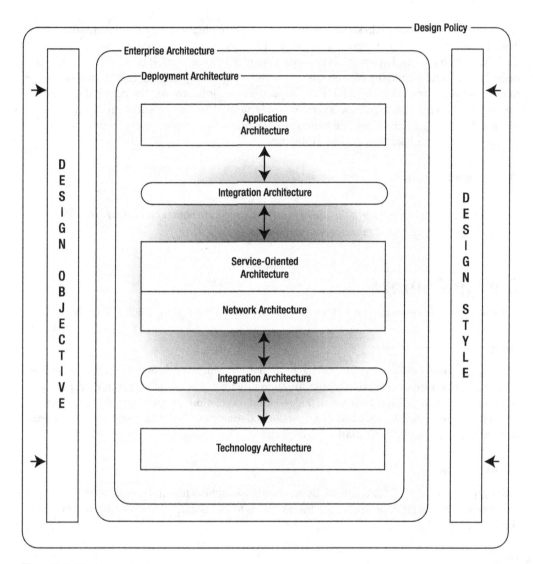

Figure 6-1. *Design context*

The Standard: Design Context

The standard acknowledges that the design workspace has to be identified, so that appropriate resources may be organized. In practice, not all of the functionality of an enterprise may be included within an enterprise context.

Enterprise Design Framework

While the design context defines the workspace, it is the framework that transposes the concept of architecture into concrete layers (e.g., application or enterprise services layer) in which to design a composition of interrelated modules of functionality.

Note The tiers or layers of the enterprise framework may follow industry best practices, which, for example, are articulated in the Open Groups' Architecture Framework (TOGAF 8.1 Enterprise Edition). TOGAF derives from TAFIM, an architecture framework developed by the U.S. Department of Defense. You can review TOGAF at www.opengroup.org/architecture.

What

An enterprise design framework is a blueprint that defines the structures or layers of an enterprise. The structures or layers map conceptually, although not always physically, to a given architecture.

Where

The enterprise design framework is used where there are many structures that need to be blended or unified into a systematic whole.

Why

Enterprise design embodies purpose and discipline, so it requires a framework on which to guide it to that end.

Note The design framework is itself a design that evolves from a synthesis of community ideas and practices. Once an idea or practice becomes accepted, then it is inevitable that it will find favor in a design policy.

How

The framework is mapped to layers or tiers of functionality. For practical purposes, the deployment architecture is shown conceptually, although it is a concrete layer on which all other concrete layers are deployed. The enterprise architecture remains a concept that acts as the outer boundary of the framework. Figure 6-2 illustrates an enterprise design framework. Note that it shows the mapping of respective architectures to layers (except for the deployment). The framework is implemented in various summarized forms, where typically reference is limited to layers or tiers of "architecture" that exclude reference to the surrounding architectures (e.g., deployment and enterprise); the framework is commonly summarized as an "n-tier" architecture.

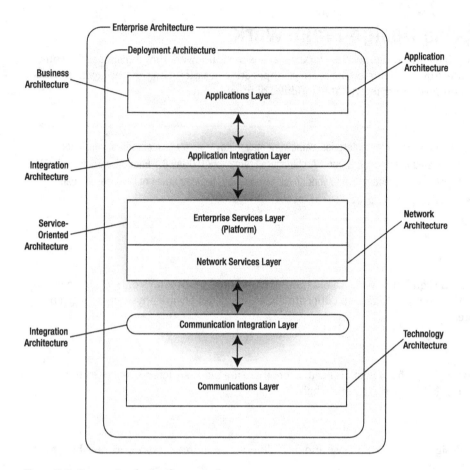

Figure 6-2. *Enterprise design framework*

The Standard: Enterprise Design Framework

The standard acknowledges the use of an enterprise design framework where there are many structures that need to be managed as a cohesive composite.

Application Layer

An application layer represents the software functionality of an enterprise. It may comprise in-house and outsourced functionality that is seamlessly presented to a user.

What

The application layer is a conceptual repository of applications that may be deployed across many networks and accessible locally, regionally, or globally. For example, a Web application would reside in the application layer, and it may through an application services layer consume security, transaction, and data services from the enterprise services layer.

Where

The application layer resides in an enterprise framework and leverages an integration layer to access enterprises services (or platform services).

Why

The design, development, and maintenance of software is a specialized skill with its own set of dynamics. Encapsulating software into a layer is an efficient and convenient way to manage the special needs of application development.

How

An application layer is built up as a composite of domain applications. Application integration and common functionality are abstracted into application integration and enterprise services layers, respectively. That has several benefits: it maximizes decoupling, minimizes the effect of change, and minimizes development in a domain application.

The Standard: Application Layer

> *The standard acknowledges that the design, development, and maintenance of software is a specialized skill with its own set of dynamics. Encapsulating domain software into a layer is an efficient and convenient way to manage the special needs of application development.*

Application Design Types

Essentially, there are three application design types: domain, enterprise, and services. The different application design types complement the nature of the business, which is classified as domain and enterprise. A domain dynamic is functionality that originates from within the organization and is custom to a given domain, whereas an enterprise dynamic is common throughout an industry, or common throughout industry generally. While it is obvious what constitutes a services application, the same cannot be said about a domain or enterprise application. The following tip illustrates what constitutes "enterprise applications."

Tip Martin Fowler gives some good examples of what he considers to be "enterprise applications," including payroll, accounting, and customer service applications. He considers that the following types of applications are *not* "enterprise applications": automobile fuel injection, operating systems, compilers, and games. Refer to Martin Fowler, *Patterns of Enterprise Application Architecture* (Addison-Wesley, 2003), p. 3.

Domain Application

Organizations and their departments require applications to manage domain-specific functionality.

What

A domain application is an application that fulfills the custom requirements of a given domain (e.g., an organization or department or activity). For example, a domain application may be one developed in-house to meet the requirements of the assembly line domain, or it may be a new game for the domain of game enthusiasts.

Where

A domain application resides within the enterprise framework, in the application layer. (Note this refers to a domain within an organization rather than an activity domain, such as game domain.)

Why

Domain applications cater to requirements that are not universal and fulfill domain requirements.

How

Domain applications are developed according to requirements that are not universal; in other words, they are quite specific to a given domain. For example, Model T production managers have a domain requirement for an application that monitors production efficiently at each stage of their mass-production assembly lines.

Note A domain application can cross over and become an enterprise application if the functionality becomes universal.

The Standard: Domain Application

The standard acknowledges the design and development of domain applications to service the custom or non-universal requirements of a domain.

Enterprise Application

While organizations are different in many respects, they are similar in other respects: an enterprise application fulfills common industry or multiple industry standard requirements.

What

An enterprise application is an application that encapsulates functionality common or standard to an industry type or industry in general (e.g., a payroll application).

Where

An enterprise application resides within the enterprise framework in the application layer.

Why

A significant part of an organization's functionality is routine and without a domain impera-tive. In such a circumstance, it is often preferable to adopt a successful industry application than to develop the functionality as a "domain" application by "reinventing the wheel."

How

Generally, an enterprise application is developed by a vendor to meet industry or multi-industry requirements. They are commonly developed as Web or Windows application types, which follow a three-tier or five-tier design architecture (refer to the section "Application Design Architectures" later in this chapter). Examples of an enterprise application include payroll or accounting applications.

The Standard: Enterprise Application

> *The standard acknowledges the use of enterprise applications to provide functionality that is routine or universal and is without a domain imperative.*

Services Application

A feature of an enterprise framework is the abstraction of common functionality into a pub-lished service (e.g., user authentication or application integration services).

What

A services application is an application that publishes functionality or services that is made available to other applications or services.

Where

A service application is commonly found in an application integration layer, enterprise serv-ices layer (or platform), network services layer, or communications integration layer.

Why

Encapsulating functionality as services to distribute throughout an enterprise is an effective and efficient way to manage functionality.

How

Functionality is encapsulated into assemblies and deployed as published services located on a server (LAN, WAN, or Web server).

The Standard: Services Application

> *The standard acknowledges the use of services applications to distribute functionality across an enterprise as an effective and efficient way to manage functionality.*

Application Design Architectures

In this section, we discuss application design architecture and examine the following: two-tier, three-tier, five-tier, and enterprise architectures. Is one design architecture *better* than the other? While there is much debate, the more relevant issue is when is one design architecture more *appropriate* than another. The essence of good design is to match the most appropriate solution to the requirements. Thus, on a site, much can be gained by using a range of design architectures, rather than shoe-horning all applications into one architecture type. For example, in a given situation, it may be inappropriate to be conservative and use a three-tier architecture when a more expensive five-tier architecture has a lower total cost of ownership. On the other hand, unnecessary cost and overhead may result from developing functionality as a three-tier application when a two-tier application would have been equally technically appropriate.

Two-Tier Design

We commence our reexamination of application design architectures by examining the two-tier architecture, which is a simple C# application.

Note The simplest application design is the one-tier application (e.g., many Windows and Console applications)—that design has not been illustrated in this chapter. Its distinguishing characteristic is that all functionality resides in one layer or tier.

What

A two-tier design is an application architecture that compacts all of the functionality or application logic into a single tier that resides on one server, while data resides on a second tier (e.g., a database server). The two-tier design is suitable for Web and Windows applications.

Where

Where there is a requirement for an application that features low overhead and high performance, then the two-tier application is a common solution. It may, however, present integration inefficiencies, scalability issues, and maintenance overhead.

Why

The two-tier design can be built rapidly, offers high performance, and may be a cost-effective solution.

How

All of the functionality is encapsulated in one layer, which resides on one server (see Figure 6-3), and the data on a second server. Commonly, websites or Windows applications have used this design to rapidly develop functionality and to minimize performance overhead. However, the tight coupling between the UI, business, and data classes, which is implicit in the design, may be problematic if there is a change to data schema, for example. In this case, a solution may be to use an Adapter design pattern (refer to Chapter 11) as a short-term solution.

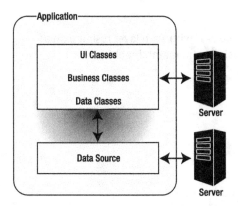

Figure 6-3. *Two-tier design structure*

The Standard: Two-Tier Design

The standard acknowledges the use of a two-tier design where there is a need for rapid development and high performance. It does caution, however, that over the medium to long term the design may encounter integration inefficiencies, and scalability, coupling, and maintenance issues.

Three-Tier Design

The three-tier design is generally considered to be the most popular design architecture in use today.

What

A three-tier design is an application architecture that separates functionality into two tiers (UI and business) that reside on separate servers, while access to data is via a third server. The three-tier design is suitable for Web and Windows applications.

Where

Where there is a requirement for an application that features high performance with a medium-to-long life expectancy, then the three-tier application is a popular solution. It supports integration efficiencies, scalability, and stability, and carries a relatively low maintenance overhead, while mildly reducing coupling concerns.

Why

The three-tier design is an alternative to a two-tier or five-tier design: it has a good mix of the advantages of the two- and five-tier architectures, but with relatively inferior de-coupling design features compared with a five-tier solution. While in theory, the user interface may be swapped between presentation types (Web or Windows), in practice, however, that is easier said than done. Commonly, problems arise because the user interface is coupled to the business layer, and the business layer is coupled to the data layer.

How

The functionality is divided over three layers (see Figure 6-4) with each layer residing on a separate server. Each layer is readily accessible, extensible, and maintainable.

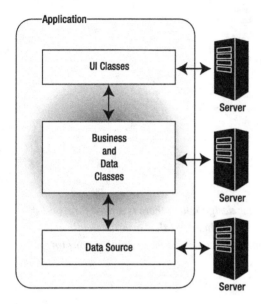

Figure 6-4. *Three-tier design structure*

The Standard: Three-Tier Design

> *The standard acknowledges the use of a three-tier design where there is a requirement for an application that features high performance with a medium-to-long life expectancy. It cautions, however, that the business and data classes may be tightly coupled implementations to the user interface and datastore, which may cause future concern.*

Five-Tier Design

The five-tier design is the elegant solution that overcomes the disadvantages of the three-tier model.

What

A five-tier design is an application architecture that separates functionality over four tiers that reside on two servers: a presentation tier resides on one server, while the UI, business, and data classes reside on a second server, and the fifth tier—the data source—is accessed via a third server. The cost of extra layers may be offset by the gain from encapsulating the UI, business, and data classes on the one server (which compares with the two-tier design and contrasts with the three-tier design). The five-tier design is suitable for Web and Windows applications.

Where

Where there is a requirement for an application that features high performance with a long life expectancy, then the five-tier application is a solution. It supports integration efficiencies, scalability, stability, and loose coupling, and carries a relatively low maintenance overhead.

Why

The five-tier design has all of the advantages of the three-tier design, but with a solution to the problem of coupling the business and data classes to the implementation of the user interface and data source. These benefits are supported by the merging of the logic functionality on to one server. However, developing a five-tier application may be more expensive than a three-tier application.

How

The functionality is divided over five layers (see Figure 6-5) with a presentation layer on its own server and the UI, business, and data classes residing on the same server, a feature that not only assists in decoupling, but also aids performance, as most of the grunt work is done on the same server. The data source is accessible via a third server. With this design, the functionality classes are decoupled from the presentation and data source. The UI classes are able to cater to the special needs of Web or Windows representation, and the data classes shelter the business functionality from changes to the underlying data source.

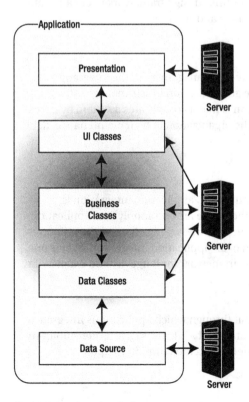

Figure 6-5. *Five-tier design structure*

The Standard: Five-Tier Design

The standard acknowledges the use of a five-tier design where there is a requirement for an application that requires high performance, presentation, and data source flexibility with a long life expectancy.

Application Integration Layer

A further safeguard of using an enterprise framework to manage design is that it mandates that integration be a design consideration implicit not only in application design, but also in the design of services and communication layers.

What

An application integration layer is a common layer through which applications are integrated. Commonly, applications are members of a system in which they must integrate and cooperate. Application integration design recognizes that integration is a systematic design consideration and is better managed through a common layer than discretely at application level.

Where

Application integration design resides within an enterprise design framework to encapsulate the task of managing connectivity between applications and services.

Why

It is more efficient, economic, and flexible to delegate the management of the integration of applications to a specialist layer, rather than require an application to self-manage integration. A major risk posed by self-management of integration is that it complicates a system by necessitating point-to-point integration, which exposes the organization to high maintenance, tight coupling, and duplication costs.

How

Within the context of the enterprise architecture framework, application integration is managed as a service to which applications subscribe. There are commonly four application integration designs that leverage an integration layer: XML messaging, dynamic link libraries (DLL), remoting, and XML Web services. The design of an application integration layer is one of the most critical stages in preparing an enterprise framework for longevity and extensibility.

XML Messaging

Messaging relies on a message bus to act as a conduit through which applications integrate to publish and subscribe to functionality, using open-standard XML messages. It offers ubiquity and asynchronous integration (refer to "Service-Oriented Architecture" in Chapter 5).

Dynamic Link Libraries

Application integration may be designed using DLLs (assemblies) that are deployed centrally on servers and referenced by subscribing applications. It is a synchronous binary solution; however, it is generally considered in situations that favor efficiency at the expense of integration ubiquity. DLLs commonly support a hub-and-spoke architecture (refer to "Service-Oriented Architecture" in Chapter 5).

Remoting

Application integration that uses remoting is an extension of the use of DLLs to integrate, with the added feature that integration outside of the immediate domain is managed through the partnership of a remotely deployed DLL acting as a proxy to communicate through a transport protocol to a server DLL, with a little help from .NET CLR at either end (refer to "Remote-Proxy Pattern Code" in Chapter 11).

XML Web Services

Web services is a solution for application integration that leverages Internet distribution functionality to offer synchronous and ubiquitous integration (refer to "Service-Oriented Architecture" in Chapter 5).

The Standard: Application Integration Layer

The standard acknowledges the use of an application integration layer to avoid the cost of high maintenance, duplication, and tight coupling.

Enterprise Services Layer

An enterprise services layer exposes or publishes common functionality that is accessible across the enterprise.

What

The enterprise services layer is a common layer through which enterprise functionality is published. It refers to a portfolio of services that act as an application platform from which applications are serviced, through an interposed integration layer, with common functionality.

Where

The enterprise services layer is located between the application integration layer and network services layer within an enterprise framework.

Why

Enterprise services enable an organization to manage application resources that are common. The objective is to standardize resource availability, usability, adaptability, and stability, while preventing or removing duplication and redundancy of functionality.

How

The enterprise services layer (see Figure 6-6) is the engine room of an enterprise framework; how it is designed is influenced by a range of factors, including implied requirements of the design policy, decisions made in terms of the enterprise-domain dichotomy (refer to the section "The Standard: Design Dichotomy" earlier in this chapter), the size of the organization, the nature of the industry, and the requirements of stakeholders. The choice of design centers around what services are defined as enterprise and what services are native to a domain. Generally, enterprise services include services that are more efficiently or effectively utilized, from an organizational perspective, outside of a domain, for example, security services, application services, data management and warehouse services, transaction management services, operating system services, and network management services.

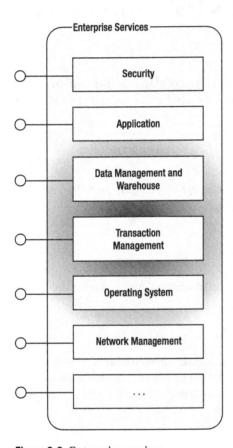

Figure 6-6. *Enterprise services*

The Standard: Enterprise Services Design

> *The standard acknowledges the use of enterprise services that seek to standardize resource availability, usability, adaptability, and stability while preventing or removing duplication and redundancy.*

Communications Integration Layer

The previously discussed standards relate very much to software services; however, software needs to run on fixed hardware and the ever-increasing array of mobile communication devices.

What

A communication integration layer encapsulates or abstracts to an interface layer the responsibility to integrate the enterprise services layer (the application platform) with the hardware and communication functionality.

Where

The communications integration layer lies in between the enterprise services layer and the communication layer in an enterprise framework.

Why

The wisdom of a communication integration layer mirrors that of an application integration layer by centralizing and coordinating the integration of multiple artifacts that may enable a more efficient, maintainable, and loosely coupled solution.

How

The integration focuses on the development of core functionality that commonly wrap IP-based networks, which enables connectivity between the enterprise services layer and Internet and other communication channels.

The Standard: Communications Integration Layer

> *The standard acknowledges the use of a communication's integration layer to centralize and coordinate the integration of multiple artifacts that may enable a more efficient, maintainable, and loosely coupled solution.*

Communications Infrastructure Layer

The portfolio of services that enable the interconnection or communication between systems is referred to as a communications infrastructure.

What

The communications infrastructure represents the local and extended software and hardware transport components, which enable data exchange and network switching. The design of the infrastructure will be driven by the requirements of the application, integration, and enterprise services layers and the deployment architecture.

Where

The communications infrastructure is accessed through the communications integration layer that houses in the enterprise framework.

Why

To participate in the benefits of network computing, be it a Local Area Network (LAN), Wide Area Network (WAN), Virtual Private Network (VPN), or Internet network, an enterprise requires a hardware layer to manage and encapsulate communication functionality within an enterprise framework.

How

A portfolio of hardware artifacts is assembled as a network of communication devices that plug in to other communication systems to access and expose functionality.

The Standard: Communication Infrastructure Layer

The standard acknowledges the use of a communication infrastructure layer to manage and encapsulate communication functionality within an enterprise framework.

CHAPTER 7

■ ■ ■

Design Development

The previous chapter discussed using structural design techniques to develop a framework—the enterprise design framework—to structure the design of the enterprise. The framework was then transformed from representing architectures (e.g., application architecture) to representing layers (e.g., application layer). In this chapter, the focus is on developing designs of functionality that reside within three of those layers: the application, application integration, and enterprise services layers. When talking about "design development," reference is made to implementing design through code, and as you shall see, each of the layers serves different roles, and note that requires code to follow different design imperatives. For example, in the application layer, you may design specialized code to meet specific requirements of a domain, whereas in the enterprise services layer, you design generalized code to meet the generic demands of domains.

As discussed in the previous chapter, there is an enterprise-domain dilemma: Which functionality is enterprise and which is domain? While it was noted that an organization may determine a rule, it was also noted that addressing the question early (*proactively*), rather than later (*reactively*), was preferable. In this chapter, we explore the way that we perceive design, and discuss how it may impact our ability to pick functionality, which should be written generically as enterprise functionality. Commonly, two methodologies are used to design functionality: design it from a layer or tier perspective (*horizontally*) or from an application perspective (*vertically*). With layer or tier development (*horizontal development*), it is an intuitive part of the design process to consider whether design should be generalized or specialized; however, that is not the case when developing design from an application perspective (*vertical development*), where intuitively design is developed from a specialized domain perspective.

The text then progresses to discussing the important role that *object collaboration* plays in developing design, and in so doing, identifies a number of problems. The problems are presented as three dichotomies: *abstract-interface* dichotomy, *composition-inheritance* dichotomy, and *abstraction-implementation* dichotomy. The abstract-interface dichotomy recognizes the dilemma of choosing between an abstract class and an interface type. The composition-inheritance dichotomy recognizes the dilemma of choosing between objects that acquire an interface through composition or inheritance. And the abstraction-implementation dichotomy recognizes the dilemma of choosing between programming against an interface (abstract class) or an implementation (concrete class). The choices made will impact the usability, maintainability, and longevity of the design, by affecting the flexibility of objects to adapt to changes made in the domain. A solution to the problem of inflexibility is to leverage design patterns, which will be briefly introduced.

Note Design patterns are comprehensively discussed in Chapters 9 through 12.

Finally, the chapter concludes by discussing two methodologies for implementing design in applications: *start-from-scratch* and *frameworks*. As you know, a start-from-scratch approach is, as the name implies, an application that is designed and developed from scratch using an empty solution, whereas a framework approach leverages a partly prebuilt solution or application template that contains application integration and enterprise services functionality. Now, let's kick off the chapter by implementing the design framework introduced in the previous chapter.

Implementing Design in the Design Framework

In the last chapter, we developed an enterprise design framework that transposed the architectures into layers, as presented again in Figure 7-1.

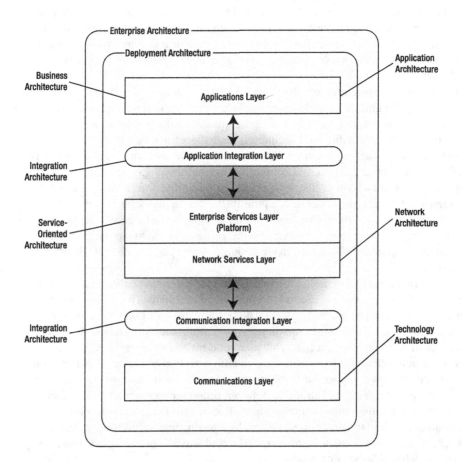

Figure 7-1. *Enterpise design framework*

We now want to narrow our focus to those layers that are of immediate interest to C# architects and developers: the application, application integration, and enterprise services layers. Refer to Figure 7-2, where the layers that are out of scope for our discussion have been crossed through.

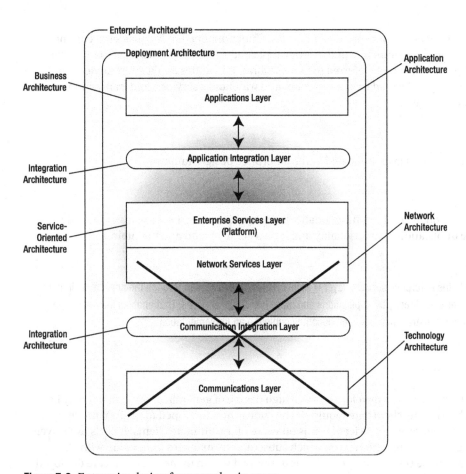

Figure 7-2. *Enterprise design framework—in scope*

Implementing Design in Layers

We know that each layer has a different role and dynamics; for example, the application layer contains applications or functionality that are enterprise applications (e.g., payroll) or domain applications (e.g., ModelT website), while the enterprise services layer contains functionality that provides support to the application software (enterprise and domain). These two layers are isolated by an integration layer that decouples applications from the services. The enterprise services layer is the first layer to be discussed.

Design of Enterprise Services Layer

As mentioned previously, the enterprise services layer is designed to service the common functionality requirements of applications.

What

The enterprise services layer contains the code or functionality that is considered common across applications or common within a given application; in other words, it acts as a platform—hence the layer is commonly referred to as a *platform*. It includes application services, for example, security services, data management and warehouse services, and transactions management services, etc.

Where

An enterprise services layer is located in the enterprise design framework.

Why

The centralization of common functionality leads to efficiencies, because it significantly reduces the duplication of functionality and it is easier to extend and maintain.

■**Note** While the enterprise services layer is highly visible, it is accessed through the application integration layer, rather than directly by applications and other enterprise services. That enables the enterprise services to remain abstract and not itself become coupled to an implementation.

How

Enterprise services code is developed with a high degree of generalization so that it may be consumed by as many clients are required. The code is not developed for a given implementation. In fact, the enterprise services layer is unaware of the ultimate clients; it deals exclusively with the application integration layer, which subsequently manages integration with clients. Typically, enterprise services functionality is developed within namespaces that are deployed in nonlocal assemblies to a network server, .NET's General Assembly Cache (GAC), Microsoft's Internet Information Server (IIS), or enterprise Windows or ASP.NET server controls.

The Standard: Design of Enterprise Services Layer

> *The standard acknowledges the design of an enterprise services layer and its role to publish generic functionality that is highly visible and accessible to enable functionality to be managed more effectively and efficiently throughout the enterprise.*

Design of Application Integration Layer

The application integration layer code serves the functionality requirements of applications that may reside within the enterprise or externally (e.g., stakeholders).

What

All applications that are integrated into the environment do so through code residing in the application integration layer. The code in this layer directly accesses the enterprise services layer on behalf of subscribing applications that reside within the applications layer or are external to the environment.

Tip An application integration layer not only acts to integrate applications that reside within the enterprise, but it also acts as an integration channel through which vendor and stakeholder functionality integrates into the enterprise. Centralizing integration into a common layer simplifies the complexity associated with designing code that has multiple integration requirements.

Where

An application integration layer is located in an enterprise design framework, as an interposed layer between enterprise services and application layers.

Why

The integration of functionality requires transparency and enterprise visibility. It is more effectively and efficiently managed as a central service that is accessible to in-house, vendor, and stakeholder applications.

How

Integration code is written that consumes enterprise services and customizes it, where necessary, for a domain or enterprise application requirement, and then republishes it, making it accessible to applications in the applications layer or accessible externally. It is also the layer in which vendor functionality is accessible for integration. Functionality may be accessed through COM+ services, GAC, and web services, for example.

Note While stakeholder functionality is external to an organization, it is commonly included as part of the organization's enterprise. However, there is a contrary view, which argues that functionality should only be shown as part of the enterprise where the organization has some form of control over design or development or a legal right.

The Standard: Design of Application Integration Layer

The standard acknowledges the design of an application integration layer, and its role is to satisfy domain and vendor requirements by providing a service that offers integration functionality that is customizable, transparent, and highly visible.

Design of Application Layer

The application layer is designed to represent the code encapsulated in domain and enterprise applications.

What

The application layer designs code to be coupled to the implementation of the application (domain or enterprise). Generally, code is designed specifically or specialized for a given application.

Where

An application layer is located in an enterprise design framework.

Why

By segregating application code from integration and services code, tight coupling is limited, which maximizes portability and minimizes the impact of change.

How

Application code is written or purchased to meet domain or enterprise requirements. Commonly, functionality may be accessed through ASP.NET, Windows, and Console application types.

The Standard: Design of Application Layer

The standard acknowledges the design of an application layer and that its role enables isolation of application code from integration and services code, which maximizes portability and minimizes the impact of change.

Horizontal and Vertical Design Methodologies

As discussed in the previous chapter, there is an enterprise-domain dilemma: Which functionality is enterprise and which is domain? While it was noted that an organization may determine a rule, it was also noted that addressing the question early (*proactively*), rather than later (*reactively*), was preferable. Maybe the dilemma is associated with the way that we approach design. Generally, there are two ways to design functionality: from a layer or tier perspective (*horizontally*) and subsequently referenced by an application, or from an application perspective (*vertically*) and subsequently migrated through the layer hierarchy, where appropriate. With layer or horizontal design development, it is an intuitive part of the design process to consider whether design should be generalized or specialized; however, that is not the case when developing design from an application perspective, which is done vertically, where it is intuitive to design from a domain perspective. Perhaps a key to maximizing design and code reuse is to favor horizontal in preference to vertical design?

Horizontal Design Development

Horizontal design development refers to developing functionality within layers or tiers: each layer is seen as a distinct yet coordinated development.

What

Horizontal design development supports the notion that each layer is autonomous and collaborates with other layers through an interface. While functionality in all layers is designed to ultimately support applications, nevertheless an application is seen as a facade or a container through which layer functionality is accessed by clients.

Where

Horizontal design development occurs *along* each layer: the application, application integration, and enterprise services layers (and the other three layers, which have been excluded for convenience—see Figure 7-2 earlier).

Why

By regulating design development through layers, each layer may remain true to its inherent purpose and avoid becoming biased or coupled to any given application implementation or interface.

How

Typically, the driving force for development comes from the domains; however, the design and development of each of the layers is managed by developers who specialize in a given layer. As horizontal design follows a layer imperative, a domain application, for example, is seen as a consumer of services or client. Although layer developers are not developing for a given implementation, they need to be conscious that their development not only has to enable application developers to easily access functionality, but also needs to be presented in such a way that consuming layer functionality improves development efficiency. Figure 7-3 illustrates the autonomous nature of the layers that are developed horizontally and that an application is a facade through which functionality from the layers is accessed.

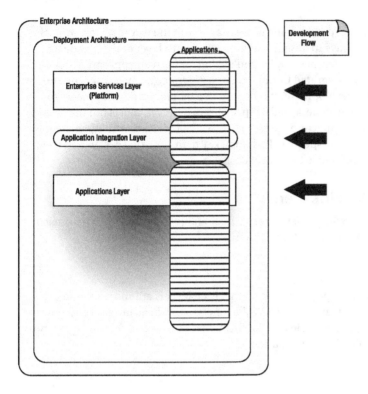

Figure 7-3. *Horizontal design development*

The Standard: Horizontal Design Development

> *The standard acknowledges horizontal design development as a method to regulate design development through layers, which seeks to ensure that the inherent purpose of the layer does not become biased or coupled to an application implementation.*

Vertical Design Development

Vertical design development recognizes that functionality can be developed across layers to fulfill the requirements of a domain or enterprise application.

What

Vertical design development supports the notion that development commences in the application layer and progresses through the other layers, as appropriate. In other words, the layers are developed as part of, or as a consequence of, an application project and not autonomously.

Where

Vertical code development occurs *across* layers: the application, application integration, and enterprise services layers.

Why

By regulating design development from an application perspective, applications may be developed more quickly, and only functionality that is known to have an integration or enterprise value is migrated to those respective layers.

■**Caution** An inherent risk in developing code in the application layer and then migrating it to the application integration and enterprise services layers is that the code may be *too* coupled to the domain. Excessive domain coupling is often quoted as a reason why so many applications are developed from scratch, because the code that is developed in applications commits the design to an implementation, and it is not viable to transpose it to an abstraction so that it may be reused.

How

An application is developed from a domain perspective with functionality being added or migrated to the application integration and enterprise services tiers, as appropriate. Generally, functionality is commenced in the application layer and moves up the hierarchy (see Figure 7-4). However, design development could commence in the enterprise services layer and progress downward. In such cases, it would mimic horizontal development and address the issue of excessive domain coupling or bias, which may improve design and code reuse.

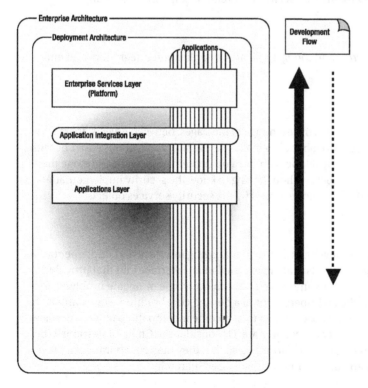

Figure 7-4. *Vertical design development*

The Standard: Vertical Design Development

The standard acknowledges vertical design development as a method to regulate domain development, but cautions that code and design may be excessively coupled to a domain, which may make it a poor candidate to migrate to other layers for reuse.

Object Collaboration

Designing applications is really about designing collaborations between objects; it is collaborating objects that perform the requirements of a domain.

▪**Note** Professor Trygve Reenskaug presents a most interesting discussion on the role of object collaboration; refer to the "Role Modeling" and "UML-VM" discussions (`http://heim.ifi.uio.no/~trygver/index.html`).

What

The functionality of an application may be expressed as a set of collaborations between objects. The ability of an object to collaborate is determined by its interface and its implementation, which impact its ability to form associations or relationships with other objects.

Where

Object collaboration occurs *across* and *along* application, application integration, and enterprise services layers.

Why

Collaboration is important because it is the exchange of messages, between objects, that yields the functionality of an application. Collaboration makes developing applications easier because, for example, a domain application developer can develop domain objects that leverage the functionality of security services objects without having to know the security implementation, only how to program against the interface exposed by the security services objects.

How

Collaboration between objects is developed through managing interface and implementation. Objects communicate through methods that are exposed in an interface and that provide functionality for a client object to consume. Often, we can overcome or negate problems that arise because an interface may be an impediment to a desired collaboration. For example, the Adapter design pattern uses an interposed object to overcome incompatible object interfaces and enables two incompatible objects to collaborate. Or consider the Chain of Responsibility design pattern, which enables objects to be arranged so that they may collaborate in a previously unforeseen manner: as an authoritative or specialized hierarchy.

Note The Adapter and Chain of Responsibility design patterns are discussed in Chapters 10 and 12, respectively.

The Standard: Object Collaboration

The standard acknowledges the importance of the role of object collaboration because it is the collaboration of exchanging messages between objects that yields the functionality of an application.

The Abstract-Interface Dichotomy

Often it is not obvious when to use class or interface inheritance to design the interface of an object: Why should we use an interface type when it has no functionality?

What

The dichotomy recognizes the problem that arises when designing code for objects that collaborate: Do we develop the interface as an abstract class or as an interface type? The dilemma is a manifestation of the underlying problem of choosing between class and interface inheritance.

Where

The dilemma occurs across application, application integration, and enterprise services layers.

Why

In nontrivial situations, it is not obvious whether an abstract class or an interface type is the best candidate for a base type: this really requires a case-by-case evaluation. The problem is complicated by the fact that C# supports single class inheritance, which means that in any hierarchy there can only be one base or super class. That contrasts with an interface type, which supports multiple inheritance, but does not implement functionality. There is a tendency to favor an abstract class, which may implement functionality, only to discover subsequently that the choice is inappropriate because it becomes too inflexible and cannot accommodate the collaborative demands of other types.

Note Abstract classes cannot be instantiated. They are conceptual; however, they may define functionality that a derived class may implement or specialize.

How

A key to the dilemma lies first in understanding the purpose of an interface type within the context of object collaboration. Once that is understood, then the role of the abstract class becomes obvious. The purpose of an interface type is to *signify a role* that an object can perform, which is encapsulated in a list of generic methods that do not impose an implementation, and are therefore able to be utilized by a wide range of objects. For example, in the Model T domain, we may introduce an `IServiceable` interface that lists service functionality. A wide range of objects may inherit that role, for example, `Engine`, `Radiator`, and `Brakes`, and each service interface will be implemented differently. By analyzing collaborative roles, we can get a feel for the roles which are generic; *a generic role suggests that the functionality is suited to be encapsulated in an interface type*. Conversely, *functionality that is dominate or common to a given class type is a likely candidate to be encapsulated in an abstract class*.

The Standard: Object Collaboration (Abstract-Interface Dichotomy)

> *The standard acknowledges that it is not always obvious when to use class or interface inheritance to design the interface of an object. A key to the dilemma is that an interface type is used to signify a role that an object can perform—an interface type is suitable to perform generic roles.*

The Composition-Inheritance Dichotomy

While objects are abstractions of real-life or logical entities and expose an interface through which other objects can collaborate, it is not always obvious how they should acquire that interface: through composition or inheritance.

What

The dichotomy recognizes the problem that arises when designing objects because there are two ways to acquire an interface, i.e., through composition or inheritance (an example is shown in the upcoming "How" section), and commonly it is not obvious which method to use.

Where

The dilemma occurs across application, application integration, and enterprise services layers.

Why

The dilemma arises because of the different abilities of class inheritance and composition to accommodate change in a domain. Class inheritance is more sensitive to change: it is statically defined at design time, and because a subclass implements functionality of the class hierarchy, it is additionally exposed to changes higher in the hierarchy. Composition, however, is less sensitive to change: it is defined at run time, and a consuming object may replace an object, at runtime, with a more suitable object.

How

A key to the dilemma is to be aware that, generally, class inheritance is more sensitive to change than is composition. GoF propose a principle: "Favor object composition over class inheritance."[1]

---

1. Gamma, Helm, Johnson, and Vlissides, *Design Patterns: Elements of Reusable Object-Oriented Software* (Addison-Wesley, 1994), p. 20.

Listing 7-1 and Listing 7-2 demonstrate the difference between acquiring functionality through composition and inheritance, respectively.

Listing 7-1. *Composition*

```
class ModelT
{
  ...
  //Model T is composed of these two objects
  private object aObject;
  private object bObject;
  ...

  //ModelT leverages functionality
  //of contained objects
  public string MethodOne()
  {
    return aObject.DoSomething();
  }

  public string MethodTwo()
  {
    return bObject.DoSomethingElse();
  }
}
```

Listing 7-2. *Inheritance*

```
class Automobile
{

  //functionality is developed within
  //the class hierarchy
  public string MethodOne()
  {
    return "...";
  }

}


class Car: Automobile
{

  public string MethodTwo()
  {
```

```
    return "...";
  }
.
}

class ModelT: Car
{

  //ModelT inherits functionality
  //from the class hierarchy
  this.MethodOne();
  this.MethodTwo();

}
```

In either example, the ModelT acquires the same functionality; however, it is the ease with which composition manages change that distinguishes it from inheritance. For example, to add new functionality, a ModelT built on composition merely adds another specialist object to do the new work; however, the ModelT built on inheritance requires the inheritance hierarchy to be modified. That may be problematic, as a change to a hierarchy has to consider all derived types that use the hierarchy and not just the ModelT.

The Standard: Object Collaboration (Composition-Inheritance Dichotomy)

The standard acknowledges that there is a dilemma when designing objects because there are two ways to acquire an interface: through composition or inheritance. A key to the dilemma is that class inheritance is more sensitive to change than is composition. GoF propose a principle: "Favor object composition over class inheritance."

The Abstraction-Implementation Dichotomy

It is beneficial to use class inheritance to leverage the "free" functionality of a hierarchy; however, as the composition-inheritance dichotomy illustrated, class inheritance is sensitive to change. This, unfortunately, gives rise to another dilemma: When is it appropriate to reference a type as an abstract (interface) or as a concrete class (implementation)?

What

The dichotomy recognizes the problem that is associated with deciding whether to commit to reference a type through its interface (abstract class) or through its implementation (concrete class).

Where

The dilemma occurs across application, application integration, and enterprise services layers.

Why

The dilemma arises because at some point in time a design has to commit to an implementation; however, it needs to balance the cost of commitment against the need for flexibility in a dynamic domain.

How

A key to the dilemma lies in using *polymorphism*, which enables an object to be treated as an object (implementation) or as a member of its type (interface) at run time. Polymorphism preserves flexibility after an interface has committed to an implementation. The solution is articulated by GoF in a principle: "Program to an interface, not an implementation."[2] It works like this: a variable is declared as an abstract class or type (e.g., Mammal) and instantiated as a given subclass (e.g., Dog) of the type:

```
Mammal majorBarker = new Dog();
```

rather than

```
Dog majorBarker = new Dog();
```

This aids flexibility because it enables the object (majorBarker) to be referenced as an implementation (Dog) or through its interface (Mammal). Additionally, the concrete class (Dog) may be substituted by any class of the same type, for example, by a quiet Cat.

The Standard: Object Collaboration (Abstraction-Implementation Dichotomy)

The standard acknowledges that problems arise because at some point a design has to commit to an implementation; however, it needs to balance the cost of commitment against the need for flexibility in a dynamic domain. A key to the dilemma lies in using polymorphism, which enables an object to be treated as an implementation or as an interface at run time. GoF propose a principle: "Program to an interface, not an implementation."

Design Patterns

It is not easy to orchestrate a society of objects in a collaboration; there are always problems at design time and run time, after an application has been deployed. Design patterns are commonly used as a design and maintenance tool to solve collaborative problems.

What

A design pattern is a methodology that cleverly arranges class interfaces and implementations to overcome collaborative problems.

---

2. Gamma, et al., *Design Patterns*, p. 18.

■**Tip** There are hundreds of design patterns—GoF cataloged only 23. Acknowledged authorities
on design patterns include Martin Fowler, Gregor Hohpe, and Bobby Woolf. These authors commonly
use Java and C# examples. You can check out their websites for more information: Martin Fowler's
site is at `www.martinfowler.com` and Gregor Hohpe and Bobby Woolf's is at
`www.enterpriseintegrationpatterns.com`.

Where

Design patterns may be used across application, application integration, and enterprise services layers. They have become particularly useful in overcoming enterprise issues in enterprise
application architecture (refer to Fowler) and enterprise integration (refer to Hohpe and Woolf).

Why

Design patterns are a structured, efficient, and universal way to design object collaborations.

How

A design pattern solves a problem within a given context; therefore it is necessary to identify a
problem type and apply the appropriate design pattern. Generally, patterns are written generically and are not constrained by layers.

■**Note** Chapters 10 through 12 discuss many contextual problems that the GoF design patterns solve.

Design patterns are successful in solving problems because they are able to manage
interfaces and implementations in such a way that they remove an impediment in an object
collaboration.

The Standard: Collaborative Code (Design Patterns)

*The standard acknowledges the role that design patterns play in solving problems of
objects collaborating in a dynamic domain.*

Implementing Design in Applications

There are two common ways that applications are designed: using the *start-from-scratch*
method or using an application *framework*. An application that is started from scratch is,
as the name implies, an empty solution (an empty Visual Studio template solution, e.g., an
ASP.NET template). An application framework, on the other hand, is a partially built Visual

Studio solution that includes wiring to functionality that will be used by the application (e.g., application integration and enterprise services functionality).

Start-from-Scratch Application Solution

Commonly, where an organization does not leverage an enterprise development framework, applications are developed from scratch. There are two reasons cited: an application may be a "one-off," or the pressures of Rapid Application Development (RAD) may be unsympathetic to the time required to develop and maintain an infrastructure of common functionality.

What

A start-from-scratch application solution is a methodology whereby functionality is developed as new functionality (green fields), and reuse of existing functionality is nonexistent or trivial. The methodology is inefficient: it maximizes development time; and it condones duplication, high maintenance, and uncertainty.

Where

Start-from-scratch applications are developed in the application layer.

Why

To reuse functionality, it has to be written generically and be relevant to a wide range of application requirements; however, the reality is that the pressures of RAD development work against developing generic functionality and commit developers to developing functionality that is tightly coupled to the domain implementation. Consequently, there is very little code that may be reused, and so developers start from scratch.

How

An empty Visual Studio template solution will be used, and functionality for a given domain project will be added in accordance with the technical and functional specifications. Commonly, code reuse, if there is any, is limited to trivial data access and business functionality.

The Standard: Start-from-Scratch Application Solution

The standard acknowledges that a start-from-scratch application is used where there is very little code to reuse, and so developers start from scratch. It cautions that such a practice is generally inefficient as it may result in duplication of functionality and higher maintenance (compared with the use of a framework).

Application Framework Solution

To overcome the inefficiencies of starting an application from scratch, organizations invest in developing generic functionality that can be specifically implemented in application frameworks or solution templates.

What

An application framework is a prebuilt template that includes integration and enterprise services functionality or wiring. There are two common categories of application frameworks: domain and project frameworks. A *domain framework* is one that is prebuilt to accommodate domain requirements: for example, an eCommerce website framework or inventory framework. A *project framework* is a framework that is prebuilt to accommodate an application project type: for example, an ASP.NET or Windows application project. While implementing an application within an application framework avoids the problems of starting from scratch every time and should significantly reduce development time, it does however, require an up-front and continuous investment in infrastructure.

Where

Application frameworks may be used across application, application integration, and enterprise services layers.

Why

Application frameworks are an efficient and effective way to reuse proven design and functionality. They have many benefits, including minimizing development time by reducing the functionality that has to be developed; and reducing maintenance costs, duplication, and uncertainty. However, the net benefit is subject to the amount of reuse of the infrastructure.

How

A type of framework is defined, for example, a corporate intranet application template. It is developed in Visual Studio and wired up with the necessary enterprise and integration functionality. The framework is copied, and copies are made available to domain developers.

The Standard: Frameworks Application Solution

The standard acknowledges the use of application frameworks, which are partially prebuilt solution templates, as an efficient and effective way to reuse proven design and functionality.

CHAPTER 8

■■■

Design Documentation

In this chapter we examine standards on documenting application design. It is one of a pair of chapters on documentation; the other is Chapter 4. Design documentation is managed through a documentation policy, which seeks to ensure that procedures are in place to safeguard an investment in software.

Documentation Policy

A documentation policy is a statement that contains a set of rules and controls that manage the way design is documented. It covers documenting application specifications, application architecture, and enterprise (framework) architecture.

What

The policy seeks to harmonize documentation across all development by requiring architects and developers to follow a set of common guidelines. Devising a policy can be a difficult task because the policy has to balance the time demands on application architects and developers; however, that difficulty may be addressed by making documentation an integral part of development and not a discrete task. The following is a template of a documentation policy based on the policy presented in Chapter 4; it may be modified to suit your situation.

Design Documentation Policy Template

- The policy is the responsibility of the IT governance committee.

- There is one design documentation policy for all development.

- The policy is reviewed every six months.

- A documentation manual (hardcopy or online) is developed and distributed.

- All architects and developers are to be trained in design documentation and made familiar with the in-house documentation policy.

- Documentation is not delegated but incorporated into the design and development tasks of architects and developers. The exception is application specification documentation that is prepared before development commences and may limit architects and developers to a consultation role. Specification documentation may be the responsibility of project management, or shared between development and analyst teams, for example. Documenting an application has three aspects: documenting the technical and functional requirements; documenting the application from a code design perspective; and documenting the application from the perspective of how it fits within the enterprise.

- Documentation is to be signed off and subject to peer group or independent auditor review.

- Documentation is to be housed where it is accessible to stakeholders (e.g., on an intranet portal or in a hierarchy of folders on the network), with appropriate read/write permissions.

Where

A design documentation policy is appropriate for all development sites.

Why

A design documentation policy minimizes the risk of knowledge degradation and all that it encompasses. For example: developers may introduce bugs because the intention of the founding developers was not explicit or documented.

How

A policy is the result of a consultation process between stakeholders (IT governance; development managers, architects, analysts, and developers). Once agreed on, it may be distributed as part of a documentation manual (hardcopy or online).

The Standard: Application Design Documentation Policy

The standard acknowledges the implementation of a single application design documentation policy across all projects within a given site.

Application Specification Documentation

There are two types of specifications that are documented—technical and functional specifications—but it is not quite clear who has the responsibility of developing the documentation. Obviously, the answer will vary according to in-house policy, yet it is likely that in all scenarios the developers and architects will play a significant role in the development or consultation process. Technical and functional specification documentation is a rather unusual type of documentation, in that it is prepared long before development commences, and in reality such documentation drives the design and development process. Commonly, application specification forms part of the contract between the software development team (or organization) and the client. Although a breach of an in-house "contract" made between an IT department and a functional department may have fewer implications than a legally enforceable contract with an external client, which may impose financial penalties, nevertheless, any type of breach reflects poorly on the team.

As technical and functional specifications may form part of a legally enforceable contract, they are not to be taken lightly. The form of the specifications will be determined by your situation. In the following two standards, there are template outlines that illustrate the type of content found in such specifications.

Technical Specification Documentation

An application requires technology to be configured to its requirements, and a technical specification details that requirement in technical terms.

What

A technical specification is a document that precisely details the minimum technical requirements for an application to meet its functional specifications.

Where

Technical specification documentation should be readily accessible to architects, developers, network and database administrators, testers, and project managers. It may be written in text and graphical format and stored in a development and/or project portal or in a set of folders on the network.

Why

A technical specification is relied on by application architects and developers in designing and coding an application. It establishes the technical environment that is necessary to support—or restrain—the functionality of an application. It is also relied on by clients to configure their environment or to evaluate an application (and other stakeholders).

How

There is no set way to document a technical specification; however, it is of most value when presented using precise technical terminology. The following template illustrates a brief outline.

Technical Specification for XYZ Application

- Hardware requirements

  - Processor and memory (e.g., processor Intel 2.20 GHz; memory 512 MB)

  - Disk space (e.g., minimum 50 MB to maximum 350 MB)

  - Screen (e.g., resolution SVGA 800 x 600; size 17")

- Printers

- Devices

  - PDAs

- Software requirements

    - Word processor (e.g., Microsoft Word 2003)

    - Internet browser (e.g., Microsoft Internet Explorer 4+)

    - Database (e.g., Microsoft SQL Server 2000+)

The Standard: Technical Specification Documentation

The standard acknowledges the role of technical specification documentation and its importance in supporting the functional specification of an application.

Functional Specification Documentation

An application represents a set of functional requirements and is specified in terms of user requirements.

What

A functional specification is a document that precisely details the functionality and tolerances of an application.

Where

Functional specification documentation should be readily accessible to business analysts, architects, developers, testers, and project managers. It may be written in text and graphical format and stored in a development and/or project portal or in a set of folders on the network.

Why

A functional specification is relied on by business analysts, application architects, and developers in application development. It establishes the functional requirements against which the design and the application are measured. It is also relied on by clients to evaluate and verify the suitability of an application to meet their requirements.

How

There is no set way to document a functional specification, but it is of most value when presented using precise functional terminology; when it is contextually categorized; and when requirements are clearly identified—for example, by using a requirements numbering system. The following template illustrates a brief outline:

- Functional overview

- Lists of feature requirements

    - List of use case (user functionality) requirements

    - List of performance requirements and tolerances

- List of scalability requirements and tolerances

- List of load requirements and tolerances

- List of user interface requirements

- List of middleware requirements

- List of interface requirements (e.g., software and hardware)

- List of security requirements

- List of quality requirements (e.g., downtime)

- List of assumptions, dependencies, and constraints

- Definitions, acronyms, and abbreviations

The Standard: Functional Specification Documentation

The standard acknowledges the role of functional specification documentation and its importance in directing the design and development of an application and in evaluating and verifying that an application meets client requirements.

Application Design Documentation

In documenting an application design, the focus is on documenting the architecture of the application and how the application fits into the enterprise (e.g., enterprise design framework). Documenting application design differs from documenting code: (1) code is documented by developers, whereas design is documented by an application architect and a technical lead developer; (2) application design focuses on code from an abstract or strategic perspective (e.g., identifying architecture strategies); and (3) application design documentation targets a wider technical audience—for example, project sponsors, project managers, enterprise architects, application architects, lead developers, developers, network architects, database administrators, business analysts, testers, and technical auditors. By contrast, code documentation has a more limited audience, including application architects, lead developers, developers, and technical auditors.

What

Application design documentation documents the architecture of an application and how the application fits within the enterprise (e.g., enterprise design framework). Figure 8-1 illustrates where application design is in the documentation hierarchy.

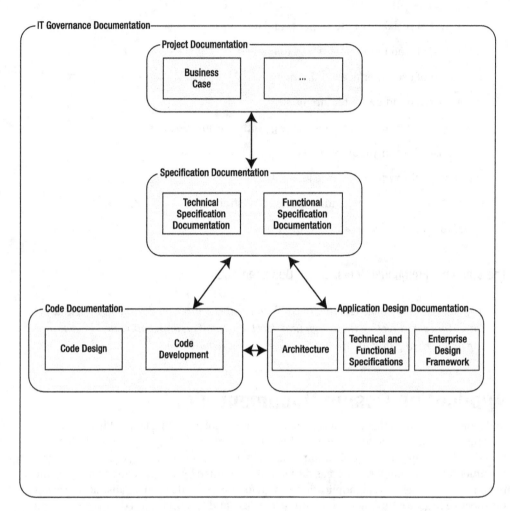

Figure 8-1. *Application design documentation*

Where

Application design documentation should be readily accessible to architects and developers. It may be written in text and graphical format and stored in a development portal or in a set of folders on the network.

Why

> *Application design documentation enables a team to retain and share critical application design knowledge that identifies and explains the underlying intention of the architects and development team. The standard acknowledges the role of technical specification documentation and its importance in supporting the functional specification of an application.*

How

The documentation is written by application architects and technical lead developers. It is written in document format and in four stages: preapplication development; application development; postapplication development; and life-cycle development. In the preapplication development stage, the application architecture is prepared based on the technical and functional specifications, by the application architect and lead developer in consultation with the enterprise architect. During the application development stage, the documentation is prepared and modified as the implementation realities are identified. Modifications to architecture are prepared in consultation with the enterprise architect, project manager, and, if necessary, the project sponsor. In the postapplication development stage (i.e., once the application has been developed and released), any additional documentation is added, such as documentation relating to testing and subsequent modification. The final phase of documentation refers to life-cycle documentation, that is, documenting service packs and versions of the application. It is updated for as long as the application is supported.

The Standard: Application Design Documentation

> *The standard acknowledges the documentation of application design and observes that it should be readily accessible to architects and developers.*

Application Architecture Documentation

Documenting an application architecture requires the systematic arrangement of information, which provides an overview and a detailed explanation of the structure of an application. If an organization uses an application framework, then the focus of the documentation is limited to explaining the specialization of the architecture within the framework (an application framework is documented as a separate application).

What

Application architecture documentation is a living document that identifies and explains the key aspects of the architecture of a given application, in summary and detail formats. It is a technical document, composed of text, figures, and tables, and written for a technical audience.

Where

Application architecture documentation forms part of application design architecture and design documentation; it should be readily accessible to architects and developers—for example, in a development portal or in a set of folders on the network.

Why

Application architecture documentation enables a team to retain and share critical architecture design knowledge that identifies and explains the underlying intention of the application architect and the lead developer.

How

An effective way to produce application architecture documentation is by developing it from a template. An example template is illustrated next. The template may be conveniently prepared as a set of HTML pages and graphics posted to a portal, or alternatively as a set of Word documents and graphics stored within a hierarchy of folders on a network.

1. **Preliminaries**
   a. Objective—identify the object of the document
   b. Ownership—identify ownership and responsibilities
   c. Version history—list version history
   d. Outline—prepare a document index
2. **Document overview**—prepare a brief overview of the document
3. **Specifications**
   a. Functional—prepare a summary of functional specifications
   b. Technical—prepare a summary of technical specifications
4. **Architecture strategy**—prepare a description of the key design decisions, reasons, and compromises, as well as insights into key features of the architecture; identify extensibility, vulnerabilities, and constraints, etc.
5. **Application architecture**
   a. Application layers—identify and explain layers: e.g., five layers or tiers
      - Summary
      - Detail
   b. Enterprise layer mapping—identify and explain mapping or interfacing of application architecture layers to layers within the enterprise application framework (application integration layer)
6. **Design topology**
   a. Methodology—identify and explain methodologies, e.g., development sequence; reuse of enterprise services functionality
   b. Dependencies and assumptions—identify architecture dependencies (e.g., enterprise services accessed via the application integration layer) and key assumptions (e.g., critical statements made in functional and technical specifications)
   c. Risks—identify risks and tolerances, etc.
7. . . . (more content)

8. Glossary

    a. Terms—define key terms used in the document

    b. Acronyms—define acronyms used in the document

9. . . . (more references)

The Standard: Application Architecture Documentation

The standard acknowledges the documentation of application architecture and that it should be readily accessible to architects and developers. Documentation enables a team to retain and share critical architecture design knowledge that identifies and explains the underlying intention of the application architect and lead developer.

Enterprise Framework Documentation

Documentation of an application architecture doesn't end with the documentation of the application; it is also necessary to document how it fits within the enterprise design framework.

What

Although the application architecture also documents the interface between the application and the application integration layer, it is also necessary to understand its relationship with other layers within the enterprise design framework (e.g., network services and communication layers)—which is the purpose of enterprise framework documentation.

Where

Enterprise framework documentation forms part of application design architecture and design documentation and should be readily accessible to architects and developers—for example, in a development portal or in a set of folders on the network.

Why

Enterprise framework documentation and application architecture documentation enable a team to retain and share critical knowledge of how an application integrates and impacts an enterprise.

How

An effective way to produce enterprise framework documentation is by developing it from a template. An example template is illustrated next. It may be conveniently prepared as a set of

HTML pages and graphics posted to a portal, or alternatively as a set of Word documents and graphics stored within a hierarchy of folders on a network.

1. Preliminaries

    a. Objective—identify the object of the document

    b. Ownership—identify ownership and responsibilities

    c. Version history—list version history

    d. Outline—prepare a document index

2. Document overview—prepare a brief overview of the document

3. Enterprise integration

    a. Summary

    b. Detail

    - Application integration layer

    - Enterprise services dependencies—identify enterprise services dependencies (e.g., security functionality)

    - Network layer—identify deployment architecture; network impact analysis, etc.

    - Communication layer

    - Assumptions—list key assumptions (e.g., critical statements made in functional and technical specifications)

    - Risks—identify risks and tolerances, etc.

4. Glossary

    a. Terms—define key terms used in the document

    b. Acronyms—define acronyms used in the document

5. ... (more references)

The Standard: Enterprise Framework Documentation

The standard acknowledges the documentation of application design as it relates to the enterprise architecture and that it should be readily accessible to architects and developers. Documentation enables a team to retain and share critical architecture design knowledge that identifies and explains the underlying intention of the enterprise and application architects and lead developer.

PART 3

■ ■ ■

Pattern Standards

In this part of the book we discuss pattern standards by looking at a selection of design patterns that were cataloged by Drs. Gamma, Helm, Johnson, and Vlissides (GoF). They are presented in Chapters 10 to 12; however, before we discuss them we introduce pattern language and design patterns.

CHAPTER 9

■ ■ ■

Patterns

In this chapter we introduce *patterns* and discuss the role they play in solving recurring software problems. There are three aspects of patterns of interest to us: *pattern language, design patterns,* and *talking patterns.*

Pattern Language

A pattern language is a technical vocabulary that we use to communicate design problems and solutions in a given domain. It has a simple grammar that consists of *problem* and *solution types* (as we shall soon see, a design pattern is a solution type). In other words, a pattern language is an intelligent way to discuss and solve problems: it is structured, efficient, and universal.

Design Patterns

A *design pattern* is a generic or template solution to a given problem type or genre, in a given context. In a domain, when a new problem exhibits distinctive characteristics, it is identified as a *problem type*; for example, in a road management pattern language, the problem of cars colliding at an uncontrolled intersection is identified as problem type: *uncontrolled intersection.* After considering the uncontrolled intersection problem, a generic solution is identified, tested, and proven; the result of this process is the creation of the *intersection controller* design pattern, which is then applied to solve the given problem.

A design pattern is a generic solution because it will be implemented in a variety of ways; for example, in the previous scenario, we applied the intersection controller design pattern to solve an uncontrolled intersection problem, in which cars collided. However, if we had another uncontrolled intersection problem that involved cars and trains, then we would implement the intersection controller design pattern differently: in the car scenario, we might implement four sets of traffic lights, whereas in the car–train scenario we might implement four sets of traffic lights and a set of crossing gates.

Talking Patterns

Patterns are not monuments that we place on a pedestal and admire from afar. They need to be part of our everyday working vocabulary; they allow us to map our thoughts and skills into structured solutions. To become articulate we have to talk in patterns habitually—that is, talk about problems and solutions in terms of design patterns.

Earlier, it was said that a pattern language is structured, efficient, and universal. From the intersection scenarios discussed in the previous section, we can see the efficiency of a structure that frames problems and maps them to solutions (a given design pattern). Once the grammar of the pattern language is understood by people working in the given domain, then it can be used universally; for example, management can talk with developers and be understood, which would be a refreshing novelty.

If we were asked to design and develop a computer traffic program that simulated the intersection scenarios, then by learning the pattern language we would be talking design very quickly and successfully. An architect could converse with a developer at a high level of abstraction without ever knowing anything about code and yet be understood. For example, the architect might say to the lead developer: "In this application we have two uncontrolled intersection problems, one with cars only and the other with cars and trains. So, please implement an intersection controller for each problem." From this brief dialogue, the lead developer will know exactly what the architect wants and can leave the meeting with a clear vision of the problem and solution.

From this introduction we can already see great value in using a pattern language:

- It requires us to articulate problems and solutions in a structured format.

- It is universal.

- It helps us to communicate in an efficient manner.

- It enables us to discuss low-level implementation in a high-level, abstract manner.

- It enables us to apply a proven solution (design pattern).

- It is expandable—a domain can create new design patterns for new problem types.

Using a pattern language and design patterns is a relatively new practice in computer science, and they have their origins in building architecture and city planning.

The Origins: Pattern Language and Design Patterns

In 1995, a pattern language and a catalog of design patterns were articulated by Drs. Gamma, Helm, Johnson, and Vlissides—commonly known as the "Gang of Four" (GoF)—in their book *Design Patterns: Elements of Reusable Object-Oriented Software* (Addison-Wesley, 1995). In the book they discuss a foundation set of 23 design patterns that they observed were commonly found in software development. The GoF adapted the ideas of Dr. Christopher Alexander and others, who had applied the concept in the fields of city planning and building architecture. In 1975, Alexander authored *The Oregon Experiment,* which was followed in 1977 by *A Pattern Language,* coauthored with S. Ishikawa, M. Silverstein, M. Jacobson, I. Fiksdahl-King, and S. Angel. And in 1979, Alexander authored *The Timeless Way of Building.*

Note The works of Christopher Alexander may be reviewed at his website: `www.patternlanguage.com`.

It is understood that the first sighting of a design pattern in computer science was in 1978–79, when Professor Trygve Reenskaug, while at Xerox PARC, articulated *the* design pattern: Model-View–Controller (MVC). Subsequently, a version of the MVC pattern was implemented by Jim Althoff and others in the Smalltalk-80 class library. As history has unfolded, MVC has turned out to be not only a design pattern, but with its ability to efficiently manage coupling, it is also considered to be an architecture pattern. We will revisit MVC at the end of this chapter and use it as a fitting way to bridge this brief historical introduction and lead us into subsequent chapters, in which we examine many of the design patterns cataloged by GoF.

Note The works of Professor Reenskaug may be reviewed at his website: `http://heim.ifi.uio.no/ ~trygver/index.html`.

In his books, Alexander observes that in architecture throughout the world, there is a regularity with which design problems are solved by variations of a common set of design patterns. He articulates a language that uses building patterns as a grammar to enable architects and builders to discuss design problems and solutions. It is worthwhile to spend a little time familiarizing ourselves with Alexander's concept so that we can see how the pattern language works in its original setting. To appreciate a pattern language, we need to think and talk in the language.

Thinking and Talking in a Pattern Language

In *The Timeless Way of Building*, Alexander asserts that the design of a building or town needs to be "alive" and that this can be achieved by defining a sequence of patterns that gives "life" to the building or town. Alexander refers to this concept as a "quality without a name." For example, a town can be given life by structuring it around a *town center* or *marketplace* from which *narrow cobblestone lanes* can be affixed and adorned with *quaint shops*. Such a design enables people to have a pleasant walk through atmospheric narrow lanes, passing one quaint shop after another to arrive at a marketplace abuzz with activity.

In this vision, the town center or marketplace, narrow cobblestone lanes, and quaint shops are design patterns that have been carefully sequenced to create a town with a life, which is timeless and abuzz with pleasant activities. That "timeless way of building" is an obvious solution to the problem of an anti-shopping attitude, which bugs many consumers when shopping in enclosed shopping centers surrounded by acres of parking lots.

From this brief introduction, we can see how easy it is for us to visualize the same problem domain as we both think and talk in the pattern language—it's little wonder that Alexander's ideas have excited so many people!

In computer science it is a little more difficult to become fluent and visualize problems and solutions, yet, as in learning any language, this short-term bump is soon smoothed over with persistence and practice.

Tip   To appreciate pattern languages and design patterns, it is beneficial to read the original material. Much can be learned from reading *A Pattern Language or The Timeless Way of Building* and the GoF's *Design Patterns: Elements of Reusable Object-Oriented Software*. (Note: the GoF's book does *not* show .NET language examples, and the models predate UML.)

Pattern Language in Computer Science

In the 26 years since the arrival of MVC, design patterns have substantially influenced computer science. MVC, for example, has been implemented in Smalltalk, NextSTEP, OPENSTEP, Cocoa, Java Swing library, Jakarta Struts, and Microsoft Foundation Classes (MFC). Design patterns have also found their way into many other implementations, including the .NET Framework. For example, the Facade pattern is used in ADO.NET—in the DataAdapter class—to hide the complexity of dealing with different database types. This means that the DataAdapter class is presented to us as a simple and consistent interface regardless of database type: SQL Server, Oracle, MySQL, and so forth.

Unfortunately, many .NET professionals have found design patterns to be complex, so in this book we have sought to address the problem by applying our own little Facade design pattern to simplify the "learning interface" of design patterns. Each design pattern is presented using the same simple format that presents the following brief sections: "What," "Where," "Why," and "How." These sections are followed by a Model T example that includes a discussion of the problem, a UML diagram, a list of Key Code Ingredients, code listing with explanations, and a printout of the console output. A copy of the full code listings is available as a download from Apress (www.apress.com/book/download.html).

Design Patterns

Design patterns have been cataloged by GoF into three categories of problem types: *creational*, *structural*, and *behavioral*.

- A creational pattern refers to the design of a given entity. For example, a template method is a creational pattern that we use to make copies of a given design. We could use a creational pattern to make jeans or shoes or iPods.

- A structural pattern refers to the shape of a given design. For example, a Mac Mini computer is designed to ship without a keyboard or mouse or monitor, whereas a PC has a different structure and is designed to ship with a box, keyboard, mouse, and monitor.

- A behavioral pattern refers to the recurrence of a given behavior, usually in response to an action or stimulus. For example, when you feel a hunger pang (stimulus), you get something to eat (behavior).

In this book, we present a subset of 12 of 23 design patterns from the GoF catalog, plus the classic MVC pattern. We have limited our focus to the design patterns that we understand are the most commonly used in the C# community. One popular pattern that has been omitted is the *Iterator* pattern, because C# 2.0 introduces its own iterator. The C# 2.0 Iterator implementation is relatively simple compared with the design pattern: it does not require an enumerator for each type, and it leverages *generics* and the new `yield` statement in the Iterator block, which returns to the calling `foreach` statement. The *Observer* pattern varies from that articulated by GoF and is simplified by leveraging a `delegate` class, which is a feature of the C# language and was not available to GoF. We have also divided the *Proxy* pattern into *Surrogate-Proxy* and *Remote-Proxy* design patterns to acknowledge the two distinct ways that a proxy is used in the workplace.

As with any language, a pattern language is fluid, which means that a conversation is characterized by a discussion that links patterns into a "sentence," as was shown in the earlier example of the town vision. Advanced design-pattern practitioners will converse about including a number of design patterns in an application. However, in this book, our goal is to lower the design-patterns learning curve, which means that our focus is on standards that communicate the basics of design patterns, from which you can advance. The subset of design patterns we discuss are as follows:

Creational Patterns

- Abstract Factory

- Abstract Method

- Singleton

Structural Patterns

- Surrogate-Proxy

- Remote-Proxy

- Adapter

- Composite

- Facade

Behavioral Patterns

- Chain of Responsibility

- Observer

- Strategy

- Template Method

Design Patterns: Tricks of the Trade

There are a few tricks to working with design patterns:

- Think in terms of *design problems* and *solutions* (remember the earlier example about the uncontrolled intersection problem and traffic-light controller design pattern or solution).

- Think about a pattern in terms of *how* it overcomes a given problem in a given context.

- Familiarize yourself with a *category* of design patterns before moving to the next category—for example, understand all of the behavioral patterns before moving on to structural patterns. Otherwise, it is very easy to become disoriented.

- Start with the category of design patterns that best suits you.

- Practice drawing and coding the design patterns presented in this book until they become second nature, and then substitute the examples for scenarios in your workplace.

- Actively think about patterns—get into a pattern habit!

We now continue by introducing the MVC pattern, as a forerunner to the following three chapters on design patterns. The MVC is arguably *the mother of all design patterns*.

Note To run the Console application, if you press **F5** in Visual Studio 2005, the **Quick Console** will appear; if you press **Ctrl+F5**, then the **Windows Console** will appear. It is only in the **Windows Console** that you will see the `Press any key to continue` notice, at the bottom of the Console window.

MVC

An MVC pattern encapsulates a design feature where *controller* objects play a decoupling role by enabling clients to choose a *view* of information, while minimizing or preventing change to the *model*, which outputs the information in one format only. In everyday life, examples of a MVC pattern include a translation tool that translates code from Java to C#, or an integration layer that interposes two layers of architecture.

What

The MVC pattern is a design that seeks to minimize the impact that results from fulfilling the requirements of clients to control how they view information from the model.

Where

An MVC is used where there is a requirement to vary perspectives or views (output) without disturbing, or while minimizing the disruption to, the underlying information source (model) that publishes the information used in the views. It may be used not only in an information-view scenario, but also in architecture—for example, to offer platform independence.

A platform controller object (controller) may be used to transpose functionality of an application (model) that runs on an incompatible platform to an application (view) running on another platform. The pattern may natively be extended to include multiple controllers.

Why

MVC prevents the model from being coupled to an expensive association with clients, while maintaining a relatively low-cost association between the model and the respective controllers—who return the view to the client(s). In other words, the technical and economic rationale is that it is more manageable and less expensive to encapsulate change in a set of controller objects than it is to disfigure the model object through constant reengineering. In many domains clients want to have control over the way information is presented to them, but this presents a problem because it would place additional responsibility on the object that publishes the information, in one standard format, and would directly couple many views to that one publisher (model).

How

The MVC overcomes the multiview problem by encapsulating the client requirements in a controller object that transposes the information from the model object into the variety of formats required by the client. The client gets what it wants, and the model is left undisturbed or requires relatively minor reengineering. We do this by creating a model object (model) and a view interface (IView), or abstract class, if you prefer; then deriving any number of views (AmericanView and NorwegianView classes) from the interface; then creating a controller object (controller), to represent each view; and then wiring up the functionality. The client accesses the views it wants from the controllers, and the model may be none the wiser or only a little inconvenienced. In a nontrivial example, unlike the following, the controller would normally associate with the model through a publisher–subscriber relationship. The model would publish an event against which the controller would subscribe or register. So, scaling the MVC may require minimal change to the model, if new events are required for new views.

Caution Although it may be tempting to encapsulate the control of all views within one controller object, it is a design that doesn't scale and that is contrary to object-oriented design best practices.

Pattern Example

In the Model T domain, we have an application that is used to look up the price of spare parts. The problem that we have is that the information is displayed to the screen in only the English language: it was unforeseen when the application was designed that there would ever be a need for another display language. But now the men in suits have decided to permit dealers from other countries to access the system and look up the price in their native language. To accommodate this, we are required to come up with yet another cunning little plan, this time a design that permits the application to display the text in various languages, while quoting the price in U.S. dollars.

The part of the problem we are focusing on is how to add variability to client views without reengineering the object that returns the content of that view (i.e., the price of the part). Given that we are expected to add 35 languages (or views), we have decided to develop a proof of concept using two language view controllers (American and Norwegian).

We shall now look at the MVC pattern (see Figure 9-1) in a UML diagram and then implement the pattern in code.

UML

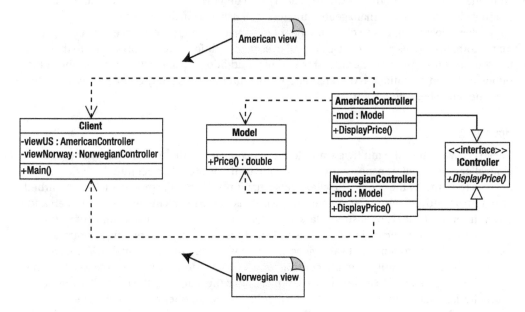

Figure 9-1. *MVC pattern*

Key Code Ingredients

The code for MVC has the following key ingredients:

- A Model class (Model)—with some functionality.

- A View interface type (IView).

- A set of controller classes that implement the IView interface (AmericanController and NorwegianController classes), for each view.

- Client code (Client) that decides which views are called.

Now let's code the MVC pattern.

Pattern Code

The essence of the design lies in delegating responsibility and managing the placement of coupling. The Model is an independent class; it just returns a price when asked—it is decoupled. Two ordinary classes (AmericanController and NorwegianController) implement the IController interface, making them controller types. They are coupled to the Model class, and the client (Client) is, in turn, lightly coupled to the controller objects (AmericanController and NorwegianController). We have made the controllers inherit from an interface type rather than an abstract class to illustrate the flexibility of interface types: a class can implement many interfaces. Alternatively, we could have used a controller abstract class and overridden the DisplayPrice() method. However, the trade-off between the two methodologies is that by using an interface type we do more wiring (i.e., cut–paste and tweak) for the benefit of avoiding the restriction of using a Controller class as a base class. (The choice of a base class is a big issue with single class inheritance; perhaps there is a better candidate for a base class, in the domain, other than a Controller class?) It is the respective controller objects that manage the responsibility of preparing respective views for the client (Client). It is ultimately the client who chooses which view to display—in this situation, both views have been displayed to prove the concept.

Model Class

```
public class Model
{
  public double Price()
  {
    return 100;
  }
}
```

IController Interface

```
interface IController
{
  void DisplayPrice();
}
```

AmericanController Class

```
public class AmericanController: IController
{
  private Model mod;

  public void DisplayPrice()
  {
    //get price from model and add US margin
    double cost = mod.Price()*1.1;
```

```
      String message = "Price: USD " + cost.ToString();
      Console.WriteLine(message);
   }

   public AmericanController()
   {
     mod = new Model();
   }
}
```

NorwegianController Class

```
public class NorwegianController: IController
{
   private Model mod;

   public void DisplayPrice()
   {
     //get price from model and add Norwegian margin
     double cost = mod.Price() * 1.15;
     String message = "Pris: USD " + cost.ToString();
     Console.WriteLine(message);
   }

   public NorwegianController()
   {
       mod = new Model();
   }
}
```

Client Code

In the client code we see the MVC pattern at work. We test the effectiveness of the design pattern by creating instances of two controllers that return an American and Norwegian view of the price of a spare part. Each view is illustrated in English and Norwegian languages, respectively. (The price differential reflects the additional costs associated with European orders.)

```
public class Client
{
   static void Main(string[] args)
   {
     AmericanController viewUS = new AmericanController();
     viewUS.DisplayPrice();
     NorwegianController viewNorway = new NorwegianController();
     viewNorway.DisplayPrice();
   }
}
```

Console Output

```
Price: USD 110
Pris: USD 115
Press any key to continue . . .
```

The Standard: MVC Pattern

The standard acknowledges the use of the MVC design pattern where there is a require-ment to vary perspectives or views (output) without disturbing—or while minimizing the disruption to—the underlying information source (model) that publishes the information.

CHAPTER 10

■ ■ ■

Creational Patterns

Creational patterns encapsulate a design feature where the focus is on strategically manipulating the instantiation of classes. They empower design by augmenting the act of class instantiation so that it can affect the behavior of a class, as well. In everyday life, examples of a creational pattern include a bank check that can be instantiated only once, or a web application that dynamically creates a set of controls compatible with a given web browser.

What

In software design, creational patterns give the software designer a tool that can be used to bring subtlety to the creation or instantiation of classes by isolating what objects get instantiated, where, when, and how.

Where

Creational patterns are used where a design needs to exhibit flexibility of control over the creational behavior of a set of classes in a given domain.

Why

In many domains there is a requirement to configure behavioral characteristics that go beyond the bounds of encapsulating functionality in a class and require flexibility over *what*, *where*, *when*, and *how* classes are created. In most domains this requirement presents a problem, so to overcome the problem a creational pattern is incorporated into the design of the program.

How

There are commonly four features that identify how a given creational pattern is implemented: identify *what* gets created, *where* it gets created, *when* it gets created, and *how* it gets created. The functionality of a given creational pattern lies with these four features: they usually reside in one or two classes and client code.

In the Model T domain, we present three examples of creational patterns: Abstract Factory, Abstract Method, and Singleton.

■Note To run the respective Console applications, if you press **F5** in Visual Studio 2005, the **Quick Console** will appear; if you press **Ctrl+F5**, then the **Windows Console** will appear. It is only in the **Windows Console** that you will see the `Press any key to continue` notice, at the bottom of the Console window.

Abstract Factory Pattern

An *Abstract Factory* pattern encapsulates a design feature where a client associates with an abstract factory, which in turn creates a set of related objects—this enables the client to indirectly control object creation while distancing itself from coupling to a set or family of object implementations. In everyday life, examples of an Abstract Factory pattern include a human resource analyst who creates departmental job positions without needing to know the details of the incumbents; or a web application that renders a set of controls appropriate for a given web browser type or version.

What

An Abstract Factory pattern is a design that enables a client to deal with a high-level abstraction while leaving the factory abstraction to deal with coupling the implementation.

Where

An Abstract Factory pattern is used where there is a requirement not to couple the client to an implementation that creates sets or families of objects. The pattern enables the client to commit to an interface and avoid commitment to an implementation.

Why

In many domains there is a requirement for client code to avoid committing to an implementation; this design requirement enhances the client's ability to switch between a set or family of objects. In some domains switching presents a major reengineering problem, so to prevent or overcome the problem, the Abstract Factory pattern is incorporated into the design of the program.

How

Client code has an association at a high level with the interface of the factory class. It is the role of the factory objects to commit to creating the sets of objects that are indirectly manipulated by client code through the factory interface.

Pattern Example

In the Model T domain, there is client code that manages the supply of radiators fitted to the car. The part of the problem we are focusing on is how to isolate the client from the code that implements the creation of radiators and caps, yet enable the client code to indirectly control the build process.

To code this routine, we let client code deal through a factory abstraction that acts as a medium through which it can manipulate the creation of different sets of radiators and caps from different factories. In the client, a work order is used to give the build process a context; it is passed to an abstract factory that is called on to create a set of factory implementations or types (Briscoe, Detroit, and McCord). In turn, the set of factory implementations create sets of product implementations or types (Radiator and RadiatorCap). This design pattern ensures that the client can avoid coupling to an implementation and yet indirectly control the creation of objects. That is the Abstract Factory pattern!

We shall now look at the Abstract Factory pattern in a UML diagram (see Figure 10-1) and then implement the pattern in code.

UML

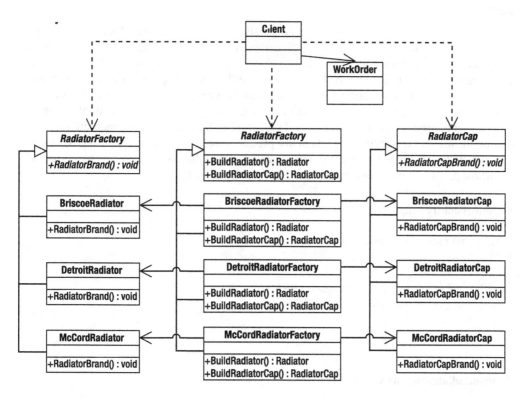

Figure 10-1. *Abstract Factory pattern*

Key Code Ingredients

The code for the Abstract Factory pattern has the following key ingredients:

- An abstract RadiatorFactory class

- A number of RadiatorFactory objects derived from the abstract RadiatorFactory class

- An abstract Radiator class

- A number of Radiator objects derived from the abstract Radiator class

- An abstract RadiatorCap class

- A number of RadiatorCap objects derived from the abstract Radiator class

- A WorkOrder class

- Client code that, through passing a set of abstract factories to an instance of a WorkOrder, is able to indirectly control the creation of sets of factories (Briscoe, Detroit, and McCord) that build sets of products (Radiators and RadiatorCaps)

Now let's code the Abstract Factory pattern.

Pattern Code

The essence of the design lies in the way in which the abstract RadiatorFactory class leverages abstract classes (Radiator and RadiatorCap), delegating or deferring implementation and coupling to RadiatorFactory objects. The WorkOrder class plays the role of a context that enables the client to distance itself from the build process. Notice that it is when the RadiatorFactory class is implemented or instantiated that there is the first commitment to a set of factories types (Briscoe, Detroit, and McCord). In turn, these factory types commit to an implementation of a set of product types (Radiators and RadiatorCaps). Observe the regimentation of control throughout the design: the sets of like products are encapsulated within a given factory, which itself is treated as an abstraction through which the client indirectly manipulates the whole process without being coupled to factory or product types.

RadiatorFactory Class

```
public abstract class RadiatorFactory
{

  public abstract Radiator BuildRadiator();
  public abstract RadiatorCap BuildRadiatorCap();

}
```

BriscoeRadiatorFactory Class

```
public class BriscoeRadiatorFactory: RadiatorFactory
{

  public override Radiator BuildRadiator()
  {
    Radiator rad = new BriscoeRadiator();
    rad.RadiatorBrand();
    return rad;
  }
```

```
  public override RadiatorCap BuildRadiatorCap()
  {
    RadiatorCap cap = new BriscoeRadiatorCap();
    cap.RadiatorCapBrand();
    return cap;
  }

  public BriscoeRadiatorFactory() {;}
 }
```

DetroitRadiatorFactory Class

```
public class DetroitRadiatorFactory: RadiatorFactory
{

  public override Radiator BuildRadiator()
  {
    Radiator rad = new  DetroitRadiator();
    rad.RadiatorBrand();
    return rad;
  }

  public override RadiatorCap BuildRadiatorCap()
  {
    RadiatorCap cap = new DetroitRadiatorCap();
    cap.RadiatorCapBrand();
    return cap;
  }

  public DetroitRadiatorFactory() {;}
}
```

McCordRadiatorFactory Class

```
public class McCordRadiatorFactory: RadiatorFactory
{

  public override Radiator BuildRadiator()
  {
    Radiator rad = new  McCordRadiator();
    rad.RadiatorBrand();
    return rad;
  }

  public override RadiatorCap BuildRadiatorCap()
```

```
  {
    RadiatorCap cap = new McCordRadiatorCap();
    cap.RadiatorCapBrand();
    return cap;
  }

  public McCordRadiatorFactory() {;}
}
```

Radiator Class

```
public abstract class Radiator
{

  public abstract void RadiatorBrand();

}
```

BriscoeRadiator Class

```
public class BriscoeRadiator: Radiator
{

  public override void RadiatorBrand()
  {
    Console.WriteLine ("Briscoe Radiator.");
  }

  public BriscoeRadiator() {;}

}
```

DetroitRadiator Class

```
public class DetroitRadiator:Radiator
{

  public override void RadiatorBrand()
  {
    Console.WriteLine ("Detroit Radiator.");
  }

  public DetroitRadiator() {;}

}
```

McCordRadiator Class

```csharp
public class McCordRadiator: Radiator
{

  public override void RadiatorBrand()
  {
    Console.WriteLine ("McCord Radiator.");
  }

  public McCordRadiator() {;}

}
```

RadiatorCap Class

```csharp
public abstract class RadiatorCap
{

  public abstract void RadiatorCapBrand();
}
```

BriscoeRadiatorCap Class

```csharp
public class BriscoeRadiatorCap: RadiatorCap
{

  public override void RadiatorCapBrand()
  {
    Console.WriteLine("Briscoe Radiator cap.");
  }

  public BriscoeRadiatorCap() {;}

}
```

DetroitRadiatorCap Class

```csharp
public class DetroitRadiatorCap: RadiatorCap
{

  public override void RadiatorCapBrand()
  {
    Console.WriteLine("Detroit Radiator cap.");
  }
```

```
  public DetroitRadiatorCap() {;}
}
```

McCordRadiatorCap Class

```
public class McCordRadiatorCap: RadiatorCap
{

  public override void RadiatorCapBrand()
  {
    Console.WriteLine("McCord Radiator cap.");
  }

  public McCordRadiatorCap() {;}

}
```

WorkOrder Class

```
public class WorkOrder
{

  public void AssembleRadiator(Factory fact)
  {
    Radiator rad = fact.BuildRadiator();
    RadiatorCap cap = fact.BuildRadiatorCap();
    this.Assemble();
  }

  private void Assemble()
  {
    Console.WriteLine ("Assembling Radiator and cap.");
    Console.WriteLine();
  }

  public WorkOrder() {;}

}
```

Client Code

In the client code, we see the Abstract Factory pattern at work. We test the effectiveness of the design pattern, which enables client code to indirectly control the build process through a set of factories and a set of products, while ensuring that it is decoupled from factory and product implementations.

```
class Client
{

  static void Main(string[] args)
  {
    Factory factoryOne = new BriscoeRadiatorFactory();
    WorkOrder workOne = new WorkOrder();
    workOne.AssembleRadiator(factory1);

    /* With the Abstract Factory pattern,
    The Model T domain can easily
    switch suppliers. It simply stops calling
    the Briscoe Radiator
    factory, and commences calling the Detroit
    and McCord Radiator
    factories, to supply radiators. For each
    new supplier, respective
    Radiator, Cap and Factory classes need to
    be added. Which is a good
    thing, because shortly after changing from
    Briscoe, The Model T
    domain made a further change and began
    to fit only Ford radiators.*/

    Factory factoryTwo = new DetroitRadiatorFactory();
    WorkOrder workTwo = new WorkOrder();
    workTwo.AssembleRadiator(factoryTwo);

    Factory factoryThree = new McCordRadiatorFactory();
    WorkOrder workThree = new WorkOrder();
    workThree.AssembleRadiator(factoryThree);

  }

}
```

Console Output

```
Briscoe Radiator.
Briscoe Radiator cap.
Assembling Radiator and cap.

Detroit Radiator.
Detroit Radiator cap.
Assembling Radiator and cap.
```

```
McCord Radiator.
MsCord Radiator cap.
Assembling Radiator and cap.

Press any key to continue
```

The Standard: Abstract Factory Design Pattern

The standard acknowledges the use of the Abstract Factory design pattern when there is a requirement not to couple the client to an implementation that creates sets or families of object, yet to let the client indirectly control the build process.

Factory Method Pattern

A *Factory Method* pattern encapsulates a design feature when a class can't foresee what objects it will be required to create and so delegates the task to subclasses. In everyday life, examples of a factory pattern include a translation service that delegates the task of translating news stories to a variety of specialist language translators; or a visual display controller that delegates the task of displaying data to display objects, which in turn display data in text or graphic format.

What

A Factory Method pattern is a design that defines an interface for creating objects but delegates the choice of what objects to create to subclasses.

Where

A Factory Method pattern is used where there is a design problem where a creator class is required to be decoupled from creating specific objects.

Why

In many domains there is a requirement for flexibility in creating a variety of objects and to localize the functionality to a set of specialized subclasses.

How

The creator class delegates to its subclasses, which override its factory method to create specific types, which in turn create content objects.

Pattern Example

In the Model T domain, there is client code that manages composing two publications: a new car catalog and an owners' technical manual.

The part of the problem we are focusing on is how to efficiently coordinate the tasks of creating different content and different arrangements in different publications: a page in a catalog is arranged with features and picture content, whereas a page in a technical manual is arranged with technical, picture, and instruction content.

To code this routine, we create an abstract page class (Page) that includes an abstract factory method (AddContent()) that the subclasses (CatalogPage and ManualPage) will override as they make a choice on which content to add to the respective page. An abstract Content class offers an interface to manage the creation of content by subclasses (FeaturesContent, InstructionContent, PictureContent, and TechnicalContent). The factory method (AddContent()), which resides in the Page sub-classes (CatalogPage and ManualPage), makes the choice of what Content classes to instantiate in the respective page. That is the Factory Method pattern!

We shall now look at the Factory Method pattern in a UML diagram (see Figure 10-2) and then implement the pattern in code.

UML

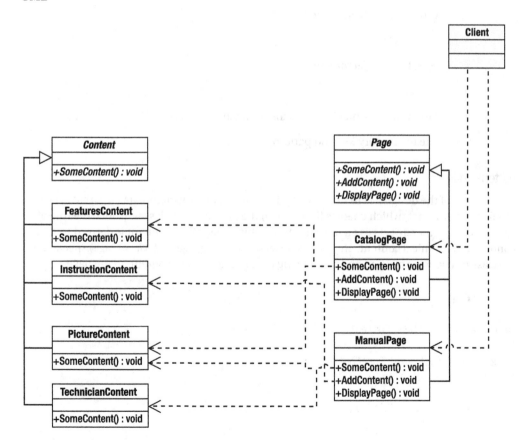

Figure 10-2. *Factory Method pattern*

Key Code Ingredients

The code for the Factory Method pattern has the following key ingredients:

- An abstract Content class
- Several classes that derive from Content class
    - FeaturesContent class
    - InstructionContent class
    - PictureContent class
    - TechnicalContent class
- An abstract Page class
    - An abstract factory method
- Several classes that derive from Page class
    - CatalogPage class
    - An override of the factory method
    - ManualPage class
    - An override of the factory method
    - Client class
    - A call to the factory method of an instantiated Page class

Now let's code the Factory Method pattern.

Pattern Code

The essence of the design lies in the Page class, where the factory method (AddContent()) is modified as abstract, which enables flexibility in the design of subclasses. Notice the role of Content class: it merely acts as an interface from which specialized content is derived (picture content and technical content, etc.). The subclasses (CatalogPage and ManualPage) specialize the class by choosing content and sequencing the arrangement of content on the page.

Content Class

```
public abstract class Content
{
  public abstract void SomeContent();
}
```

FeaturesContent Class

```
public class FeaturesContent: Content
{

  public override void SomeContent()
  {
    Console.WriteLine("Technical content.");
  }

  public FeaturesContent() {;}

}
```

InstructionContent Class

```
 public class InstructionContent: Content
{

  public override void SomeContent()
  {
    Console.WriteLine("Instruction content.");
  }

  public InstructionContent() {;}

}
```

PictureContent Class

```
public class PictureContent: Content
{

  public override void SomeContent()
  {
      Console.WriteLine("Picture content.");
  }

  public PictureContent() {;}

}
```

TechnicalContent Class

```
public class TechnicalContent: Content
{

  public override void SomeContent()
  {
    Console.WriteLine("Technical content.");
  }

  public TechnicalContent() {;}

}
```

Page Class

```
public abstract class Page
{

  //A page compositor arranges the content on the page
  protected ArrayList pageCompositor = new ArrayList();

  //This is the Factory method
  public abstract void AddContent();

  //Method to display page content
  public abstract void DisplayPage();

}
```

CatalogPage Class

```
public class CatalogPage: Page
{

  //This is the Factory method
  public override void AddContent()
  {
    this.pageCompositor.Clear();
    this.pageCompositor.Add(new FeaturesContent());
    this.pageCompositor.Add(new PictureContent());
  }

  //Method to display page content
  public override void DisplayPage()
  {
```

```
    Console.WriteLine("Catalog page contains:");
    foreach(Content c in this.pageCompositor)
      c.SomeContent();
    Console.WriteLine();
  }


  public CatalogPage()
  {
    this.AddContent();
  }
}
```

ManualPage Class

```
public class ManualPage: Page
{


  //This is the Factory method
  public override void AddContent()
  {
    this.pageCompositor.Clear();
    this.pageCompositor.Add(new TechnicalContent());
    this.pageCompositor.Add(new PictureContent());
    this.pageCompositor.Add(new InstructionContent());

  }

  //Method to display page content
  public override void DisplayPage()
  {
    Console.WriteLine("Manual page contains:");
      foreach(Content c in this.pageCompositor)
        c.SomeContent();
    Console.WriteLine();
  }

  public ManualPage() {;}

}
```

Client Code

In the client code, we see the Factory Method pattern at work. We test the effectiveness of the design pattern, which shelters client code from the details of page composition—it is required only to create an instance of the respective Page types and call their respective factory methods (AddContent()) to set in motion the creation of different content, page types, and arrangements.

```
class Client
{

    static void Main(string[] args)
    {
        //1. Compose content on a page of a Catalog
        Page p = new CatalogPage();
        p.AddContent(); //calling the Factory method
        p.DisplayPage();

        //2. Compose content on a page of a Manual
        p = new ManualPage();
        p.AddContent(); //calling the Factory method
        p.DisplayPage();

    }

}
```

Console Output

```
Catalog page contains:
Technical content.
Picture content.

Manual page contains:
Technical content.
Picture content.
Instruction content.

Press any key to continue
```

The Standard: Factory Method Design Pattern

The standard acknowledges the use of the Factory Method design pattern where there is a design problem when a creator class is required to be decoupled from creating specific objects.

Singleton Pattern

A *Singleton* pattern encapsulates a design feature when something can be done only once or when there can be only one instance of an object. In everyday life, examples of a Singleton pattern include a bank check that can be instantiated only once; or a game of tennis, where there can be only one winner.

What

A Singleton pattern is a design that ensures a given class is instantiated only once.

Where

A Singleton pattern is used where there is a design problem when there can be only one instance of a given object and where there is a requirement for client code to trigger the creation of the object.

Why

In many domains it is illogical to have more than one instance of an entity. A class has a design constraint: its constructor is natively scoped `public`, which means that the class can't control how many times its constructor is called. In some domains this constraint presents a problem, so to overcome the problem the Singleton pattern is incorporated into the design of the program.

How

In a given class, its constructor is scoped `private`, which is placed in a `public` method in which it is wrapped in an `if` statement. This ensures that no matter how many times client code calls the `public` method, only one instance of the class is created.

Pattern Example

In the Model T domain, there is client code that manages the task of installing the engine into the car. The process requires that only one engine is created per car.

The part of the problem we are focusing on is how to prevent more than one engine from being returned to client code (note: there is other code that manages the task of matching the engine to the car).

To code this routine, we need to answer two questions: How do we prevent client code calling the engine constructor more than once? and which piece of code should be responsible for controlling the quantity that is returned to client code? In "normal" class design, the constructor can be called many times by client code—the class can't, natively, restrict client code from calling it more than once. The answer to the first question lies in creating an "abnormal" class design that restricts the use of the class constructor. Given that, we can then answer the second question: we assign the responsibility for controlling the quantity to the engine class itself.

We modify the engine constructors' visibility to `private`, so that it can't be called by client code, then we wrap the `private` constructor (`private Engine()`) in a `public` method (e.g., public GetEngine()), which can be called by client code. Then, in the public method (GetEngine()), we write code that prevents the private constructor from being called, by internal code, more than once. This ensures that the engine is created once by client code, regardless of how many times it calls the GetEngine() method. That is the Singleton pattern!

We shall now look at the Singleton pattern in a UML diagram (see Figure 10-3) and then implement the pattern in code.

UML

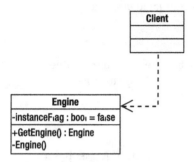

Figure 10-3. *Singleton pattern*

Key Code Ingredients

The code for the Singleton pattern has the following key ingredients:

- A class modified as sealed

- A private member variable that acts as a flag

- A private constructor

- A public static member that holds the private constructor

- An if statement that sets the flag to false once it has called the constructor

Now let's code the Singleton pattern

Pattern Code

The essence of the design lies in manipulating the control of the Engine constructor. Notice that the Engine() constructor is scoped private and how the static public method GetEngine() uses an if statement to prevent the constructor from being called more than once, while offering client code one opportunity to indirectly create an Engine. The Engine is modified sealed to prevent cloneability from being added in a subclass.

```
//note: sealed - prevent cloning
sealed class Engine
{
   //flag used in constructor: set to false when constructor
   //has not been called then set to true when called first time.
```

```
private static bool instanceFlag = false;


//Uses 'if' to set instanceFlag to truefirst time GetEngine()
//called. Subsequent calls fail to return an engine as InstanceFlag
//been re-set from false to true.
public static Engine GetEngine()
{
  if (!instanceFlag)
  {
    instanceFlag = true;
    return new Engine();
  }
  else
  {
    throw new Exception("An engine has already
    been created!");
  }
}

  private Engine()
  {
    Console.WriteLine("An Engine");
  }
}
```

Client Code

In the client code, we see the Singleton pattern at work. We test the effectiveness of the design pattern by instructing the client code to attempt to return two engines. On the first attempt an engine is returned; however, on the second attempt an exception is returned to the client, from the Engine class, informing it of the error.

```
class Client
{

  static void Main(string[] args)
  {
    // 1st attempt to get an engine
    Console.WriteLine("Attempting to get first engine");
    try
    {
      Engine eng = Engine.GetEngine();
    }
    catch (Exception e)
    {
      Console.WriteLine(e.Message);
    }
```

```csharp
    // 2nd attempt to get an engine
    Console.WriteLine("Attempting to get second engine");
    try
    {
      Engine eng = Engine.GetEngine();

    }

    catch (Exception e)
    {
      Console.WriteLine(e.Message);
    }

  }
}
```

Console Output

```
Attempting to get first engine
An Engine
Attempting to get second engine
An engine has already been created!
Press any key to continue
```

The Standard: Singleton Design Pattern

The standard acknowledges the use of the Singleton design pattern where there is a design problem when there can only be one instance of a given object and where there is a requirement for client code to trigger the creation of the object.

CHAPTER 11

■ ■ ■

Structural Patterns

Structural patterns encapsulate a design feature such that the focus is on the strategic manipulation of classes into a structure. They leverage a design where the structure of the class enables it to represent (e.g., Proxy pattern) or to integrate (e.g., Adapter pattern) with another structure, for example. In everyday life, examples of a structural pattern include a reservation sign, placed on a restaurant table, that acts as a placeholder until the patrons arrive; or an adapter that enables a U.S.-compliant electricity plug to make use of a European-compliant power point.

What

In software design, structural patterns give the software designer a tool that can be used to enhance classes: behavior or functionality may be varied by manipulating the structure of participating classes.

Where

Structural patterns are used where a design needs to vary or enhance the behavior of classes. For example, arranging classes in a strategic structure (e.g., Remote-Proxy pattern) enables communication across a domain.

Why

In some domains there is a requirement to reconfigure structures to give effect to behavioral characteristics that are not native to a given design or arrangement of classes. In those domains, that requirement presents a problem, so to overcome the problem, structural patterns are incorporated into the design of the program.

How

Commonly, a structural pattern is a manipulation process that centers around the implementation of an interface.

■**Note** To run the respective Console applications, if you press **F5** in Visual Studio 2005, the **Quick Console** will appear; if you press **Ctrl+F5**, then the **Windows Console** will appear. It is only in the **Windows Console** that you will see the Press any key to continue notice, at the bottom of the Console window.

Pattern Examples

In the Model T domain, we present five examples of structural patterns: Proxy (Surrogate and Remote), Adapter, Composite, and Facade.

Proxy Pattern

A *Proxy* pattern encapsulates a design feature where a placeholder or surrogate is used to represent or regulate access to a principal. In everyday life, examples of a proxy pattern include an icon on a Web page that acts as a placeholder while an image is being downloaded, or an ambassador who represents or regulates access to a head of state in a foreign country.

What

A Proxy pattern is a design that represents or regulates access to a principal that is scarce or remote.

Where

A Proxy pattern is used where there is a design problem such that access to a principal (e.g., scarce resource) needs to be regulated or access to a principal needs to be distributed through representation (e.g., remote access).

Why

In many domains, it is, or soon becomes, problematic to allow client code unfettered access to a given resource; additionally, in some situations remote access to functionality is desirable. To accommodate these requirements, the Proxy pattern is incorporated into the design of the program.

How

A principal class is enriched with functionality, then a proxy class is derived from the same base class as the principal class. The proxy class uses *composition*—it creates a member instance of the principal—to expose the functionality of the principal through a set of wrapper methods or properties. The client code creates an instance of the proxy class that regulates or distributes access to the functionality of the principal.

Proxy Pattern Examples

Over time, the community has taken a shine to the Proxy pattern, so much so that there is now a small commune of variants. Two popular types of Proxy patterns are the *Surrogate-Proxy* and the *Remote-Proxy* patterns: they fulfill similar yet distinct roles. The Surrogate-Proxy pattern, articulated by GoF, plays the role of regulating access to the principal, whereas the Remote-Proxy pattern plays the role of distributing access to the principal, through remote representation. Full examples of the Surrogate- and Remote-Proxy patterns follow.

Pattern Example: Surrogate-Proxy

In the Model T domain, we have client code that manages the task of responding to technical queries from the workshop managers employed by major dealers. Generally, some technical queries deal with matters more advanced than those covered in manuals and require expert knowledge. To accommodate this requirement, it has been decided to permit the major deal-ers, for a limited time, to have access to the chief design engineer to ask advanced technical queries. The part of the problem we are focusing on is how to regulate access to the chief design engineer and channel the queries in a systematic manner.

To code this requirement, we build a design engineer interface (IDesignEngineer), which is inherited and enriched by the chief design engineer (ChiefDesignEngineer) through imple-menting a set of inherited knowledge methods (DesignKnowledge(), StressTestKnowledge(), MechanicalKnowledge(), and PerformanceKnowledge()). Then we create a proxy chief design engineer (ChiefDesignEngineer), which also implements the IDesignEngineer interface. Within the proxy chief design engineer we use composition~~to~~ create a private member instance of the chief design engineer~~and~~ override the knowledge methods by wrapping them around the methods of the member instance of the ChiefDesignEngineer object. How-ever, as the proxy seeks to filter the non-advanced or run-of-the-mill questions from going to the principal (ChiefDesignEngineer), it has *not* wrapped all of the knowledge methods of the member instance; instead it has substituted default answers (refer: PerformanceKnowledge() and MechanicalKnowledge() in ProxyChiefEngineer) to handle them. That is the Surrogate-Proxy pattern, or one variant of it!

We shall now look at the Surrogate-Proxy pattern in a UML diagram (see Figure 11-1) and then implement the pattern in code.

UML

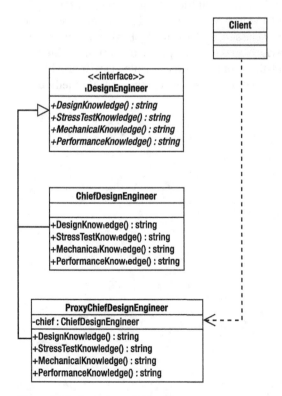

Figure 11-1. *Surrogate-Proxy pattern*

Key Code Ingredients

The code for the Surrogate-Proxy pattern has the following key ingredients:

- An interface type (IDesignEngineer).

- A principal class (ChiefDesignEngineer) that implements IDesignEngineer interface.

- A proxy class (ProxyChiefDesignEngineer) that also implements the IDesignEngineer interface, which

  - has a member instance of the principal class (ChiefDesignEngineer).

  - implements the methods inherited from IDesignEngineer that wrap the methods of the member instance of the principal class (ChiefDesignEngineer) and further specializes two of them (PerformanceKnowledge() and MechanicalKnowledge()).

- Client code that instantiates the proxy class (ProxyChiefDesignEngineer), then calls the methods of the ProxyChiefDesignEngineer class.

  Now let's code the Surrogate-Proxy pattern.

Surrogate-Proxy Pattern Code

The essence of the design lies in the way that a proxy class (ProxyChiefDesignEngineer) selects composition or containment rather than inheritance to regulate access to the functionality of the principal (ChiefDesignEngineer). Notice that the IDesignEngineer interface type provides the interface, which is inherited and implemented by ChiefDesignEngineer and ProxyChiefDesignerEngineer classes. The proxy class (ProxyChiefDesignEngineer) wraps the methods of the principal class (ProxyChiefDesignEngineer), except where it wants to shield the principal from the nonadvanced or run-of-the-mill questions, in which case it provides its own implementation (see PerformanceKnowledge() and MechanicalKnowledge() methods).

DesignEngineer Interface

```
public interface IDesignEngineer
{
  string DesignKnowledge();
  string StressTestKnowledge();
  string MechanicalKnowledge();
  string PerformanceKnowledge();
}
```

ChiefDesignEngineer Class

```
public class ChiefDesignEngineer: IDesignEngineer
{

  public string DesignKnowledge()
  {
    return "The Model T is designed to...";
```

```
  }

  public string StressTestKnowledge()
  {
    return "We found in stress-testing, the...";
  }

  public string MechanicalKnowledge()
  {
    return "The mechanical features include...";
  }

  public string PerformanceKnowledge()
  {
    return "The performance characteristics include...";
  }

  public ChiefDesignEngineer() {;}
}
```

ProxyChiefDesignEngineer Class

```
public class ProxyChiefDesignEngineer: IDesignEngineer
{
  private ChiefDesignEngineer chief;

  public string DesignKnowledge()
  {
    return this.chief.DesignKnowledge();
  }

  public string StressTestKnowledge()
  {
    return this. chief.StressTestKnowledge();
  }

  //The proxy can also be used to save "over-use" of the principal,
  //by encapsulating a means to handle queries internally.
  public string MechanicalKnowledge()
  {
    return "A supplement has been added to the mechanical manual.";
  }

  public string PerformanceKnowledge()
  {
    return "Performance information is in the manual.";
  }
}
```

```
//constructor - instantiates local copy of ChiefDesignEngineer.
public ProxyChiefDesignEngineer()
{
  this.chief = new ChiefDesignEngineer();
}

}
```

Client Code

In the client code, we can see the Surrogate-Proxy design pattern at work. We test the effectiveness of the design pattern by instructing the client code to deal directly through two proxies of the principal (caProxyChief and nyProxyChief). Although the client has access to the principal, it does so through the proxies, which act as surrogates for the principal (ChiefDesignEngineer).

```
public class Client
{

  static void Main(string[] args)
  {
    //Create a proxy ChiefDesignEngineer
    //to handle Californian State technical queries
    ProxyChiefDesignEngineer caProxyChief = ➥
new ProxyChiefDesignEngineer();

    //Setup the console
    Console.WriteLine("*** Answer(s) for CA State ***");

    //Ask a stress-test question of the ProxyChief
    Console.WriteLine(caProxyChief.StressTestKnowledge());

    //Ask a performance question of the ProxyChief
    Console.WriteLine(caProxyChief.PerformanceKnowledge());

    //Create a proxy ChiefDesignEngineer
    //to handle NewYork State technical queries
    ProxyChiefDesignEngineer nyProxyChief = ➥
new ProxyChiefDesignEngineer();

    //Setup console
    Console.WriteLine();
    Console.WriteLine("*** Answer(s) for NY State ***");

    //Ask a mechnical question of the ProxyChief
    Console.WriteLine(nyProxyChief.MechanicalKnowledge());

  }
}
```

Console Output

```
*** Answer(s) for CA State ***
We found in stress-testing, the . . .
Performance information is in the manual.

 *** Answer(s) for NY State ***
A supplement has been added to the mechnical manual.
Press any key to continue
```

The Standard: Surrogate-Proxy Design Pattern

> *The standard acknowledges the use of the Surrogate-Proxy design pattern where there is a design problem such that access to a principal (e.g., scarce resource) needs to be regulated.*

Pattern Example: Remote-Proxy

In the Model T domain, the policy of allowing workshop managers to ask advanced questions of the chief design engineer has been so successful that the policy is to be extended, for a limited time, to major dealers in the United Kingdom (UK). We have been asked to do the wiring.

The part of the problem we are focusing on is how to extend access to the remote UK workshop managers so they can channel their queries in a systematic manner to the chief design engineer and receive the answers. The solution requires implementing an architecture that relies on *TCP transport protocol* and *.NET Remoting*. The following code example extends the business case introduced in the Surrogate-Proxy example, although it is a self-contained example. We will reuse `IDesignEngineer`, which is inherited by `ChiefDesignEngineer` and `ProxyChiefDesignEngineer`; however, we also make the two classes inherit from the `MarshallByRef` class, so that they can be transported using TCP. The multiple inheritance is not a problem: .NET permits single class inheritance to be combined with (multiple) interface inheritance.

■Note In Appendix A, there is a step-by-step example on setting up this pattern using the command line. Preferably, you may continue to read through this discussion, get an overview of the pattern, and then go to the appendix and set up the example. (Use the download code or key in the code, as there are respective code listings following.) Also, to do the example you will need to know a little bit about environment variables and command-line programming—primers can be found in Appendix A, if you need them (see "Environment Variables" and "Remote-Proxy Pattern Example—Using the Command Line").

Architecture

This pattern has a *server* and a *remote client*, which reside in separate domains and are connected using transport protocol (TCP). The following diagram (Figure 11-2) illustrates the architecture. Note that both domains have a local copy of RemoteProxyServer.dll and access to .NET Remoting (from the .NET Framework).

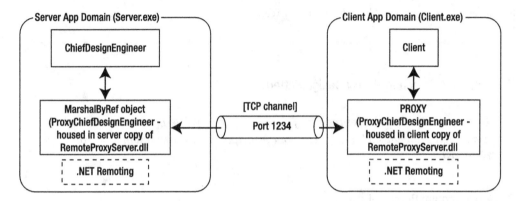

Figure 11-2. *Remote-Proxy architecture*

Code

We code two sets of functionality (server and client), and both sets will have access, within their respective domains, to a copy of the same class library (ProxyRemoteServer.dll), that defines the actors (e.g., ProxyChiefDesignEngineer). The client needs a local copy of the class library so that it can create an association with the ProxyChiefDesignEngineer. Let's now examine each of the new classes in turn.

ProxyRemoteServer.cs

This class plays the role of an "interface" class; it is through this class that the client will interface with the ChiefDesignEngineer. (This class will eventually be compiled into a class library file—ProxyRemoteServer.dll.)

Server.cs

ProxyRemoteServer is an "interface" class, whereas the Server class fulfils the role of a server "plumber" class: it encapsulates all of the functionality to create a *TCP Server Channel*. In the code, use is made of *port 1234*; this number is chosen because it is a *Well Known Port*. The .NET Remoting configuration is used to register a *Well Known Service* and it is passed the name of the proxy class (ProxyChiefDesignerEngineer), a service name ("RemoteProxy"), and uses the *SingleCall* option of the *Well Known Object Mode*. The code writes a message to the console and stays open waiting for a call from the client application (which is discussed next).

Client.cs

The Client class plays two roles: it acts as a client "plumber" class, mirroring the role of Server, and it also fires off questions to the ProxyChiefDesignerEngineer. We register a *TCP channel* with .NET channel services, and then we configure .NET's remoting to register use of the *RegisterWellKnownClientType* configuration option. .NET's remoting configuration is passed the type of proxy object (ProxyChiefDesignerEngineer) and the address of the service (tcp://localhost:1234/RemoteProxy). If we were to use this service outside of the example environment, then we would modify the *localhost* setting.

Having made connection through the transport protocol, the code then instantiates a local proxy instance of the ProxyChiefDesignEngineer class, through which .NET Remoting calls on the ProxyChiefDesignEngineer object, located on the remote server, to call the methods of the ChiefDesignEngineer object (also located on the remote server). The response is seen on the client console. We shall now look at the Remote-Proxy pattern in a UML diagram (see Figure 11-3) and then discuss the code.

UML

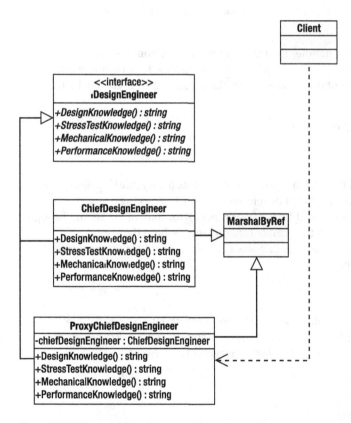

Figure 11-3. *Remote-Proxy pattern*

Key Code Ingredients

The code for the Remote-Proxy pattern has the following key ingredients:

- An interface type (IDesignEngineer).

- A principal class (ChiefDesignEngineer) that inherits from MarshalByRefObject class, so that it can be transported across a domain, and that implements IDesignEngineer interface.

- A proxy class (ProxyChiefDesignEngineer) that inherits from MarshalByRefObject class, so that it can be transported across a domain, and that implements the IDesignEngineer interface.

    - A member instance of the principal class (ChiefDesignEngineer).

    - Implements the methods inherited from IDesignEngineer, which wrap the methods of the member instance of the principal class (ChiefDesignEngineer), and further specializes two of them (PerformanceKnowledge() and MechanicalKnowledge()).

- Server code (Server.cs) that handles the transport plumbing, from the server perspective.

- Client code (Client.cs) that handles the transport plumbing, from the client perspective; instantiates a local proxy class (ProxyChiefDesignEngineer), and through this interface calls the methods of the remote ProxyChiefDesignEngineer class (which is located on the server).

Now let's code the Remote-Proxy pattern.

Remote-Proxy Pattern Code

The essence of the design lies in the way that an instance of class (ProxyChiefDesignEngineer), which is resident on the server, is marshaled by reference by .NET Remoting using TCP transport and a remote proxy interface (ProxyChiefDesignEngineer), located on the client, through which the client (Client.exe) accesses the remote functionality. Behind the scenes, .NET Remoting manages transporting the functionality via a TCP port (port 1234 on the localhost), shielding us from that complexity.

ProxyRemoteServer Class

The ProxyRemoteServer class is a container class that stores the interface type and classes: IDesignEngineer, ChiefDesignEngineer, and ProxyChiefDesignEngineer. The ProxyRemoteServer class will be complied into a class library (ProxyRemoteServer.dll).

DesignEngineer Interface

```
public interface IDesignEngineer
{
  string DesignKnowledge();
  string StressTestKnowledge();
  string MechanicalKnowledge();
  string PerformanceKnowledge();
}
```

ChiefDesignEngineer Class

```
public class ChiefDesignEngineer: MarshalByRefObject, IDesignEngineer
{
  public string DesignKnowledge()
  {
    return "The Model T is designed to...";
  }

  public string StressTestKnowledge()
  {
    return "We found in stress-testing, the...";
  }

  public string MechanicalKnowledge()
  {
    return "The mechanical features include...";
  }

  public string PerformanceKnowledge()
  {
    return "The performance characteristics include...";
  }

  public ChiefDesignEngineer() {;}
}
```

ProxyChiefDesignEngineer Class

```
public class ProxyChiefDesignEngineer: MarshalByRefObject, IDesignEngineer
{

  private ChiefDesignEngineer chief;

  public string DesignKnowledge()
  {
    return this.chief.DesignKnowledge();
  }

  public string StressTestKnowledge()
  {
    return this.chief.StressTestKnowledge();
  }

  //The proxy can also be used to save "over-use" of the principal,
  //by encapsulating a means to handle queries internally.
  public string MechanicalKnowledge()
```

```
  {
    return "A supplement has been added to the mechanical manual.";
  }


  public string PerformanceKnowledge()
  {
    return "Performance information is in the manual.";
  }


  //constructor - instantiates local copy of ChiefDesignEngineer.
  public ProxyChiefDesignEngineer()
  {
    this.chief = new ChiefDesignEngineer();
  }


}
```

Here is the complete code listing of ProxyRemoteServer.cs, which will be compiled into ProxyRemoteServer.dll:

```
using System;

namespace Patterns.ProxyRemoteServer
{
  public interface IDesignEngineer
  {
    string DesignKnowledge();
    string StressTestKnowledge();
    string MechanicalKnowledge();
    string PerformanceKnowledge();
  }

  public class ChiefDesignEngineer: MarshalByRefObject, IDesignEngineer
  {
    public string DesignKnowledge()
    {
      return "The Model T is designed to...";
    }

    public string StressTestKnowledge()
    {
      return "We found in stress-testing, the...";
    }

    public string MechanicalKnowledge()
    {
      return "The mechanical features include...";
    }
```

```csharp
    public string PerformanceKnowledge()
    {
      return "The performance characteristics include...";
    }

    public ChiefDesignEngineer() {;}
  }


  public class ProxyChiefDesignEngineer: MarshalByRefObject, IDesignEngineer
  {
    private ChiefDesignEngineer chief;

    public string DesignKnowledge()
    {
      return this.chief.DesignKnowledge();
    }

    public string StressTestKnowledge()
    {
      return this.chief.StressTestKnowledge();
    }

    //The proxy can also be used to save "over-use" of the principal,
    //by encapsulating a means to handle queries internally.
    public string MechanicalKnowledge()
    {
      return "A supplement has been added to the mechanical manual.";
    }

    public string PerformanceKnowledge()
    {
      return "Performance information is in the manual.";
    }

    //constructor - instantiates local copy of ChiefDesignEngineer.
    public ProxyChiefDesignEngineer()
    {
      this.chief = new ChiefDesignEngineer();
    }

  }
}// end namespace
```

Server Class

The Server class initiates the service (RemoteProxy), making it available to client code.

```
public class Server
{
  static void Main(string[] args)
  {
    TcpServerChannel channel = new TcpServerChannel (1234);
    ChannelServices.RegisterChannel (channel);

    RemotingConfiguration.RegisterWellKnownServiceType
    (typeof (ProxyChiefDesignEngineer), "RemoteProxy", ➥
WellKnownObjectMode.SingleCall);

    Console.WriteLine ("Press [Enter] to terminate server...");
    Console.ReadLine();
  }
}
```

Here is the complete code listing of Server.cs, which will be compiled into Server.exe:

```
using System;
using System.Runtime.Remoting;
using System.Runtime.Remoting.Channels;
using System.Runtime.Remoting.Channels.Tcp;
using Patterns.ProxyRemoteServer;

public class Server
{
  static void Main(string[] args)
  {
    TcpServerChannel channel = new TcpServerChannel (1234);
    ChannelServices.RegisterChannel (channel);

    RemotingConfiguration.RegisterWellKnownServiceType ➥
(typeof (ProxyChiefDesignEngineer), "RemoteProxy", ➥
WellKnownObjectMode.SingleCall);

    Console.WriteLine ("Press [Enter] to terminate server...");
    Console.ReadLine();
  }
}
```

Client Code

In the client code, we see the Remote-Proxy pattern at work. We test the effectiveness of the design pattern by instructing the client code to deal through the ProxyChiefDesignEngineer interface while .NET Remoting manages the transporting of the query to the server and the response from the proxy chief design engineer.

```
public class Client
{
  static void Main(string[] args)
  {
    TcpClientChannel channel = new TcpClientChannel ();
    ChannelServices.RegisterChannel (channel);

    RemotingConfiguration.RegisterWellKnownClientType ➥
(typeof(ProxyChiefDesignEngineer), "tcp://localhost:1234/RemoteProxy");

    ProxyChiefDesignEngineer ukProxyChief = new ProxyChiefDesignEngineer();

    Console.WriteLine("*** Answer for UK Dealers from ➥
US Chief Design Engineer ***");
    Console.WriteLine("Question: Not on an advanced topic - ➥
filtered to Proxy US Chief Design Engineer");
    Console.WriteLine("Answer:" + ukProxyChief.PerformanceKnowledge());
    Console.WriteLine("Question: Was on an advanced topic - ➥
answered by the US Chief Design Engineer");
    Console.WriteLine("Answer:" + ukProxyChief.DesignKnowledge());
    Console.WriteLine("Press [Enter] to terminate client...");
    Console.ReadLine();
  }
}
```

Here is the complete code listing of Client.cs, which will be compiled into Client.exe:

```
using System;
using System.Runtime.Remoting;
using System.Runtime.Remoting.Channels;
using System.Runtime.Remoting.Channels.Tcp;

//Note that Client.cs is placed in the ProxyRemoteServer namespace.
namespace Patterns.ProxyRemoteServer
{
  public class Client
  {
    static void Main(string[] args)
    {
      TcpClientChannel channel = new TcpClientChannel();
      ChannelServices.RegisterChannel(channel);

      RemotingConfiguration.RegisterWellKnownClientType
        (typeof (ProxyChiefDesignEngineer), "tcp://localhost:1234/RemoteProxy");
      ProxyChiefDesignEngineer ukProxyChief = new ProxyChiefDesignEngineer();
```

```
        Console.WriteLine("*** Answer for UK Dealers from US Chief ➡
Design Engineer ***");
        Console.WriteLine("Question: Not on an advanced topic filtered ➡
to Proxy US Chief Design Engineer");
        Console.WriteLine("Answer: " + ukProxyChief.PerformanceKnowledge());
        Console.WriteLine("Question: Was on an advanced topic - answered ➡
by the US Chief Design Engineer");
        Console.WriteLine("Answer: " + ukProxyChief.DesignKnowledge());
        Console.WriteLine("Press [Enter] to terminate client...");
        Console.ReadLine();
    }
  }
}//end namespace
```

There are two sets of console output in this example. First, we run Server.exe:

Console Output: Server.exe

```
Press [Enter] to terminate server . . .
```

And second, we run Client.exe.

Console Output: Client.exe

```
*** Answer for UK Dealers from US Chief Design Engineer ***
Question: Not on an advanced topic - filtered to Proxy US Chief Design Engineer
Answer: Performance information is in the manual.
Question: Was on an advanced topic - answered by the US Chief Design Engineer
Answer: The Model T is designed to . . .
Press [Enter] to terminate client . . .
```

The Standard: Remote-Proxy Design Pattern

> *The standard acknowledges the use of the Remote-Proxy design pattern where there is a design problem such that access to a principal needs to be distributed through representation.*

Adapter Pattern

An *Adapter pattern* encapsulates a design feature where an interface can be supplemented to comply with the interface expected by another entity. In everyday life, examples of an Adapter pattern include an electric plug adapter that enables a U.S.-compliant electricity plug to make use of an European power point; or a pair of pliers that enables a hand to pick up minute screws.

What

An Adapter pattern is a design that enables a noncompliant interface to be superimposed by an intermediary, which manages an adaptation process to effect compliance.

Where

An Adapter pattern is used where there is a requirement to integrate with a noncompliant interface or where there is a requirement for one design to leverage the functionality of another design.

Why

In many domains, it is advantageous to reuse or integrate existing functionality, or there may be a change in business requirements that necessitates reengineering design or functionality. In those domains this presents a problem, so to overcome the problem the Adapter pattern is incorporated into the design.

How

An intermediary class or set of classes is used to map the desired functionality from the source interface to that required by the target interface.

Pattern Example

In the Model T domain, the purchasing department has some client code that is now required to handle the task of converting U.S. dollars into foreign currencies. The enterprise architect is on notice to maximize opportunities to reuse reliable code. The enterprise architect has advised us that the accounting department has a class (ForeignExchange) that has most of the functionality we require; however, it has an incompatible interface.

The part of the problem we are focusing on is to prepare a solution that maps as much functionality as possible, from ForeignExchange into our class (FX). In the design meeting the enterprise architect informed us that ForeignExchange was sealed—it cannot be derived from—and so the adapter will need to use composition.

Tip Composition acquires functionality from member objects rather than from class inheritance—in best practices, composition is favored over class inheritance.

We have identified in ForeignExchange that we can leverage two methods: UStoUK() and UStoCAN(). (With FX we plan on a different naming convention, based on purpose and currency code—for example,   FX_USD_XXX()). This requirement impacts the interface, as does the requirement to support an extra currency: the Australian dollar.

To code this routine, we need to design the FX interface, then compare it with the interface of the source class (ForeignExchange). We will then prepare an adapter (Adapter) to map the source interface and add any enrichments (e.g., code to handle U.S. to Australian conversion). The target interface (FX) will then be implemented using an Adapter object to map the functionality to the required interface. That is the Adapter pattern!

We shall now look at the Adapter pattern in a UML diagram (see Figure 11-4) and then implement the pattern in code.

UML

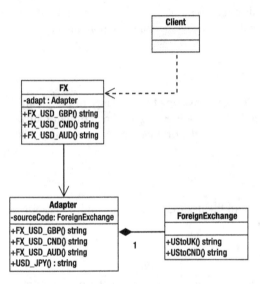

Figure 11-4. *Adapter pattern*

Key Code Ingredients

The code for the Adapter pattern has the following key ingredients:

- A source interface (ForeignExchange) from which functionality is to be leveraged

- A target interface (FX) that seeks to leverage functionality of the source interface (ForeignExchange)

- An adapter class (Adapter) that encapsulates the mapping of the interfaces between the source (ForeignExchange) and target (FX) interfaces

Now let's code the Adapter pattern.

Adapter Pattern Code

The essence of the design lies in creating an adapter class (Adapter) that uses composition or containment to include an instance of the source interface (ForeignExchange), which wraps the methods into an implementation expected by the target interface (FX). Notice how the source interface (ForeignExchange) is incompatible with the target interface (FX): the method names are different and the source interface (ForeignExchange) doesn't have a method for converting Australian dollars to U.S. dollars. However, it does have functionality to convert British pounds and Canadian dollars to U.S. dollars. Notice in the adapter class (Adapter) how the source interface (ForeignExchange) is mapped into the interface required by the target interface (FX).

ForeignExchange Class (Source Interface)

```
public sealed class ForeignExchange
{
  public string  UStoUK()
  {
    return "USD to GBP is...";
  }

  public string  UStoCAN()
  {
    return "USD to CND is...";
  }

  public ForeignExchange() {;}
}
```

FX Class (Target Interface)

```
public class FX
{
  private Adapter adapt;

  public string FX_USD_GBP()
  {
    return this.adapt.USD_GBP();
  }

  public string FX_USD_CND()
  {
    return this.adapt.USD_CND();
  }

  public string FX_USD_AUD()
  {
    return this.adapt.USD_AUD();
  }

  public FX()
  {
    adapt= new Adapter();
  }
}
```

Adapter Class

```csharp
public class Adapter
{
  private ForeignExchange sourceCode;

  public string USD_GBP ()
  {
    return  "Conversion " +this.sourceCode.UStoUK();
  }

  public string  USD_CND()
  {
    return "Conversion " + this.sourceCode.UStoCAN();
  }

  public string  USD_AUD()
  {
    return "Conversion USD to AUD is...";
  }

  public string USD_JPY()
  {
    return "Conversion USD to JNY is...";
  }

  public Adapter()
  {
    sourceCode= new ForeignExchange();
  }
}
```

Client Code

In the client code, we see the Adapter design pattern at work. We test the effectiveness of the design pattern by instructing the client code to use the interface of the FX class. The client code calls the FX class and is unaware that its functionality is sourced through an adaptation process.

```csharp
public class Client
{

  static void Main(string[] args)
  {
    FX afx = new FX();
    Console.WriteLine(afx.FX_USD_GBP());
    Console.WriteLine(afx.FX_USD_CND());
```

```
        Console.WriteLine(afx.FX_USD_AUD());
    }
}
```

Console Output

```
Conversion USD to GBP is . . .
Conversion USD to CND is . . .
Conversion USD to AUD is . . .
Press any key to continue
```

The Standard: Adapter Design Pattern

The standard acknowledges the use of the Adapter design pattern where there is a design problem, where there is a requirement to integrate with a noncompliant interface, or where there is a requirement for one design to leverage the functionality from one design into another design.

Composite Pattern

A Composite pattern encapsulates a design feature where all entities in a hierarchy expose the same interface regardless of whether the entity is a single entity or a composite. In everyday life, examples of a Composite pattern include a society in which citizens are organized as individuals and as groups, or a treeview control that is organized as individual and parent nodes.

What

A Composite pattern is a design that ensures that an entity and a composite of entities expose the same interface.

Where

A Composite pattern is used where there is a hierarchy of entities and a requirement for a simple, nonconditional methodology to manage single and composite entities.

Why

In many domains there is a requirement to organize entities into hierarchies. Hierarchies contain single entities and composite entities, both of which need to be managed and iterated. In some domains this presents a problem, so to overcome the problem the Composite pattern is incorporated into the design of the program.

How

A common interface is inherited by a composite and an entity, with each implementing the interface in its own way.

Pattern Example

In the Model T domain, we have client code that manages the task of presenting a hierarchy that represents the offices that handle Model T sales inquiries. The part of the problem that we are focusing on is how to manage (add, remove, and iterate) through a hierarchy of single offices and branches, which are a composition of offices.

To code this routine we need to ensure that the Office and Branch classes implement the same interface and yet allow the Branch class to be composed of Office classes and prevent an Office class from being added or removed from Office—which would be illogical. We derive Office and Branch from the same interface (Entity), and the trick to overcome the issue of treating an Office, which *is not* a composite of other Offices, in the same manner as a Branch, which *is* a composite of Offices, lies in the way the GetChild() method is overridden—and to a lesser extent in the way that the Add() and Remove() methods are overridden. In the Branch class, the GetChild() method is implemented using a ListArray object to manage the adding and removing of Office objects. The Office class, by contrast, implements the GetChild() method without an array and relies simply on leveraging name in the base class (Entity) to return its name. Also, in the Office class the Add() and Remove() methods are stubs with no functionality, which differs from the way that Branch implements these methods. That is the Composite pattern!

We shall now look at the Composite pattern in a UML diagram (see Figure 11-5) and then implement the pattern in code.

UML

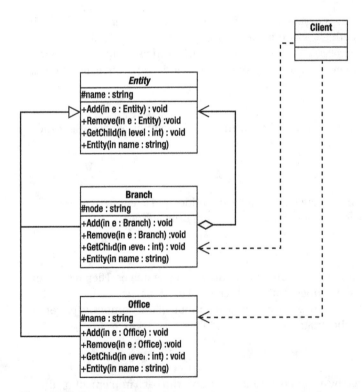

Figure 11-5. *Composite pattern*

Key Code Ingredients

The code for the Composite pattern has the following key ingredients:

- An interface (Entity class) with some default behavior (name)

- A node class (Office) that derives from Entity and implements the interface

- A node composite class (Branch) that derives from Entity and implements the interface and stores a collection of node (Office) objects

- Client code that manages the hierarchy of nodes and composite nodes

Now let's code the Composite pattern.

Composite Pattern Code

The essence of the design lies in deriving the Office and Entity classes from the same interface (Entity) and then varying the way that each implements the common interface; this enables them to be treated in the same manner by client code yet behave appropriately. Notice how the Entity class defines the interface that is inherited and implemented by Office and Branch. The Entity class also includes some default behavior (setting name). Also note that in the Entity class, the use of name has its accessor set to protected—this enables the subclasses to use this default functionality rather than having to implement it.

Contrast the Office class with the Branch class: the Branch class may hold a composite of Office classes, so it includes an array (node) to hold these objects. However, as the Office class is a single entity, it has no need for an array. Also note how the Remove() and Add() methods in the Office class are implemented as stub code—it is illogical for an   Office to add or remove an Office. The stub code feature is one of the consequences of implementing a common interface across a class that is a composite and a class that is not: it is a small price to pay for enabling client code to avoid the complication of conditionally treating nodes pending whether or not they are composites.

Entity Class

```
public abstract class Entity
{
  protected string name;
  public abstract void Add(Entity e);
  public abstract void Remove(Entity e);
  public abstract void GetChild(int level);

  public Entity(string name)
  {
    this.name = name;
  }
}
```

Office Class

```
public class Office: Entity
{
  public override void Add (Entity c)
  {
    Console.WriteLine("Can't use 'Add' in Office!");
  }

  public override void Remove (Entity e)
  {
    Console.WriteLine("Can't use 'Remove' in Office! ");
  }

  public override void GetChild (int level)
  {
    Console.WriteLine(new string ( '*', level) + this.name);
  }

  public Office(string name): base (name) {;}
}
```

Branch Class

```
using System.Text;
using System.Collections;

public class Branch: Entity
{
  private ArrayList node = new ArrayList();

  public override void Add (Entity e)
  {
    node.Add(e);
  }

  public override void Remove (Entity e)
  {
    node.Remove(e);
  }

  public override void GetChild (int level)
  {
    Console.WriteLine(new String ( '#', level) + this.name);
    foreach (Entity e in this.node)
      e.GetChild(level + 1);
```

```
  }

  public Branch (string name) : base (name) {;}
}
```

Client Code

In the client code, we see the Composite pattern at work. We test the effectiveness of the design pattern by instructing the client code to manage the adding and removing of offices and branches that expose the same interface. Notice how we attempt to add a dummy Office to another Office, which is illogical; however, we have coded the Office class to handle this eventuality. When displaying name, note that the Branch class has implemented iteration functionality (foreach statement), whereas the Office, which is a single entity, has no need to iterate.

```
public class Client
{
  static void Main(string[] args)
  {
    //build a hierarchy from a root
    Branch root = new Branch("US (Root)");

    Office ny = new Office("New York Office (Entity)");
    Office ca = new Office("California Office (Entity)");

    //add an entity, in the same way as a branch
    root.Add(ny);
    root.Add(ca);

    //add a branch to the root, in the same way as an entity
    Branch rootHawaii = new Branch("Hawaii Branch (Branch)");
    root.Add(rootHawaii);

    //build and add another branch and add to offices (entities)
    Branch branchUK = new Branch("UK Branch  (Branch)");
    Office ldnc = new Office("London City Office (Entity)");
    Office ldnw = new Office("London West Office (Entity)");
    branchUK.Add(ldnc);
    branchUK.Add(ldnw);
    //add branch to the root
    root.Add(branchUK);

    //we now try to add an dummy office to another office - which is
    //illogical so we should get a warning message.
    Office dummy = new Office("Dummy Office - we should not see this!");
    lndc.Add(dummy);
```

```
    //get root level and all branches and offices
    root.GetChild(0);

    //remove a branch in the same way as a entity
    root.Remove(rootHawaii);
    //remove a entity in the same way as a branch
    branchUK.Remove(ldnc);
    Console.WriteLine();
    Console.WriteLine("Remove Hawaii branch and London City office");
    Console.WriteLine();
    root.GetChild(0); //get first level
  }
}
```

Console Output

```
Can't use 'Add' in Office!
US (Root)
*New York Office (Entity)
*California Office {Entity)
#Hawaii Branch (Branch)
#UK Branch (Branch)
**London City Office (Entity)
**London West Office (Entity)

Remove Hawaii branch and London City office

US (Root)
*New York Office (Entity)
*California Office (Entity)
#UK Branch (Branch)
**London West Office (Entity)
Press any key to continue
```

The Standard: Composite Design Pattern

The standard acknowledges the use of the Composite design pattern where there is a design problem where there is a hierarchy of entities and a requirement for a simple nonconditional methodology to manage single and composite entities.

Facade Pattern

A Facade pattern encapsulates a design feature where there is a simple interface that acts as a central point of reference for many interfaces. In everyday life, examples of a Facade pattern include a travel-agent clerk who manages the booking of several holiday services (e.g., airline booking, rental-car booking, hotel booking, and insurance) or a website portal that acts a central point from which to access many other websites.

What

A Facade pattern is a design that ensures the complexity of many interfaces is hidden behind a simple and uniform interface.

Where

A Facade pattern is used where there is a requirement, by client code, for a high-level abstraction that is simple to use.

Why

In many domains, software becomes complex as it seeks to interact with many interfaces, systems, or subsystems. When complexity is thrust upon a client, it puts at risk the usability of the software. In most domains this presents a problem, so to overcome the problem, the Facade pattern is incorporated into the design of the program.

How

The complexity of managing multiple interfaces is delegated to a facade class that hides the complexity from client code and instead presents it with a simple interface.

Pattern Example

In the Model T domain, we have client code that manages information associated with the acquisition of a Model T; presently, a dealer has to interact with six of our departments to get all of the information for a customer. The part of the problem that we are focusing on is how to simplify the process for the dealer.

To code this routine, we need to push the complexity from the dealer to a dealer representative, which takes on the role of the facade class. We build a facade class (DealerRepresentative) and assign it the burden of interacting with the six departments. This results in client code (the dealer) merely having to call on the one-method DealerRepresentative to get all of the information from the six departments. That is the Facade pattern!

We shall now look at the Facade pattern in a UML diagram (see Figure 11-6) and then implement the pattern in code.

UML

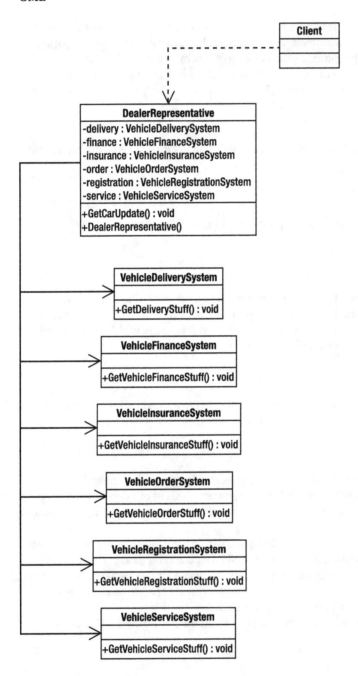

Figure 11-6. *Facade pattern*

Key Code Ingredients

The code for the Facade pattern has the following key ingredients:

- A facade class that interacts with multiple interfaces and exposes a simple interface to client code

- Multiple interfaces (e.g., VehicleDeliverySystem and VehicleFinanceSystem, etc.)

  Now let's code the Facade pattern.

Facade Pattern Code

The essence of the Facade pattern is simplifying the interface presented to a client by delegating the task of managing the complexity to a facade class (DealerRepresentative class). Notice how the DealerRepresentative class acts as a facade that shelters the client from the burden of dealing with six systems: the DealerRepresentative class exposes a simple interface (one method—GetCarUpdate()) to client code.

VehicleDeliverySystem Class

```
public class VehicleDeliverySystem
{
  public void GetDeliveryStuff()
  {
    Console.WriteLine ("Vehicle Delivery stuff.");
  }

  public VehicleDeliverySystem() {;}
}

public class VehicleFinanceSystem
{
  public void GetVehicleFinanceStuff()
  {
    Console.WriteLine("Vehicle Finance stuff.");
  }

  public VehicleFinanceSystem() {;}
}
```

VehicleInsuranceSystem Class

```
public class VehicleInsuranceSystem
{
  public void GetVehicleInsuranceStuff()
  {
    Console.WriteLine("Vehicle Insurance stuff.");
```

```
    }

    public VehicleInsuranceSystem() {;}
}
```

VehicleOrderSystem Class

```
public class VehicleOrderSystem
{
  public void GetVehicleOrderStuff()
  {
    Console.WriteLine("Vehicle Order stuff.");
  }

  public VehicleOrderSystem() {;}
}
```

VehicleRegistrationSystem Class

```
public class VehicleRegistrationSystem
{

  public void GetVehicleRegistrationStuff()
  {
    Console.WriteLine("Vehicle Registration stuff.");
  }

  public VehicleRegistrationSystem() {;}
}
```

VehicleServiceSystem Class

```
public class VehicleServiceSystem
{

  public void GetVehicleServiceStuff()
  {
    Console.WriteLine("Vehicle Service stuff.");
  }

  public VehicleServiceSystem() {;}
}
```

DealerRepresentative Class

```
public class DealerRepresentative
{
  private VehicleDeliverySystem delivery;
  private VehicleFinanceSystem finance;
  private VehicleInsuranceSystem insurance;
  private VehicleOrderSystem order;
  private VehicleRegistrationSystem registration;
  private VehicleServiceSystem service;

  public void GetCarUpdate()
  {
    this.delivery.GetDeliveryStuff();
    this.finance.GetVehicleFinanceStuff();
    this.insurance.GetVehicleInsuranceStuff();
    this.order.GetVehicleOrderStuff();
    this.registration.GetVehicleRegistrationStuff();
    this.service.GetVehicleServiceStuff();  }

  public DealerRepresentative()
  {
    delivery = new VehicleDeliverySystem();
    finance = new VehicleFinanceSystem();
    insurance = new VehicleInsuranceSystem();
    order = new VehicleOrderSystem();
    registration = new VehicleRegistrationSystem();
    service = new VehicleServiceSystem();
  }
}
```

Client Code

In the client code, we see the Facade design pattern at work. We test the effectiveness of the design pattern by examining the simple interface exposed to the client and the way in which the facade class (DealerRepresentative) shelters the client code from complexity and offers it a simple central point from which to gain access to six systems.

```
public class Client
{
  static void Main(string[] args)
  {
    DealerRepresentative gopher = new DealerRepresentative();
    gopher.GetCarUpdate();
  }
}
```

Console Output

```
Vehicle Delivery stuff.
Vehicle Finance stuff.
Vehicle Insurance stuff.
Vehicle Order stuff.
Vehicle Registration stuff.
Vehicle Service stuff.
Press any key to continue
```

The Standard: Facade Design Pattern

The standard acknowledges the use of the Facade design pattern where there is a requirement, by client code, for a high-level abstraction that is simple to use.

CHAPTER 12

■ ■ ■

Behavioral Patterns

Behavioral patterns encapsulate a design feature that focuses on communication, responsibility, and algorithm. In everyday life, examples of a behavioral pattern include a football team, on which responsibility is assigned according to skill or task specialty; or a university that administers a course entrance strategy based on a set of business rules.

What

In software design, behavioral patterns orchestrate objects, enriching them with behavioral traits to enable them to participate in an intelligent, purposeful, and cohesive society of objects.

Where

Behavioral patterns are used where a design needs objects to exhibit the intelligent traits of coordination and cooperation.

Why

In many domains there is a requirement to simulate intelligence, among objects, by introducing communication, responsibility, and algorithm variation. In these domains this requirement presents a problem, so to overcome the problem, behavioral patterns are incorporated into the design of the program.

How

Commonly, a behavioral pattern is identified by classes coordinating or cooperating in an intelligent manner. It is likely that client code may play an active role in the intellectual process. For example, in the Chain of Responsibility pattern, client code identifies the start of the chain and determines the hierarchy of objects.

■Note To run the respective Console applications, if you press **F5** in Visual Studio 2005, the **Quick Console** will appear; if you press **Ctrl+F5**, then the **Windows Console** will appear. It is only in the **Windows Console** that you will see the Press any key to continue notice, at the bottom of the Console window.

Behavioral Pattern Examples

In the Model T domain, we present four examples of behavioral patterns: Chain of Responsibility, Observer, Strategy, and Template Method.

Chain of Responsibility Pattern

A Chain of Responsibility pattern encapsulates a design feature in which a set of responsibilities or links joins to form a chain of responsibility, and each link is presented as an object that is responsible for a given task. A client requirement is passed along the chain until a link (object) in the chain can handle the requirement. In everyday life, examples of a Chain of Responsibility pattern include a call center or a corporate hierarchy, in which responsibility is assigned according to specialty or rank.

What

A Chain of Responsibility pattern is a replication of the business or functional process of delegating responsibility within a hierarchy.

Where

A Chain of Responsibility pattern is used where there is a requirement to manage tasks by coordinating objects and have them cooperate within a hierarchical structure.

Why

In many domains, it is convenient to manage responsibilities or activities by lines of authority or specialty that are delegated to a set of participating individuals or entities. In object-oriented development, this arrangement presents a problem because a class is not natively aware of its responsibility or place in a hierarchy. To overcome the problem, the Chain of Responsibility pattern incorporates responsibility and hierarchy into the design of the program.

How

An abstract class that represents a participant or link is subclassed into a set of links, and then the subclassed links implement the functionality that represents their limit of responsibility and they can trigger the passing on of a requirement, if it is outside their responsibility or specialty. The client determines the hierarchy among the links and initiates passing the requirement to the chain.

Pattern Example

In the Model T domain, we have client code that handles the requirements arising from customer inquiries. The part of the problem we are focusing on is how to model a business policy that advocates customer requirements being managed by a hierarchy of specialized staff, yet avoid burdening the customers with having to know which specialist they need to deal with, in the customer department. In other words, the customer department needs to have the intelligence to know what requirements it is responsible for and which specialist is responsible for servicing the requirement of a given customer.

To code this routine, we need to establish a chain of responsibility that passes the customer requirement up the chain until it is dealt with by the appropriate customer specialist. We instantiate a set of links that forms a chain of responsibility, making each Link object aware of its responsibility and of which is the next Link object in the chain. If a Link object is passed a requirement outside of its responsibility, which is determined using a switch statement, then it passes the requirement to the next Link object, higher in the chain, and so on until the requirement is handled. The client code determines the order of the Link objects in the chain of responsibility and passes the requirement to the first Link object, and then leaves it to the chain to manage the process. That is the Chain of Responsibility pattern!

We shall now look at the Chain of Responsibility pattern in a UML diagram (see Figure 12-1) and then implement the pattern in code.

UML

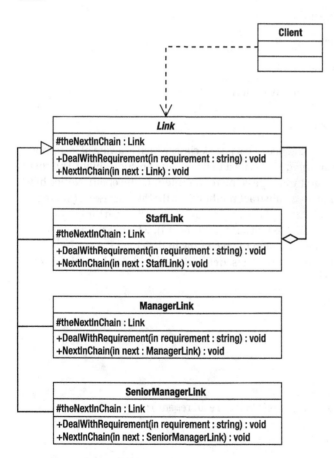

Figure 12-1. *Chain of Responsibility pattern*

Key Code Ingredients

The code for the Chain of Responsibility pattern has the following key ingredients:

- An abstract `Link` class.

- An abstract method (`DealWithRequirement(string requirement)`) that deals with a requirement that is implemented in subclasses.

- A method to assign the next `Link` in the chain (`NextInChain()`).

- A number of `Link` objects.

- Each `Link` object overrides the `DealWithRequirement(string requirement)` method and implements functionality within a given delegated authority (encapsulated in a `switch` statement).

- Client code that

   - instantiates the `Link` objects;

   - assigns the chain hierarchy;

   - submits requirements to the chain.

Now let's code the Chain of Responsibility pattern.

Chain of Responsibility Pattern Code

The essence of the design lies in the intelligence of each `Link` class, which is aware of its responsibility, via a `switch` statement, and of which `Link` is next in the chain of responsibility. The client code is relied on to establish the hierarchy and pass the requirement to the chain. Notice how the `Link` class, which is abstract, houses an abstract method (`DealWithRequirement(string requirement)`), which subclasses (`StaffLink`, `ManagerLink`, and `SeniorManagerLink`) will override. The `Link` class also houses a method (`NextInChain(Link next)`), which is inherited by subclasses that implement functionality to assign the next `Link` in the chain.

The client code creates an instance of the objects, determines the hierarchy of the links, and initiates a series of requirements.

Link Class

```
public abstract class Link
{

  protected Link theNextInChain;
  public abstract void DealWithRequirement(string requirement);

  public void NextInChain(Link next)
  {
    this.theNextInChain = next;
  }

}
```

StaffLink Class

```
public class StaffLink: Link
{
  public override void DealWithRequirement(string requirement)
  {
    switch (requirement)
    {
      case "Commercial Corporates":
        Console.WriteLine ("{0} has managed the Commercial Corporate ➡
requirement.", this);
        break;
      default:
        if (theNextInChain != null)
          theNextInChain.DealWithRequirement(requirement);
          break;
    }
  }
}
```

ManagerLink Class

```
public class ManagerLink: Link
{
  public override void DealWithRequirement(string requirement)
  {
    switch (requirement)
    {
      case "Dealers":
        Console.WriteLine ("{0} has managed the Dealer requirement.", this);
        break;
      default:
        if (theNextInChain != null)
          theNextInChain.DealWithRequirement(requirement);
          break;
    }
  }
}
```

SeniorManagerLink Class

```
public class SeniorManagerLink: Link
{
  public override void DealWithRequirement(string requirement)
  {
    switch (requirement)
    {
```

```
    default: Console.WriteLine("{0} has managed the " + requirement + ➡
" requirement.", this);
      break;
    }
  }

  public SeniorManagerLink() {;}

}
```

Client Code

In the client code we see the Chain of Responsibility pattern at work. We test the effectiveness of the design pattern by instructing the client code to submit four customer requirements to the chain. Two of the requirements (Commercial Corporates and Dealers) have specialist customer representatives (StaffLink and ManagerLink), which deal with the appropriate customer requirement. Also note that there are two customer requirements from two previously unknown customer groups (Not For Profit Corporates and Government Agency), which by default are attended to by the SeniorManager.

```
class Client
{
  static void Main(string[] args)
  {
    //Build the links
    Link staff = new StaffLink();
    Link manager = new ManagerLink();
    Link seniorManager = new SeniorManagerLink();

    //Assign chain hierarchy
    staff.NextInChain(manager);
    manager.NextInChain(seniorManager);


    //submit four requirements to be dealt with by the chain
    staff.DealWithRequirement("Not For Profit Corporates");
    staff.DealWithRequirement("Commercial Corporates");
    staff.DealWithRequirement("Dealers");
    staff.DealWithRequirement("Government Agency");
  }
}
```

Console Output

```
Patterns.ChainOfResponsibility.SeniorMangerLink has managed ➡
the Not For Profit Corporates requirement.
Patterns.ChainOfResponsibility.StaffLink has managed the ➡
```

```
Commercial Corporate requirement.
Patterns.ChainOfResponsibility.ManagerLink has managed ➡
the Dealer requirement.
Patterns.ChainOfResponsibility.SeniorMangerLink has managed ➡
the Government Agency requirement.
Press any key to continue
```

The Standard: Chain of Responsibility Design Pattern

> *The standard acknowledges the use of the Chain of Responsibility design pattern where there is a requirement to manage tasks by coordinating objects and have them cooperate within a hierarchical structure.*

Observer Pattern

An Observer pattern encapsulates a subscriber–publisher relationship where a subscriber (an observer object) registers, with a publisher, an interest in being notified when the publisher (a subject object) fires a given event. In everyday life, examples of an Observer pattern include when we register with a website to send us an SMS message of the final football scores; or a cruise control system which clicks in when the car has reached a given speed.

What

An Observer pattern is a design based on a *one-to-many* relationship, where *one* is a publisher that publishes an event against which *many* subscribers register an interest.

Where

An Observer pattern is used where there is a requirement to initiate and manage communications among a society of objects.

Why

In domains, objects need to communicate or collaborate. The Observer pattern is a way to programmatically establish and manage a set of relationships among objects at run time. The Observer pattern allows us to mimic dynamic relationships such that object relationships can be managed in an elegant and efficient manner.

How

Create a subject object (publisher) and any number of observer objects (subscribers), and then wire an event handler in the observer objects to an event in the subject object. In .NET we use a delegate event-handling model to wire the observer objects to the publisher's eventdelegates simplify the architecture articulated by GoF.

Pattern Example

In the Model T domain, we have a car delivery department and car dealers that are interested in knowing when cars roll off the assembly line. The car delivery department wants to be informed when all cars roll off the assembly line, so that it can send a truck to collect the cars and deliver them to car dealers. However, a given car dealer wants to be notified only when a car that they have ordered rolls off the assembly line. When the given car has rolled off the assembly line and the car dealer has been notified, then the dealer wants to deregister its interest in the event until it places another order.

The part of the problem we are focusing on is how to standardize the way in which we handle the communication between the observer objects (car dealers and car delivery department) and the subject object (assembly line). The subject object will need to publish an event against which the observer objects can register and deregister: to do this we create a delegate type event (Changed) that is fired or published by a subject object (ObservedAssemblyLine) and subscribed to by many observer objects (ObserverCarDealer and ObserverDelivery). The delegate event can be registered and deregistered, programmatically, at run time.

Let's look at the Observer pattern in a UML diagram (see Figure 12-2) and then implement the pattern in code.

UML

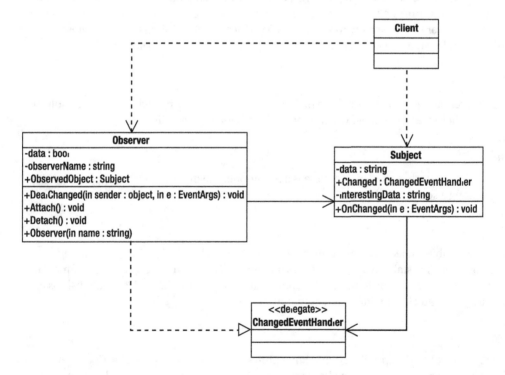

Figure 12-2. *Observer pattern*

Key Code Ingredients

The code for the Observer pattern has the following key ingredients:

- A `Delegate` class.
- A `Subject` class, comprising
    - an event of type `delegate`;
    - a method to invoke the `event`;
    - a property to hold data.
- An `Observer` class, which comprises
    - a property to hold data;
    - an event handler with the same signature as the `delegate`;
    - a method to attach to the event of the `Subject`;
    - a method to detach from the event of the `Subject`.
- A `Client` code, which comprises
    - a `Subject` class;
    - two `Observer` classes;
    - calls to the respective methods of the `Subject` and `Observer` objects.

Now let's code the Observer pattern.

Observer Pattern Code

The essence of the design lies in the delegate class model, which programmatically enables an observer object (`Observer`) to register and deregister an interest in an event (`Changed`) published by a subject object (`Subject`). Notice that the delegate class is placed in the same code file (`Subject.cs`) as the `Subject` class; this is done for programmatic convenience. Also note its unique class signature (it has no braces). While looking at the `Subject` class, study the relationship between the `InterestingData` property and the `OnChanged` event. It is when the set accessor method of the `InterestingData` property is called that it triggers the calling of the `OnChanged` event, which is logical because the `InterestingData` has changed. Also note, in the `Observer` class, the elegant way in which .NET's delegate allows registration (`Attach()` method) and deregistration (`Detach()` method) of the event (`OnChanged`) in the `Subject` class.

Delegate Class and Subject Class

```
//delegate class included in same code (cs) file as Subject class, for convenience
public delegate void ChangedEventHandler(object sender, EventArgs e);

public class Subject
{
```

```csharp
  private string data;
  public event ChangedEventHandler Changed;

  public string InterestingData
  {
    get{return data;}
    set
    {
      data = value;
      this.OnChanged(EventArgs.Empty);
    }
  }

  protected virtual void OnChanged (EventArgs e)
  {
    if (Changed !=null)
      this.Changed(this, e);
  }

  public Subject() {;}
}
```

Observer Class

```csharp
public class Observer
{
  private Subject data;
  private string observerName;

  public Subject ObservedObject
  {
    get {return data;}
    set {data = value;}
  }

  private void DataChanged (object sender, EventArgs e)
  {
    Console.WriteLine("Notification to {0}, the car {1}",➡
observerName, data.InterestingData);
  }

  public void Attach()
  {
    data.Changed += new ChangedEventHandler(DataChanged);
  }

  public void Detach()
```

```
  {
    data.Changed -= new ChangedEventHandler(DataChanged);
  }

  public Observer (string name)
  {
    observerName = name;
  }
}
```

Client Code

In the client code, we see the Observer pattern at work. We test the effectiveness of the design by instructing the client code to create a subject and two observer objects.

The client code creates instances of the subject object (ObservedAssemblyLine) and two observer objects (ObserverCarDealer and ObserverDelivery) in this example, we create two observer objects so that we can we can show the effect of deregistering one of them. Then the client code assigns the instance of the subject object (ObservedAssemblyLine) to the ObservedObject property of the respective observer objects (ObserverCarDealer and ObserverDelivery). The observer objects' ObservedObject property is required to be called by the client code, so that it knows which object is being observed.

Next, the client code calls the Attach() method of the observer objects (ObserverCarDealer and ObserverDelivery), and this step registers the event handler (ChangedEventHandler) with the delegate event (Changed) of the subject object (ObservedAssemblyLine). Then the client code assigns some new data to the InterestingData property of the subject object (ObservedAssemblyLine). Code within the InterestingData property fires the event (Changed) and passes it some new data. As the event handler (ChangedEventHandler) of the observer objects (ObserverCarDealer and ObserverDelivery) have been registered against the event (Changed), they are both notified of the event.

Following that, the client code calls the Detach() method of one of the observer objects (ObserverCarDealer), which causes its event handler (ChangedEventHandler) to be detached from the event (Changed); that is done because the car which the dealer is interested in has since rolled off the assembly line, and it is no longer interested in being notified of the event. Finally, the client code passes a second set of interesting data to the InterestingData property of the subject object (ObservedAssemblyLine), which will illustrate that the remaining observer object (ObserverDelivery), which is registered with the subject object (ObservedAssemblyLine), is notified of the second event.

■Tip By the way, you may have noticed that when the second car rolls off the assembly line, there is no car dealer interested in the event, which in reality wouldn't happen, as there are always car dealers waiting for cars to roll off the assembly line. To keep the example simple, we haven't added a second ObserverCarDealer object; however, if you like, you can extend the code in the client to include a second ObserverCarDealer object. To do that, just repeat the code for ObserverCarDealer, giving the variable a different name (e.g., ObserverCarDealer2), of course.

```
class Client
{
  static void Main(string[] args)
  {
    Subject observedAssemblyLine = new Subject();
    Observer observerCarDealer = new ➡
Observer("CarDealer Observer");
    Observer observerDelivery = new Observer("Delivery Observer");
    observerCarDealer.ObservedObject = ObservedAssemblyLine; ➡
observerDelivery.ObservedObject = ObservedAssemblyLine;
    observerCarDealer.Attach();
    observerDelivery.Attach();
    observedAssemblyLine.InterestingData = "# 001 ➡
is now finished!";
    observerCarDealer.Detach();
    observedAssemblyLine.InterestingData = "# 002 ➡
is now finished!";
  }
}
```

Console Output

```
Notification to CarDealer Observer, the car # 001 is now finished!
Notification to Delivery Observer, the car # 001 is now finished!
Notification to Delivery Observer, the car # 002 is now finished!
Press any key to continue
```

The Standard: Observer Design Pattern

> *The standard acknowledges the use of the Observer design pattern where there is a requirement to initiate and manage communications among a society of objects.*

Strategy Pattern

A Strategy pattern encapsulates a design feature where there is a need to contextually manage different implementations of a concept. In everyday life, examples of a Strategy pattern include a chain of international hotels that applies a regional decor strategy; or a university that administers a course entrance strategy based on a set of business rules.

What

A Strategy pattern is a design that presents a family of algorithms or business rules encapsulated in classes that can be swapped, polymorphically, within a context, which is independent of the client.

Where

A Strategy pattern is used where there is a design problem that requires the contextual implementation of different algorithms or business rules without the use of conditional code.

Why

In many domains there is a need to contextually apply a set of algorithms or business rules, and over time, as business requirements change, code that manages the choice and the implementation of algorithms or business rules can evolve into a tangled mess. The Strategy pattern prevents or overcomes this problem by presenting a design that separates the choice of algorithm or business rule from its implementation and delegates the contextual choice of algorithm or business rule to client code.

How

Design an abstract strategy class that includes an abstract method from which an algorithm may be called. For each strategy, subclass it from the *abstract strategy* class, then implement an appropriate algorithm in each of the *concrete strategy* classes. Prepare a context class to contain an abstract strategy class and then code the client to choose the strategy and inform the context class of the choice of strategy. Note that the context class acts as a liaison between the client and the strategy classes.

Pattern Example

In the Model T domain, there is client code that manages the task of handling inquiries regarding credit policy. For illustrative purposes, there is a credit policy context within which operates a credit strategy that seeks to offer favorable terms to volume purchasers (dealer and corporate customers). There are two different business rules or algorithms—one for each strategy (a corporate and a dealer strategy).

The part of the problem we are focusing on is how to apply the Strategy pattern to prevent the business rules from becoming intertwined in the choice of present and future strategies. This is tackled by implementing business rules in instances of strategy classes (objects), passing them, polymorphically, to a context class, which leverages composition to access the functionality of a strategy object. This allows client code to make the choice of which strategy to call or instantiate. That is the Strategy pattern!

We shall now look at the Strategy pattern in a UML diagram (see Figure 12-3) and then implement the pattern in code.

UML

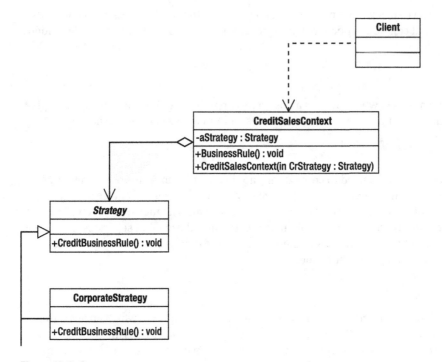

Figure 12-3. *Strategy pattern*

Key Code Ingredients

The code for the Strategy pattern has the following key ingredients:

- An abstract strategy class (Strategy), which contains an abstract or virtual method (CreditBusinessRule) to access the algorithm or business rule

- A number of strategy classes derived from the abstract strategy class

- An override, in the strategy classes (CorporateStrategy and DealerStrategy), of the method (CreditBusinessRule) that contains the algorithm or business rule

- A context class (CreditSalesContext), which includes

  - a member variable that is of type abstract strategy class;

  - a method that represents an algorithm or business rule of a strategy that can be accessed by client code;

  - a constructor that is passed a strategy type.

- Client code that makes the choice of which strategy to call or instantiate.

Strategy Pattern Code

The essence of the design lies in specializing a set of Strategy classes that can be passed poly-morphically—because they all derive from   Strategy—to a context class. It is the client which determines the context, by calling a given Context class. Notice that the Strategy class is abstract and that its only method (CreditBusinessRule()) is also abstract; that signifies that there is no default implementation in the abstract class, although that need not be the case. There may be default behavior implemented in the abstract class, but the business rule needs to be abstract or virtual so that it can be overridden in each Strategy subclass. In the case of a virtual method, if it is not overridden by any subclass, then this indicates that the Strategy pattern is an inappropriate design solution—the Strategy pattern is a design solution appropriate to situations where there is *variation* in business rules (algorithms).

Strategy Class

```
public abstract class Strategy
{

  //abstract method which subclasses will
  //implement to enable access to the strategy functionality
  public abstract void CreditBusinessRule();
  public Strategy() {;}
}
```

CorporateStrategy Class

```
public class CorporateStrategy: Strategy
{
  public override void CreditBusinessRule()
  {
    Console.WriteLine("Corporates: Allow 30 days credit.");
  }

  public CorporateStrategy() {;}
}
```

DealerStrategy Class

```
public class DealerStrategy: Strategy
{
  public override void CreditBusinessRule()
  {
    Console.WriteLine("Dealers: Allow 90 days credit.");
  }

  public DealerStrategy() {;}
}
```

CreditSalesContext Class

```
public class CreditSalesContext
{
  Strategy aStrategy;

  public CreditSalesContext (Strategy crStrategy)
  {
    this.aStrategy = crStrategy;
  }

  public void BusinessRule()
  {
    this.aStrategy.CreditBusinessRule();
  }
}
```

Client Code

In the client code, we see the Strategy pattern at work. We test the effectiveness of the design pattern by enabling the client code to choose a strategy in a given context.

```
class Client
{
  static void Main(string[] args)
  {
    //Client makes choice to call the Corporate Strategy - there
    //is an inquiry from a potential corporate customer regarding
    //the credit terms.
    CreditSalesContext cr = new CreditSalesContext(new CorporateStrategy());
    cr.BusinessRule();
  }
}
```

Console Output

```
Corporates: Allow 30 days credit.
Press any key to continue
```

The Standard: Strategy Design Pattern

> *The standard acknowledges the use of the Strategy design pattern where there is a design problem that requires the contextual implementation of different algorithms or business rules without the use of conditional code.*

Template Method Pattern

A Template Method pattern encapsulates a design feature, in an abstract class, which contains a template of an algorithm, part of which is left to be implemented by the subclass. In everyday life, examples of a Template Method pattern include a bank account application form, such that different accounts include a mix of standard questions and a few account-specific questions; or a book binder who binds all books in a given way but varies the algorithm or technique on limited editions.

What

A Template Method pattern ensures that the same structure can be subclassed to house different implementations of an algorithm and defer part of the implementation to the subclass.

Where

A Template Method pattern is used where there is a requirement for a common structure to house an algorithm, while offering some flexibility to vary the implementation of the algorithm.

Why

In many domains, there is a requirement for client code to call a common interface with a default implementation that has the flexibility for a subclass to vary the underlying algorithm within the implementation.

How

An abstract class exposes a Template Method that wraps a set of functionality or methods, part of which is overridden by a subclass.

Pattern Example

In the Model T domain, we have client code that manages the task of calling code to arrange the clock faces of different types of clocks that are fitted by a coachbuilder to the car. A requirement of the client code is that it wants a standard way to deal with this process regardless of the clock type—it simply wants to instantiate a clock type and call one method (SetupClockFace()). However, a design problem lies with the fact that not all clock faces are assembled in the same way; for example, a deluxe clock face has a label affixed to it, requiring one more step than needed to prepare a standard clockface, which doesn't have a label.

The part of the problem we are focusing on is how to satisfy the requirements of a common code structure, which the client code expects, and yet permit the clock itself to implement its own functionality.

To code this routine we develop an abstract clock class—the clock needs to perform two steps to set up the clock face. The first step is to set the clock hands to seven, which is a requirement of all clocks (seven is an arbitrary number). The second step is to position a label on the clock face. The Standard clock face does not require a label; however, to accommodate this variability, the Clock class declares the method PositionLabel() as abstract, which requires a subclass to provide an implementation. In this example, the Deluxe clock will provide an implementation, whereas the Standard clock will provide a code stub (empty code). The method that acts as a template is SetupClockFace( ), which resides in the Clock class. Notice that Step 1 is a fixed task that is handled for the subclasses by the base class Clock, but Step 2 is delegated to the subclasses to implement. That is the Template Method pattern!

We shall now look at the Template Method pattern in a UML diagram (see Figure 12-4) and then implement the pattern in code.

UML

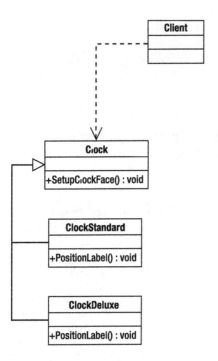

Figure 12-4. *Template Method pattern*

Key Code Ingredients

The code for the Template Method pattern has the following key ingredients:

- An abstract base class (Clock)

- An abstract method (PositionLabel())

- A template method (SetupClockFace()), which resides in the base class and wraps several steps or other methods of the class

- Any number of subclasses (ClockDeluxe and ClockStandard) that override the abstract method (PositionLabel()) called by the template method (SetupClockFace()) from the base class

Now let's code the Template Method pattern.

Template Method Code

The essence of the design lies in the use of inheritance to subclass a common interface and the structure of the algorithm contained within the template method (SetupClockFace()) in the base class (Clock). Notice that in the template method there is default behavior in the algorithm; however, within the algorithm lies the flexibility to vary an element of the algorithm—PositionLabel().

Clock Class

```
public abstract class Clock
{
  // an abstract method that all sub-classes need to code a full
  // implementation of functionality
  public abstract void  PositionLabel();

  //the template method
  public void SetupClockFace()
  {
    //step 1. set hands to 7 o'clock - this could be represented as a method
    Console.WriteLine("Clock hands set at 7 o'clock");

    //step 2. position the label on the clockface
    this.PositionLabel();
  }

  public Clock() {;}
}
```

Deluxe Clock Class

```
public class ClockDeluxe: Clock
{

  public override void PositionLabel()
  {Console.WriteLine("Deluxe clock, position the label bottom center.");}
  public ClockDeluxe() {;}
}
```

Standard Clock Class

```
public class ClockStandard: Clock
{
  //A Standard clock has no label, so the code that positions a label is not required
  public override void PositionLabel() {;}

  public ClockStandard() {;}
}
```

Client Code

In the client code, we see the Template Method pattern at work. We test the effectiveness of the design pattern by instructing the client code to instantiate a standard clock and a deluxe clock, and to call their respective SetupClockFace() methods. The template code, which resides in the base class (Clock), is implemented differently by the algorithm contained in the template method (SetupClockFace()) of the two subclasses (ClockDeluxe and ClockStandard).

```
class Client
{
  static void Main(string[] args)
  {
    //create an instance of the deluxe clock
    //and set up the clockface
    Console.WriteLine("** A DELUXE CLOCK **");
    Clock delClock = new ClockDeluxe();
    delClock.SetupClockFace();

    //create an instance of the standard clock
    //and set up the clockface
    Console.WriteLine("** A STANDARD CLOCK **");
    Clock stdClock = new ClockStandard();
    stdClock.SetupClockFace();
  }
}
```

Console Output

```
** A DELUXE CLOCK **
Clock hands set at 7 o'clock
Deluxe clock, position the label bottom center.
** A STANDARD CLOCK **
Clock hands set at 7 o'clock
Press any key to continue
```

The Standard: Template Method Design Pattern

> *The standard acknowledges the use of the Template Method design pattern where there is a requirement for a common structure to house an algorithm while offering some flexibility to vary the implementation of the algorithm.*

PART 4

■ ■ ■

References

This part of the book includes the appendix, standards index, glossary, and index.

Environment Variables and Remote Proxy Example

Environment Variables

To be able to call the C# compiler from the command line, you need to make your environment settings aware of the existence of the compiler (csc.exe). You can tell whether your computer recognizes the compiler by typing "csc" at the command prompt (accessing the command prompt is discussed in the section "Remote-Proxy Pattern Example─Using the Command Line," later in this appendix). If your settings have not been configured, then you should get a message advising that the system doesn't recognize csc, at the command prompt. If your settings have been configured, then you will get a different message advising that "no inputs have been specified," but a few lines above this you will see that the csc has been called and at least it is recognized by environmental settings, so you need take no further action.

Note In this example, we set up the environment variables to globally recognize the C# compiler (csc.exe) so that we can use it from the command prompt. However, you can access the command prompt through Visual Studio (Start ➤ All Programs ➤ Microsoft Visual Studio 2005 ➤ Visual Studio Tools ➤ Visual Studio 2005 Command Prompt), in the file location where Visual Studio resides—so you could set up the example that way. However, this example has been written using Visual Studio 2005 Beta 2 (running on Windows XP Version 5.1.2600), and that functionality was not wired at the time of writing. We have gone back to basics and set up the environment variables so that we run the example outside of Visual Studio. Although it is laborious, you do get to set all that the compiler does, which is quite interesting.

However, for people who need to set the environment variable in environmental settings, here we go.

1. Click the Start button, select Control Panel, and then select System.

2. In the System Properties dialog, click the Advanced tab, which should look like Figure A-1.

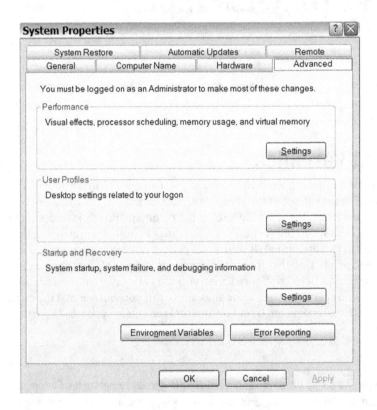

Figure A-1. *System Properties dialog*

3. Click the Environment Variables button, which will take you to the Environment Variables dialog. In the "System variables" list box, select "Path," as shown in Figure A-2.

Figure A-2. *Environment Variables dialog*

Caution Before editing Environment Variables (Path), make a local backup copy of the Path (refer to step 4).

---

4. We will shortly change the Path variable, but before proceeding we will make a backup copy of the current Path setting. While Path is highlighted, in the "System variables" list box, click the Edit button, then hold down the Ctrl button and press "C" to copy the Path to the clipboard. Now create a folder on your C drive and call it "Environment Variables" (C:\Environment Variables). Open up Notepad and press Ctrl-V; the Path variable should now be in Notepad. Save the Notepad file with a useful name: "EnvironVariablesPath_09_12_2005."

5. You can do a search (Start ➤ Search ➤ All files and folders) and type in "csc.exe" and note where your csc.exe is located. It should be located under "Windows\ Microsoft.NET\Framework*version number*." (Note: Your search will likely find multiple copies of csc.exe.)

   • Now move back to the Environment Variables dialog (you should still have the Path variable highlighted). Click on the Edit button in the Environment Variables dialog, and the Edit System Variable dialog appears (see Figure A-3). Click the path in the "Variable value" text box, and click on the text in the text box to de-highlight the variable.

- Now press the right-arrow keyboard button (or hit the End keyboard button) until you come to the end of the path, and then place a ";" immediately after the last variable (i.e., there should be no spaces between variables).

- Now enter the path where the csc.exe file is located. The following is the path that I have for v2.0 Beta 2, which I have added after the ";" C:\WINDOWS\Microsoft.NET\ Framework\v2.0.50215\. (Select the V2.0 version of csc.exe, just in case an older version causes unexpected results.) As this is the last variable in the list, it is *not* followed by a ";", which Figure A-3 illustrates.

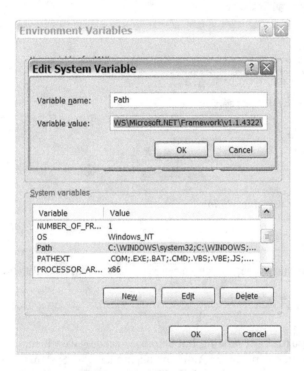

Figure A-3. *Edit System Variable dialog*

6. Click OK, OK, and OK to exit the remaining dialogs. Make sure you also close any open command windows.

7. Now open up a fresh command window and key in "csc," and hopefully csc will be recognized; however, you should receive an error message advising that "no inputs have been specified." If you don't get this message, but the previous message about csc not being recognized, then you can try a few things: revisit the entry that you keyed in the Path variable and verify that it points to where csc.exe is located on your disk; ensure that you have typed the address correctly; check to see that there are no spaces between the previous variable and the variable you entered; or try rebooting your computer. Note: csc will need to be recognized by Windows before you can advance to using the command line.

Remote-Proxy Pattern Example: Using the Command Line

In the Remote-Proxy pattern, we have chosen to use TCP as a protocol, which requires us to develop a server application (Server.exe) and not rely on IIS as the server. We are running the example outside of Visual Studio (VS). By doing it this way—even though it is laborious—we get to experience everything that is happening.

In the example, our endpoint is to have the Server.exe application run in one domain and expose the "Question-Answer service" (ProxyRemote) and have that service called by the Client.exe application, which runs in another domain. Using this setup, we can mimic what would happen if we were running the example on two computers. Now we will slowly walk through all the steps.

1. The command line is the prompt ">", which is located in the command box, which is found by clicking the Start button and then "Run . . ." on the menu. After this, the Run dialog box should appear, as shown in Figure A-4; then key in "cmd" and click OK to open the command box.

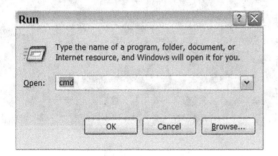

Figure A-4. *Run dialog*

2. You should now be looking at the command box with its flashing cursor. Before we continue, however, do the following:

   • Open up two instances of Windows Explorer (one for each work area: "US" and "UK") and create two folders: "C:\ModelT\US_Server" and "C:\ModelT\UK_Client."

   • In the "US_Server" folder, place a copy of `ProxyRemoteServer.cs` and `Server.cs`.

   • In the "UK_Client" folder, place a copy of `Client.cs`.

Tip If you want to key the code into the above files, the full script appears under the respective class heading in the discussion of the Remote-Proxy pattern. To enter code outside of VS, enter the script into a Notepad file and then, for example, save as: "ProxyRemoteServer.cs"—include the quote marks to prevent Notepad from saving the file as a "txt" rather than as a "cs" file.

---

3. When trying to understand what is going on, it is a good idea to open up a window for each work area. We will be working in three work areas: the US_Server folder, the UK_Client folder, and the command box. Now arrange the two instances of Windows Explorer and the command box as shown in Figure A-5.

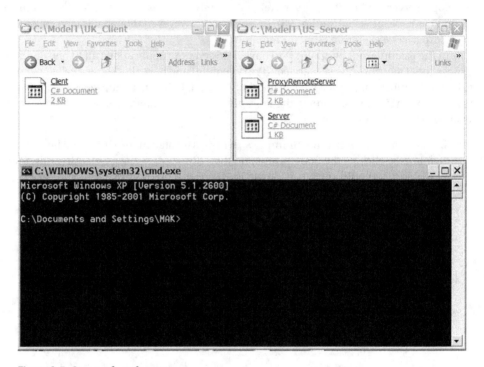

Figure A-5. *Setup of work areas*

4. Before we go any further, let's get oriented by looking at Figure A-5. We have the Client.cs resident in the UK_Client folder and ProxyRemoteServer.cs and Server.cs files resident in the US_Server folder, below which we have the command box, in which we will key in commands. Now we will key commands on the command line, and after each command we will see new files appear in the respective folders.

5. At this point I am assuming that the prompt in your command box is not within the C:\modelt\ root directory; if it is, then omit the c:\modelt\ part of the following command. We want to get the command line to point to the US_Server folder. In the command box, at the prompt enter the following:

```
cd c:\modelt\us_server
```

and then press Enter. Note that the command line is not case sensitive, so you can use lowercase rather than exact syntax, if you prefer. The command prompt should now be pointing at the US_Server folder, as Figure A-6 shows.

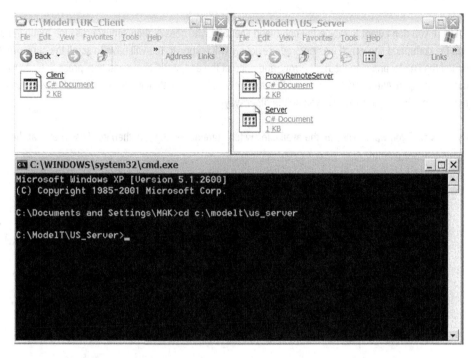

Figure A-6. *US_Server folder dialog*

6. If you look in the ProxyRemoteServer.cs file (open it using Notepad), you will find that there are three class definitions: IDesignEngineer, ChiefDesignEngineer, and ProxyChiefDesignEngineer. Also note that they are all part of the Patterns. ProxyRemoteServer namespace (which is indicated at the top of the file). The "cs" file is really just a convenient way for a developer to maintain the concept of a class definition; however, the csc allows us to place one or dozens of classes in the same file. When a cs file is compiled into Intermediate Language (IL), the cs file context is dispensed with by the complier, and the Common Language Runtime (CLR) manages classes and other types within the context of namespaces (e.g., Patterns.ProxyRemoteServer. IDesignEngineer), which reside in a given assembly (DLL). Note that once we build the ProxyRemoteServer DLL, we will no longer use any of the cs files (all of the functionality will be compiled and accessible from the ProxyRemoteServer DLL).

7. We are now ready to use the C# compiler (csc.exe) to build the ProxyRemoteServer DLL (or assembly). With the command prompt pointing at c:\modelt\us_server, key in the following:

```
csc /t:library proxyremoteserver.cs
```

and then press Enter. This will build the DLL, which you should see appear in the US_Server folder. If you missed it but would like to see it, you can delete the DLL and rerun the command line.

Tip If you don't want to retype the command line (and who does?), then simply press the function key F8, and the command line which was entered previously will reappear. You will have to scroll the cursor to the end of the line by pressing the right arrow, and once at the end of the command line, press Enter to run the command again. Alternatively, if you use the up-arrow keyboard button, it lets you go back several commands, and the down-arrow lets you go the other way.

By the way, if you want to see all the available switch statements (e.g., /t), then key "csc /help" at the command-line prompt.

8. Okay, so what exactly does `csc /t:library proxyremoteserver.cs` mean? This is a command that calls the C# compiler. The csc invokes the C# compiler (the csc stands for **c s**harp compiler). The compiler is passed a switchkey "/" followed by "t:library," which tells the compiler to build a DLL out of the **t**arget file, which is `proxyremoteserver.cs`. (To effect this in VS, you have to open a class library project, define your classes, and select the Build command from the menu. VS calls the C# compiler and puts a copy of the compiled DLL in the bin directory.) Your screen should now show the ProxyRemoteServer DLL in the US_Server folder, as shown in Figure A-7.

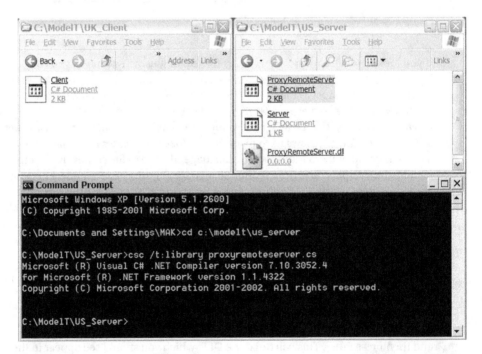

Figure A-7. *ProxyRemoteServer.cs dialog*

9. We now need to register the ProxyRemoteServer DLL against Server.cs. If you look inside Server.cs, you will see that it has the statement using Patterns.ProxyRemoteServer; this statement refers to ProxyRemoteServer DLL. Server.cs needs to reference the DLL to gain access to the functionality of IDesignEngineer, ChiefDesignEngineer, and ProxyChiefDesignEngineer. To register the DLL, we need to use the command line (which should still be pointing to the US_Server folder, as per Figure A-7). Key the following into the command line:

```
csc /r:proxyremoteserver.dll server.cs
```

and press Enter. This time the compiler has done two things instead of just one. The compiler (csc) is passed /r:proxyremoteserver.dll, which means reference the meta-data in the file proxyremoteserver.dll with server.cs file. This is all well and good, but in the US_Server folder we now have a fourth file, Server.exe, so where does that come from? Having referenced the DLL with Server.cs, the compiler then simply compiles Server.cs into an executable file, as shown in Figure A-8.

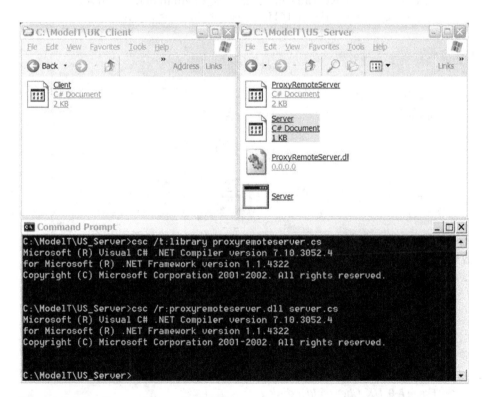

Figure A-8. *ProxyRemoteServer.dll dialog*

10. So from the perspective of the US_Server folder, our task now is complete. We have an executable server program (Server.exe) that references all the functionality in ProxyRemoteServer.dll.

11. We now need to point the command box to UK_Client folder, so on the command line key in

    cd ..\uk_client

    and press Enter. For the client to have an association with the server functionality, it needs to know about the ProxyChiefDesignEngineer—open up Client.cs and note that an instance of ProxyChiefDesignEngineer needs to be created and two of its "knowledge methods" will be called. Presently, there is nothing in the UK_Client folder to help Client.cs access ProxyChiefDesignEngineer. Herein lies the trick: make a copy of ProxyRemoteServer DLL, which is located in the US_Server folder, and place it in the UK_Client folder. We now need to associate Client.cs with the DLL and also compile it into Client.exe. This will all be done at the same time when we enter the following command on the command line:

    csc /r:proxyremoteserver.dll client.cs.

    You should now have three files in the UK_Client folder: Client.cs, ProxyRemoteServer.dll, and Client.exe, as shown in Figure A-9.

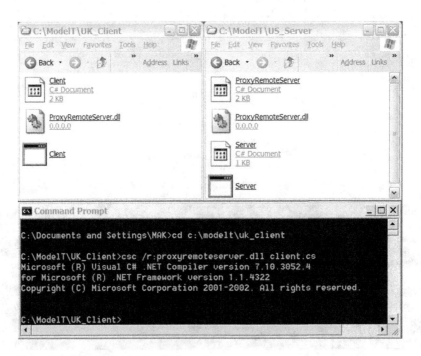

Figure A-9. *UK_Client folder dialog*

12. We have now set up both the server and client applications, so you can close the two instances of Windows Explorer that pointed to the respective folders. By the way, although this example is contrived, because we are working on a single PC, it need not be; we need only alter the TCP address in Client.cs from tcp://localhost:1234/ RemoteProxy to whatever address we choose, to allow remote client code to access the functionality exposed by Server.exe (subject to security permissions, etc.).

13. Now we are about to let the client call the service exposed by the server. Open up a second instance of the command box (see previous instructions). Align the two instances of the command boxes as shown in Figure A-10.

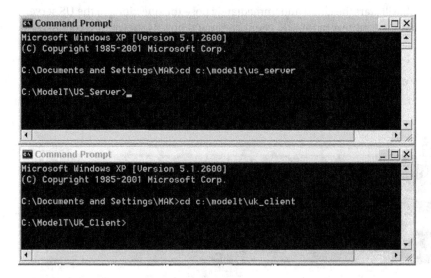

Figure A-10. *US_Server and UK_Client dialog*

14. We need to start up the service that will allow the UK technical guys to ask some questions. We do this by running server.exe from the command line. Key server.exe onto the command line that is pointed at US_Server. Calling server.exe will start the server application, as shown in Figure A-11.

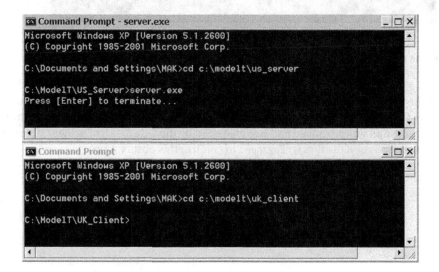

Figure A-11. *Server.exe dialog*

15. We now fire up the client application. Go to the command box that points to the UK_Client, and on the command line enter:

```
client.exe
```

which will start the client and immediately pose the questions to the US server. The answers will appear in the UK_client command box, as shown in Figure A-12.

■**Note** If server.exe is not currently running, then a SocketException will be thrown.

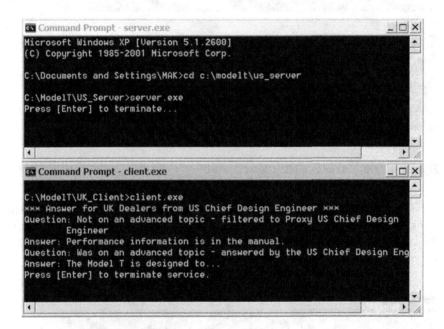

Figure A-12. *Server.exe and Client.exe dialog*

16. In the UK_Client command box, notice that the first question has been answered by ProxyChiefDesignEngineer, because it was not an advanced question, whereas the second question was advanced and was answered by the ChiefDesignEngineer (refer to the code in ProxyChiefDesignEngineer to confirm this observation).

List of Standards

This is a list of the standards that are catalogued in the respective chapters of the book.

Code Policy Standards

The following standards are the code policy standards that appear in Chapter 1.

Code Policy

The standard acknowledges that a code policy is an effective and efficient way to successfully manage code development by coordinating development across the enterprise.

Code Management

The standard acknowledges that code is a valuable resource that benefits from management throughout its development and life cycle.

Code Vision

The standard acknowledges that a code vision creates a sense of direction that unites a development team to work toward a shared technical goal.

Code Objective(s)

The standard acknowledges that code objectives are an essential part of the development process because they identify what aspects of the enterprise need to change to realize a code vision.

Code Plan

The standard acknowledges the use of a code plan to identify tasks and allocate resources to progress code from its current state to its future state.

Code Strategy

The standard acknowledges that a code strategy can be used to determine the best way to implement a code plan and achieve a set of code objectives.

Code Development Methodology

The standard acknowledges the use of code development methodologies such as XP and RUP, which are used to maximize the likelihood of developing successful code.

Peer Review

The standard acknowledges the benefits of peer review: (1) improvement of the quality of code by improving the skills of the developer, (2) knowledge sharing, (3) compliance with code policies, and (4) building team cohesion.

Unit Testing

The standard acknowledges the importance of unit testing, which is used to examine the reliability of calling the methods of an object.

Refactoring

The standard acknowledges that refactoring is a useful tool to transform the internal workings of an application without affecting its external workings.

Enterprise Imperative

The standard acknowledges that developing code with an enterprise imperative improves efficiency by minimizing code duplication and maintenance.

Domain Imperative

The standard acknowledges that a domain imperative is used where a requirement is tightly coupled to a domain or there is insufficient opportunity or incentive to develop it otherwise.

Source Code Control

The standard acknowledges that a source code security control reduces the risks associated with team development.

Obsolescence

The standard acknowledges the benefits of early warning of obsolescence. Notice should be given in a timely manner: it is considered that a notice period of one major version is a minimum.

Code Style

The standard acknowledges the use of a code style to encourage uniformity or consistency in the way that code is written. It improves understandability of code and makes it relatively easy to rotate developers from project to project or from team to team.

Pascal Notation

The standard acknowledges the use of Pascal notation for class, constant, delegate, enum type, enum value, event, event handler, exception, static member variable, interface, method, namespace, and property.

Camel Notation

The standard acknowledges the use of Camel notation for instance member variables and parameters.

Hungarian Notation

The standard acknowledges the debate about the use of Hungarian notation with Web/Windows visual controls and notes it has steadfast and wide community support, thus making its use, for a variable assigned a visual control, optional.

Case Sensitivity

The standard acknowledges that where C# and Visual Basic are supported, for consistency in naming variables, a choice is made between (1) ruling against the use of case sensitivity in C# code; or (2) prefixing variables in C# and VB code with an underscore.

Code Structure Standards

The following standards are the code structure standards that appear in Chapter 2.

Assembly

The standard acknowledges that an assembly may be used to partition specialized functionality and to control distribution and accessibility to that functionality. The choices made to structure code impact not only accessibility to code but also the flexibility and maintainability of the code.

Namespace

The standard acknowledges the use of namespaces and embedded namespaces to strategically structure code and to avoid naming conflicts.

Interface Type

The standard acknowledges the use of namespaces and embedded namespaces to strategically structure code and to avoid naming conflicts.

struct Type

The standard acknowledges a struct type may be used as a lightweight alternative to a class to structure code and leverage interface inheritance in situations where memory allocation is scarce or class-inheritance and referencing are not required.

Class Type

The standard acknowledges the use of a class type where there is a requirement to support class-inheritance or reference semantics and the overhead of a reference type is not an issue.

Partial Type

The standard acknowledges the use of partial type where there is a requirement to split a type over multiple files but cautions that once the type is compiled, it cannot be extended.

Generic Type

The standard acknowledges the use of generics to reduce overhead and increase type flexibility while retaining the protection of type safety.

Code Development Standards

The following standards are the code development standards that appear in Chapter 3.

Top-Down Method

The standard acknowledges the use of the top-down development method to develop a solution by developing an application by decomposing a domain problem.

Bottom-Up Method

The standard acknowledges the use of the bottom-up development method to develop an application by composing a domain solution.

Application Architecture

The standard acknowledges the use of application architecture, observing that an application developed using architecture is more likely to be efficient and maintainable, as well as better equipped to accommodate volatility within the domain and the enterprise, than is an application that is not developed using architecture.

Class Development

The standard acknowledges that class development is complex and is an iterative process in which many elements have to be considered to build the most appropriate concrete classes, including interface, encapsulation accessibility, functionality, design patterns, inheritance, containment, and state.

Composition

The standard acknowledges the flexibility of composition in building a class interface and that it is favored over inheritance.

Class Inheritance

The standard acknowledges the use of class inheritance and notes that it is used to strategically and progressively extend and reuse design and functionality. It cautions that inappropriate base type selection is a common cause of reengineering.

Interface Inheritance

The standard acknowledges the use of interface inheritance as a versatile means to strategically implement an interface through using multiple interface inheritance, as required.

Overriding

The standard acknowledges the use of overriding to specialize generic functionality.

Overloading

The standard acknowledges the use of overloading as a low-risk way to vary or extend functionality, where the overloaded methods implement similar functionality using different types and numbers of parameters.

abstract Modifier

The standard acknowledges that the role of an abstract class is to contain generalized functionality or an interface and that the abstract method is used to defer implementation to a subclass.

sealed Modifier

The standard acknowledges the use of sealed to indicate that it is not logical or permissible to extend a class.

new Modifier

The standard acknowledges the use of new modifier to hide a derived method or delegate.

private Modifier

The standard acknowledges the use of the private modifier where there is a requirement to limit accessibility within a given class. Note that a class field should be modified private and its value accessed through a class property, to comply with encapsulation.

protected Modifier

The standard acknowledges the use of the protected modifier where there is a requirement to limit accessibility to a class hierarchy.

internal Modifier

The standard acknowledges the use of the internal modifier where there is a requirement to limit accessibility to other classes in the same program or assembly.

protected internal Modifier

The standard acknowledges the use of the protected internal modifier where there is a requirement to limit accessibility to a class, a class(es) derived from that class, or other classes in the same assembly.

public Modifier

The standard acknowledges the use of the public modifier where there is a requirement not to limit accessibility to functionality by defining and publishing an interface against which client code can collaborate.

static Modifier

The standard acknowledges the use of static to differentiate a class member from an object member and also to leverage the ability to access class functionality without the overhead of instantiation.

Attribute

The standard acknowledges the use of Attribute, which may be used to enrich an entity with metadata that may be accessed programmatically, at runtime.

Class Header

The standard acknowledges the use of class header, which comprises the keyword `class`, modifier, and class name. It is noted that consideration may be given to using a short and generic class name that is appropriate to the domain.

const

The standard acknowledges the use of `const` in simple situations or where the underlying value has to be a string type.

delegate

The standard acknowledges the use of `delegate` for programmatic efficiency and flexibility.

enum

The standard acknowledges the use of `enum` in situations that are complex or where a `string` type is not required as the underlying type of each constant value (otherwise, a `const` may be used).

event

The standard acknowledges the use of `event` as a way for objects to collaborate.

Field

The standard acknowledges that a field is associated with a class and is commonly used to store the underlying value of a property of an object, or if modified as `static` to store a value for the class.

Indexer

The standard acknowledges the use of indexer as a default property.

Method

The standard acknowledges the use of a method to support collaboration between objects and notes for efficiency, methods are functional-specific and developed to minimize the overhead of chatty communication between objects.

Property

The standard acknowledges the preferred use of property over the use of a `public` member field, in line with the object-oriented requirement to keep the internal workings of a class or object hidden from client code.

Variable

The standard acknowledges the definition of variable as a variable that has a procedure-level association, as distinct from a member field, which is a variable that has a type-level association. A variable may be categorized as a local variable in a procedure (e.g., method); as an element of an array; or as an input or output parameter.

if

The standard acknowledges the use of if statement for simple branching.

if-else

The standard acknowledges the use of if-else statement where there is a requirement to have a single condition that explicitly identifies an alternative.

Nested if

The standard acknowledges the nested if statement. However, it is mindful of the adverse effect that deep nesting has on readability and productivity. Where a nesting exceeds two layers, consideration may be given to using a switch statement or encapsulating the logic in a method.

switch and case

The standard acknowledges the use of the switch and case statement as a conditional execution statement in any scenario where there are two or more options or conditions.

break

The standard acknowledges the use of a break statement in a switch block as an explicit way to alter the flow of execution.

default

The standard acknowledges the use of default label in a switch block to explicitly offer an option of last resort and as a way to prevent fall-throughwhich would result in a compile error.

continue

The standard acknowledges the use of continue statement to commence a new iteration at the closest iteration statement.

goto

The standard acknowledges the reluctance to use the goto statement and notes two accepted practices: using it within a switch statement to redirect the flow of control to a case statement or to a default label.

throw

The standard acknowledges the use of the throw statement to programmatically raise an exception to be handled.

try-catch

The standard acknowledges the use of the try-catch statement or block where there is not a requirement for the guarantee of a finally statement. It is mindful of the extra resources necessary to support the catch statement and the benefit of arranging them in descending likelihood of occurrence.

try-finally

The standard acknowledges the use of the `try-finally` statement as a mechanism where it is necessary to attempt to execute a block of code (in the `try` block) and, regardless of the outcome, execute a subsequent code block (in the `finally` block).

try-catch-finally

The standard acknowledges the use of `try-catch-finally` statement or block where a comprehensive exception handling methodology is a requirement. It is mindful of the extra resources necessary to support `catch` statements and the benefit of arranging them descending in likelihood of occurrence.

do-while

The standard acknowledges the use of the `do-while` statement where there is a requirement to iterate an iteration block at least once.

while

The standard acknowledges the use of `while` statement where there is a requirement for iterative flexibility: to iterate zero or more times (place `while` at the head of an iteration block) or at least once (place a `while` statement at the tail of an iteration block and a `do` statement at the head of the iteration block).

for

The standard acknowledges the use of the `for` statement where there is a requirement to test a condition, by using the value in the index variable, before entering an embedded code block.

foreach

The standard acknowledges the use of the `foreach` statement where there is a requirement to iterate a collectionfor example, objects or controls.

Code Documentation Standards

The following standards are the code documentation standards that appear in Chapter 4.

Development Documentation Policy

The standard acknowledges the importance of knowledge retention and that a documentation policy may be used to minimize the risk of knowledge degradation.

Code Design Documentation

The standard acknowledges the importance of documenting code design so that it readily identifies and explains key aspects of the underlying code design strategy, rationale, and structure.

Code Design Log

The standard acknowledges the use of a code design log as an intuitive and quick method to document code design. It may be prepared as a txt, xml, or html template and stored inside a folder within a Visual Studio solution, for example.

Line Comment

The standard acknowledges the use of the line comment, which may be used as a single line comment, a multiline comment, or an end-of-line comment.

Block Comment

The standard acknowledges the use of the block comment where documentation is extensive. However, it notes that Visual Studio's line comment tool may be a more convenient method to comment blocks.

XML Comments

The standard acknowledges the use of XML comments as a form of internal and external code documentation.

Object Browser Comments

The standard acknowledges the use of object browser comments as a form of internal and external type documentation, and notes that it conveniently publishes the documentation in the Visual Studio IDE, which makes it readily accessible for developers and application architects.

XML and Line/Block Comments

The standard acknowledges the partnership of XML and line/block comments in documenting code.

Design Policy Standards

The following standards are the design policy standards that appear in Chapter 5.

Design Policy

The standard acknowledges that a design policy is an effective and efficient way to coordinate the management of a range of interrelated architectures that have different dynamics.

Design Objectives

The standard acknowledges that design objectives are an essential part of managing the design of an enterprise because they identify in concrete terms what needs to be done.

Design Style

The standard acknowledges the use of design style, which seeks to ensure that the enterprise is and remains structured in a way that complements an organization's (dynamic) business strategy.

Architecture Framework

The standard acknowledges the use of an architecture framework to strategically use architecture to manage an enterprise.

Target Architecture

The standard acknowledges that the target architecture encapsulates and coordinates change as a version or iteration of the enterprise and avoids the high risk associated with implementing structural change in an impulsive or ad hoc manner.

Architecture Roadmap

The standard acknowledges the use of an architecture roadmap as a guide to migrating an existing architecture to a target architecture.

Architecture

The standard acknowledges the use of architecture to manage enterprise artifacts in line with technical and functional objectives.

Enterprise Architecture

The standard acknowledges the use of enterprise architecture as an efficient and effective way to manage technology, across an enterprise, in line with a business strategy.

Network Architecture

The standard acknowledges the use of network architecture as a tool to support the strategic requirements of software, technology, data, and deployment architectures, within the context of an architecture framework.

Technical Architecture

The standard acknowledges the use of technical architecture as an efficient and effective way to maximize decoupling and minimize duplication, within the context of an architecture framework.

Software or Application Architecture

The standard acknowledges the use of application architecture as an efficient and effective way to manage application design and development within the context of an architecture framework.

Data Architecture

The standard acknowledges the use of data architecture as an efficient and effective way to support information requirements within the context of an architecture framework.

Deployment Architecture

The standard acknowledges the use of deployment architecture as an efficient and effective way to deploy functionality and data throughout an enterprise within the context of an architecture framework.

Integration Architecture

The standard acknowledges the use of integration architecture as an efficient and effective way to manage the integration of functionality and data throughout an enterprise within the context of an architecture framework.

Service-Oriented Architecture

The standard acknowledges the use of service-oriented architecture as an efficient and effective way to manage the publication and subscription of functionality and data throughout an enterprise within the context of an architecture framework.

Business Architecture

The standard acknowledges the use of business architecture to identify a strategic purpose to unite and coordinate a set of architectures to manage and safeguard the enterprise.

Design Structure Standards

The following standards are the design structure standards that appear in Chapter 6.

Structural Design

The standard acknowledges the design and management of an enterprise through the use of a structural design methodology.

Design Dichotomy

The standard acknowledges that consideration may be given to determine whether functionality has an enterprise or a limited domain role. The earlier the consideration is made, the better.

Modularity

The standard acknowledges the use of modularity as a method to design, build, and maintain complex structures.

Coupling

The standard acknowledges the appropriate management of coupling and the value of decoupling where the exercise of discretion effects a net positive return on investment.

Layers

The standard acknowledges the use of layers as an efficient and effective way to design, develop, maintain, and manage complex and large structures.

Design Context

The standard acknowledges that the design workspace has to be identified, so that appropriate resources may be organized. It practice, not all of the functionality of an enterprise may be included within an enterprise context.

Enterprise Design Framework

The standard acknowledges the use of an enterprise design framework where there are many structures that need to be managed as a cohesive composite.

Application Layer

The standard acknowledges that the design, development, and maintenance of software is a specialized skill with its own set of dynamics. Encapsulating domain software into a layer is an efficient and convenient way to manage the special needs of application development.

Domain Application

The standard acknowledges the design and development of domain applications to service the custom or non-universal requirements of a domain.

Enterprise Application

The standard acknowledges the use of enterprise applications to provide functionality that is routine or universal and is without a domain imperative.

Services Application

The standard acknowledges the use of services applications to distribute functionality across an enterprise as an effective and efficient way to manage functionality.

Two-Tier Design

The standard acknowledges the use of a two-tier design where there is a need for rapid development and high performance. It does caution, however, that over the medium to long term the design may encounter integration inefficiencies, and scalability, coupling, and maintenance issues.

Three-Tier Design

The standard acknowledges the use of a three-tier design where there is a requirement for an application that features high performance with a medium-to-long life expectancy. It cautions, however, that the business and data classes may be tightly coupled implementations to the user interface and datastore, which may cause future concern.

Five-Tier Design

The standard acknowledges the use of a five-tier design where there is a requirement for an application that requires high performance, presentation, and data source flexibility with a long life expectancy.

Application Integration Layer

The standard acknowledges the use of an application integration layer to avoid the cost of high maintenance, duplication, and tight coupling.

Enterprise Services Design

The standard acknowledges the use of enterprise services that seek to standardize resource availability, usability, adaptability, and stability while preventing or removing duplication and redundancy.

Communications Integration Layer

The standard acknowledges the use of a communication's integration layer to centralize and coordinate the integration of multiple artifacts that may to enable a more efficient, maintainable, and loosely coupled solution.

Communication Infrastructure Layer

The standard acknowledges the use of a communication infrastructure layer to manage and encapsulate communication functionality within an enterprise framework.

Design Development Standards

The following standards are the design development standards that appear in Chapter 7.

Design of Enterprise Services Layer

The standard acknowledges the design of an enterprise services layer and its role to publish generic functionality that is highly visible and accessible to enable functionality to be managed more effectively and efficiently throughout the enterprise.

Design of Application Integration Layer

The standard acknowledges the design of an application integration layer, and its role is to satisfy domain and vendor requirements by providing a service that offers integration functionality that is customizable, transparent, and highly visible.

Design of Application Layer

The standard acknowledges the design of an application layer and that its role enables isolation of application code from integration and services code, which maximizes portability and minimizes the impact of change.

Horizontal Design Development

The standard acknowledges horizontal design development as a method to regulate design development through layers, which seeks to ensure that the inherent purpose of the layer does not become biased or coupled to an application implementation.

Vertical Design Development

The standard acknowledges vertical design development as a method to regulate domain development, but cautions that code and design may be excessively coupled to a domain, which may make it a poor candidate to migrate to other layers for reuse.

Object Collaboration

The standard acknowledges the importance of the role of object collaboration because it is the collaboration of exchanging messages between objects that yields the functionality of an application.

Object Collaboration (Abstract-Interface Dichotomy)

The standard acknowledges that it is not always obvious when to use class or interface inheritance to design the interface of an object. A key to the dilemma is that an interface type is used to signify a role that an object can perform—an interface type is suitable to perform generic roles.

Object Collaboration (Composition-Inheritance Dichotomy)

The standard acknowledges that there is a dilemma when designing objects because there are two ways to acquire an interface: through composition or inheritance. A key to the dilemma is that class inheritance is more sensitive to change than is composition. GoF propose a principle: "Favor object composition over class inheritance."

Object Collaboration (Abstraction-Implementation Dichotomy)

The standard acknowledges that problems arise because at some point a design has to commit to an implementation; however, it needs to balance the cost of commitment against the need for flexibility in a dynamic domain. A key to the dilemma lies in using polymorphism, which enables an object to be treated as an implementation or as an interface at run time. GoF propose a principle: "Program to an interface, not an implementation."

Collaborative Code (Design Patterns)

The standard acknowledges the role that design patterns play in solving problems of objects collaborating in a dynamic domain.

Start-from-Scratch Application Solution

The standard acknowledges that a start-from-scratch application is used where there is very little code to reuse, and so developers start from scratch. It cautions that such a practice is generally inefficient as it may result in duplication of functionality and higher maintenance (compared with the use of a framework).

Application Frameworks Solution

The standard acknowledges the use of application frameworks, which are partially pre-built solution templates, as an efficient and effective way to reuse proven design and functionality.

Design Documentation Standards

The following standards are the design documentation standards that appear in Chapter 8.

Application Design Documentation Policy

The standard acknowledges the implementation of a single application design documentation policy across all projects within a given site.

Application Specification Documentation

The standard acknowledges the role of technical specification documentation and its importance in supporting the functional specification of an application.

Functional Specification Documentation

The standard acknowledges the role of functional specification documentation and its importance in directing the design and development of an application and in evaluating and verifying that an application meets client requirements.

Application Design Documentation

The standard acknowledges the documentation of application design and observes that it should be readily accessible to architects and developers.

Application Architecture Documentation

The standard acknowledges the documentation of application architecture and that it should be readily accessible to architects and developers. Documentation enables a team to retain and share critical architecture design knowledge that identifies and explains the underlying intention of the application architect and lead developer.

Enterprise Framework Documentation

The standard acknowledges the documentation of application design as it relates to the enterprise architecture and that it should be readily accessible to architects and developers. Documentation enables a team to retain and share critical architecture design knowledge that identifies and explains the underlying intention of the enterprise and application architects and lead developer.

Pattern Standards

The following standard is the MVC design pattern standard that appears in Chapter 9note that the other pattern standards, articulated by GoF, are in subsequent chapters.

MVC Design Pattern

The standard acknowledges the use of the MVC design pattern where there is a requirement to vary perspectives or views (output) without disturbingor while minimizing the disruption tothe underlying information source (model) that publishes the information.

Creational Pattern Standards

The following standards are the creational pattern standards that appear in Chapter 10.

Abstract Factory Design Pattern

The standard acknowledges the use of the Abstract Factory design pattern when there is a requirement not to couple the client to an implementation that creates sets or families of object, yet to let the client indirectly control the build process.

Factory Method Design Pattern

The standard acknowledges the use of the Factory Method design pattern where there is a design problem when a creator class is required to be decoupled from creating specific objects.

Singleton Design Pattern

The standard acknowledges the use of the Singleton design pattern where there is a design problem when there can only be one instance of a given object and where there is a requirement for client code to trigger the creation of the object.

Structural Pattern Standards

The following standards are the structural pattern standards that appear in Chapter 11.

Surrogate-Proxy Design Pattern

The standard acknowledges the use of the Surrogate-Proxy design pattern where there is a design problem such that access to a principal (e.g., scarce resource) needs to be regulated.

Remote-Proxy Design Pattern

The standard acknowledges the use of the Remote-Proxy design pattern where there is a design problem such that access to a principal needs to be distributed through representation.

Adapter Design Pattern

The standard acknowledges the use of the Adapter design pattern where there is a design problem, where there is a requirement to integrate with a noncompliant interface, or where there is a requirement for one design to leverage the functionality from one design into another design.

Composite Design Pattern

The standard acknowledges the use of the Composite design pattern where there is a design problem where there is a hierarchy of entities and a requirement for a simple non-conditional methodology to manage single and composite entities.

Facade Design Pattern

The standard acknowledges the use of the Facade design pattern where there is a requirement, by client code, for a high-level abstraction that is simple to use.

Behavioral Pattern Standards

The following standards are the behavioral pattern standards that appear in Chapter 12.

Chain of Responsibility Design Pattern

The standard acknowledges the use of the Chain of Responsibility design pattern where there is a requirement to manage tasks by coordinating objects and have them cooperate within a hierarchical structure.

Observer Design Pattern

The standard acknowledges the use of the Observer design pattern where there is a requirement to initiate and manage communications among a society of objects.

Strategy Design Pattern

The standard acknowledges the use of the Strategy design pattern where there is a design problem that requires the contextual implementation of different algorithms or business rules without the use of conditional code.

Template Method Design Pattern

The standard acknowledges the use of the Template Method design pattern where there is a requirement for a common structure to house an algorithm while offering some flexibility to vary the implementation of the algorithm.

Glossary

****

Escape character: backslash.

!

Documentation generation ID string for "Error string."

!

An operator meaning "not."

!=

An operator meaning "not equal."

"

Double quotes.

#

An operator: examine preprocessor directive.

#define

A preprocessor directive statement that defines a preprocessor identifier.

#elif

A preprocessor directive statement that indicates an "else if" condition.

#else

A preprocessor directive statement that indicates an "else" condition.

#endif

A preprocessor directive statement that indicates the end of an "if" preprocessor directive.

#if

A preprocessor directive statement that indicates the commencement of an "if" statement.

#region

A preprocessor directive statement that indicates a comment area of text.

#undef

A preprocessor directive statement that indicates the end of a preprocessor define (#define) statement.

%

A symbol used to signify modulus or mod operator.

%=

An assignment operator that assigns the modulus.

&&

The "and" operator.

&=

The Boolean assignment operator.

'

Single quote—not a comment ("//" or "/**/.").

()

Parentheses.

*

An operator: multiply.

*=
> An assignment operator: multiply.

+
> An operator: addition.

++
> An operator: increment.

+=
> An assignment operator: addition.

–
> Operator: subtract.

–=
> Assignment operator: subtract.

.aspx.cs
> A file suffix denoting the ASP.NET code-behind file is a C# code file.

.cs
> A file suffix that denotes that a file holds C# code.

/
> An operator: division.

/*...*/
> A code comment: block.

//
> A code comment: line.

///
> An XML comment for C#.

/=
> An assignment operator: divide.

/?
> A compilation option: lists compiler options (same as "/help").

:
> Colon: used to call constructor of a base class.

;
> Semicolon: indicates an end of a statement.

<
> An operator: less than.

<=
> An operator: less than or equal to.

<c></c>
> A tag used to format text in code-style font.

<code></code>
> A tag used to format code in a font.

<example></example>
> A tag used to illustrate how a library member of method can be used.

<exception></exception>
> A tag used to document exceptions.

<include></include>
> A tag used to include an external XML document located in another code file.

<item></item>
> A tag used to define an item in a list (used with <list> and <listheader> tags).

<list></list>
> A tag used to define a list of items (used with <listheader> and <item> tags).

\<listheader>\</listheader>

A tag used to define a header (used with \<list> and \<item> tags).

\<para>\</para>

A tag used to define a paragraph (used embedded in \<return> or \<remark> tags).

\<param>\</param>

A tag used to describe a constructor parameter, an indexer parameter, or a method parameter.

\<paramref>\</paramref>

A tag used to signify text that represents a parameter.

\<permission>\</permission>

A tag used to permit documentation of the security access of a member.

\<remarks>\</remarks>

A tag used to define global or overview information about a type.

\<returns>\</returns>

A tag used to describe a method's return value.

\<see>\</see>

A tag used to define a link in the text.

\<seealso>\</seealso>

A tag used to define additional links in text.

\<summary>\</summary>

A tag used to describe a member for a type.

\<value>\</value>

A tag used to describe a property.

=

Assignment operator.

==

An operator: equals.

>

An operator: greater than.

>=

An operator: greater than or equal to.

?:

An operator: tunary.

@

Verbatim: used for a string literal.

[ ]

Square brackets.

\

Backslash for escape characters.

\"

Escape character: double quotes.

\'

Escape character: single quote.

\0

Escape character: null.

\a

Escape character: alert.

\b

Escape character: backspace.

\f

Escape character: formfeed.

\n

Escape character: newline.

\r

Escape character: carriage return.

\t

Escape character: horizontal tab.

\v

Escape character: vertical tab.

^

An operator~~logical~~: XOR.

^=

A Boolean assignment operator, e.g., int1 ^= int2: int1 is assigned the result of int1^int2.

{}

Braces.

|=

A Boolean assignment operator, e.g., int1 |= int2: int1 is assigned the result of int1|int2.

||

An operator: OR.

abstract class

A class that can't be instantiated and can only be derived from.

Abstract Factory pattern

A type of design pattern that enables a client to deal with a high-level abstraction while leaving the factory abstraction to deal with coupling the implementation.

abstract method

A method that has no implementation; if a class has an abstract method, then the class is abstract as well.

abstract-interface dichotomy

The problem that arises when designing code for objects that collaborate with other objects: Do we encapsulate the interface to access the functionality as an abstract class or as an interface type?

abstraction

Conceptualization of a real entity.

abstraction-implementation dichotomy

The problem associated with deciding whether to commit to reference a type through its interface (abstract class) or through its implementation (concrete class).

access modifier

A modifier that identifies scope.

Adapter pattern

A type of design pattern that enables a noncompliant interface to be superimposed by an intermediary which manages an adaptation process to effect compliance.

anonymous method

A method that permits blocks of code to be written inline in place of a delegate value (C# 2.0 feature).

API

Application Programming Interface: a public interface that is programmed against.

application architecture

A blueprint for application design, development, and integration.

application architecture documentation

Documentation that identifies and explains the key aspects of the architecture of a given application in summary and detail formats.

application design documentation

Documentation of the architecture of an application and how the application fits within the enterprise (e.g., enterprise design framework).

application framework

An application development methodology in which a prebuilt template includes integration and enterprise services functionality.

application integration layer

A common layer through which applications are integrated.

application layer

A conceptual repository of applications that may be deployed across many networks and accessible locally, regionally, or globally.

architecture framework

A tool that defines and strategically aligns specialist architectures (e.g., network, software, and data).

architecture roadmap

Roadmap that identifies *when*, *what*, and *how* an existing architecture can be migrated to a target architecture.

argument

A parameter passed to a method or a parameter declaration.

array

A collection of same-type variables or elements identified with an index.

ArrayList

A dynamic array class: (1.) has a default capacity of 16 objects, (2.) automatically increases in size, (3.) holds any type of object reference. When accessing the objects, they need to be cast to the appropriate type.

as

An operator used to cast the left-side operand to the type of the right-side operand.

ASCII

American Standard Code for Information Interchange: a binary code that defines a set of characters.

ASCII 0

ASCII control code: null.

ASCII 1

ASCII control code: start of heading.

ASCII 2

ASCII control code: start of text.

ASCII 3

ASCII control code: end of text.

ASCII 4

ASCII control code: end of transmit.

ASCII 5

ASCII control code: inquiry.

ASCII 6

ASCII control code: acknowledge.

ASCII 7

ASCII control code: audible bell.

ASCII 8

ASCII control code: backspace.

ASCII 10

ASCII control code: line feed.

ASCII 11

ASCII control code: vertical tab.

ASCII 12

ASCII control code: form feed.

ASCII 13

ASCII control code: carriage return.

ASCII 14

ASCII control code: shift out.

ASCII 15

ASCII control code: shift in.

ASCII 16

ASCII control code: data link escape.

ASCII 17

ASCII control code: device control 1.

ASCII 18

ASCII control code: device control 2.

ASCII 19

ASCII control code: device control 3.

ASCII 20

ASCII control code: device control 4.

ASCII 21

ASCII control code: neg. acknowledge.

ASCII 22

ASCII control code: synchronous idle.

ASCII 23

ASCII control code: end transaction block.

ASCII 24

ASCII control code: cancel.

ASCII 25

ASCII control code: end of medium.

ASCII 26

ASCII control code: substitution.

ASCII 27

ASCII control code: escape.

ASCII 28

ASCII control code: file separator.

ASCII 29

ASCII control code: group separator.

ASCII 30

ASCII control code: record separator.

ASCII 31

ASCII control code: unit separator.

ASCII 32

ASCII control code: blank space.

ASCII 33

ASCII code: !

ASCII 34

ASCII code: "

ASCII 35

ASCII code: #

ASCII 36
ASCII code: $

ASCII 37
ASCII code: %

ASCII 38
ASCII code: &

ASCII 39
ASCII code: '

ASCII 40
ASCII code: (

ASCII 41
ASCII code:)

ASCII 42
ASCII code: *

ASCII 43
ASCII code: +

ASCII 44
ASCII code: ,

ASCII 45
ASCII code: -

ASCII 46
ASCII code: .

ASCII 47
ASCII code: /

ASCII 48
ASCII code: 0

ASCII 49
ASCII code: 1

ASCII 50
ASCII code: 2

ASCII 51
ASCII code: 3

ASCII 52
ASCII code: 4

ASCII 53
ASCII code: 5

ASCII 54
ASCII code: 6

ASCII 55
ASCII code: 7

ASCII 56
ASCII code: 8

ASCII 57
ASCII code: 9

ASCII 58
ASCII code: :

ASCII 59
ASCII code: ;

ASCII 60
ASCII code: <

ASCII 61
ASCII code: =

ASCII 62
ASCII code: >

ASCII 63
ASCII code: ?

ASCII 64

ASCII code: @

ASCII 65

ASCII code: A

ASCII 66

ASCII code: B

ASCII 67

ASCII code: C

ASCII 68

ASCII code: D

ASCII 69

ASCII code: E

ASCII 70

ASCII code: F

ASCII 71

ASCII code: G

ASCII 72

ASCII code: H

ASCII 73

ASCII code: I

ASCII 74

ASCII code: J

ASCII 75

ASCII code: K

ASCII 76

ASCII code: L

ASCII 77

ASCII code: M

ASCII 78

ASCII code: N

ASCII 79

ASCII code: O

ASCII 80

ASCII code: P

ASCII 81

ASCII code: Q

ASCII 82

ASCII code: R

ASCII 83

ASCII code: S

ASCII 84

ASCII code: T

ASCII 85

ASCII code: U

ASCII 86

ASCII code: V

ASCII 87

ASCII code: W

ASCII 88

ASCII code: X

ASCII 89

ASCII code: Y

ASCII 9

ASCII control code: horizontal tab.

ASCII 90

ASCII code: Z

ASCII 91

ASCII code: [

ASCII 92

ASCII code: \

ASCII 93

ASCII code:]

ASCII 94

ASCII code: ^

ASCII 95

ASCII code: _

ASCII 96

ASCII code: `

ASCII 97

ASCII code: a

ASCII 98

ASCII code: b

ASCII 99

ASCII code: c

ASCII 100

ASCII code: d

ASCII 101

ASCII code: e

ASCII 102

ASCII code: f

ASCII 103

ASCII code: g

ASCII 104

ASCII code: h

ASCII 105

ASCII code: i

ASCII 106

ASCII code: j

ASCII 107

ASCII code: k

ASCII 108

ASCII code: l

ASCII 109

ASCII code: m

ASCII 110

ASCII code: n

ASCII 111

ASCII code: o

ASCII 112

ASCII code: p

ASCII 113

ASCII code: q

ASCII 114

ASCII code: r

ASCII 115

ASCII code: s

ASCII 116

ASCII code: t

ASCII 117

ASCII code: u

ASCII 118

ASCII code: v

ASCII 119

ASCII code: w

ASCII 120

ASCII code: x

ASCII 121

ASCII code: y

ASCII 122

ASCII code: z

ASCII 123

ASCII code: {

ASCII 124

ASCII code: |

ASCII 125

ASCII code: }

ASCII 126

ASCII code: ~

ASCII 127

ASCII code: del

assembly

A repository (e.g., .dll or .exe) to store multiple and related code constructs or functionality.

assembly metadata

An assembly's contents—also referred to as a manifest.

AssemblyInfo.cs

A file created by Visual Studio that holds assembly attributes.

assignment operator

An operator used to assign a type on the right-hand side to the left-hand side: assignment operator is "=."

asynchronous

A process that can't run simultaneously (e.g., a request and the wait for a response).

attribute class

A class that derives from class System. Attribute. It holds metadata or declarative information that is accessible, through reflection, in the assembly.

backslash

Identifier for a "\".

backward compatibility

Indicates that a successor entity is compatible with an ancestor entity.

base

Keyword used to access functionality of a parent class.

base class

A parent class.

behavioral pattern

A category of design patterns that encapsulate a design feature where the focus is on communications, responsibilities, and algorithms.

binary files

File format used to store strings of bits (e.g., images).

binary operator

An operator that performs on two operands (+, -, *, /, %, &, |, ^, <<, >>).

binding type

A process by which a variable is declared as a data type. Types are late or early bound.

bit

Binary digit.

bitwise

An operator used to perform on a set of bits in a variable.

block comment

A multilined comment format used for large comments running over multiple lines.

blocking

A term used in threading to describe a thread that has been placed into a wait state; used in conjunction with synchronization.

bool

Data type: true or false.

boolean

Form of logic devised by the English mathematician George Boole.

bootstrapper

A program that executes prior to the running of a main application program.

boxing

A process that forces a value type to act as a reference type—boxed inside an Object type.

braces

Identifier for "{ }".

brackets

Identifier for "[ ]".

branching

The process of conditional code execution: an "if" statement is an example of branching.

break

A jump statement that causes the flow of the program to exit from the immediate code block.

break mode

A program debugging technique entered by pausing a program's execution.

breakpoint

A program debugging technique that marks a point in code to enter break mode.

business architecture

The business and technical artifacts expressed through a hierarchy of architectures.

byte

Data type: unsigned values 0–255.

cache

An area of memory or disk that is used to accelerate data retrieval or execution of instructions: pronounced "cash."

Camel notation

Code notation in which first letter of the first word of a variable name is lowercase and subsequently the first letter is uppercase—e.g., thisIsCamel.

capacity

The maximum number of items that can be held in a collection.

case

Reference to uppercase or lowercase formats.

case statement

A statement that describes a branching condition in a switch statement.

case-insensitive

Insensitive to case: an uppercase "A" is the same as a lowercase "a."

case-sensitive

Sensitive to case: an uppercase "A" is different from a lowercase "a."

cast

A programming technique that forces one type to be another type: cast short to byte, for example.

catch

The part of a "try-catch-finally" block that handles a thrown exception.

Chain of Responsibility pattern

A type of design pattern in which a set of responsibilities or links joins to form a chain of responsibility and each link is presented as an object that is responsible for a given task.

char

Data type: Unicode character that holds values 0–65,535.

checked

Keyword that sets an expression's overflow checking context.

child

A derived class or subclass.

class

A complex reference type that is the definition of an object. Once instantiated, the class is known as a concrete class or an object.

class derivation

A process by which a class is derived from another class.

class header

Identifies the class; it contains the class modifier (e.g., public), the keyword class, and the name of the class.

class inheritance

Enables one class to derive functionality from a base or parent class.

class member

Valid members include fields or variables, methods, properties, and events.

class polymorphism

Object-oriented concept whereby a specialized class (child) may be passed as an instance of a generalized class (parent or ancestor).

closed type

A type that is not an open type; in other words, it does not involve type parameters (C# 2.0 feature).

code design log

A register in which key design information is stored.

code documentation

Identification of how and why code is developed in a given way.

code policy

A methodology through which to regulate the development of code. It encourages the design and development of low-risk code.

code strategy

The *how* statement: This is how we are going to implement the code plan.

collection

A type of class that holds objects; e.g., an array is a collection.

colon

Identifier (:) used to signify inheritance.

comments

Documentation text added to code that is ignored by a compiler.

communications infrastructure

Represents the local and extended software and hardware transport components that enable data exchange and network switching.

communications integration layer

Encapsulates or abstracts to an interface layer the responsibility of integrating the enterprise services layer (the application platform) with the hardware and communication functionality.

comparison operator

An operator that compares values (= =, ! =, < >,< =, >=).

compiler

An executable program that sets the rules for a given language and examines code to see that it is valid (the C# compiler is "csc.exe").

complex type

Variable type (array, structure, and enumeration).

complex types

Data types that are reference types e.g., classes.

component

Executable subprogram e.g., DLL.

composite pattern

A type of design pattern in which all entities in a hierarchy expose the same interface regardless of whether the entity is a single entity or a composite.

composition-inheritance dichotomy

The problem that arises when designing objects, because there are two ways to acquire an interface (i.e., through composition or inheritance), and commonly it is not obvious which method to use.

comprehensive namespace

Method of arranging a namespace where a hierarchy of program structures is used, commonplace in frameworks.

concurrency

A circumstance in which there are attempts to access an object simultaneously.

conditional operator

Logical operator that returns a boolean— also referred to as a ternary operator.

configuration files (.NET)

XML-formatted files for an assembly that hold rules for the .NET runtime.

const

A static modifier used on local variables or member fields; once its value is assigned, it can't be changed at runtime.

constant

Indicates that a variable's value cannot be changed: keyword const.

constructor

A special method that instantiates a class into an object.

containment

When a field of a class holds a reference to an object, the object is said to be contained in the class of the field.

context switching

Happens when a processor stops actively executing a thread to commence another thread; the immediate thread is paused and the subsequent thread is commenced.

continue

A jump statement that transfers the program flow to commence a new iteration of the closest do, for, foreach, or while statement.

copy constructor

Instantiates an object with the values copied from an existing same-type object.

CORBA

Common Object Request Broker Architecture (see www.omg.org).

coupling

The association between two or more artifacts; for example, a business object is coupled to the schema of a database table.

creational patterns

A category of design patterns that encapsulate a design feature where the focus is on strategically manipulating the instantiation of classes.

CSV

Comma-separated values: used to delimit strings.

custom exception

An exception that has been created by a developer by deriving a class from System.Exception class.

custom namespace

Methodology of arranging a namespace where it wraps custom development and separates it from code generated by an IDE.

data architecture

The structure of physical and logical data and how it is stored, accessed, and distributed within and across layers or tiers.

data binding

Methodology by which a control is bound to a data source. .NET offers dynamic data controls and data binding at runtime.

decimal

Fixed and decimal point precision to 28 digits.

declaration

Simply declares the name and the type of a field or variable.

declare

Process by which a variable is given a name and type—it may or may not be assigned a value or reference.

decouple

To remove the association between two or more artifacts.

deep copying

A technique that describes copying an object variable into another variable by value rather than by reference.

default

A statement that offers an option of last resort in a switch block.

default constructor

The constructor of the parent or base class.

delegate

A class that is a reference to a method that has a given signature (parameter list and return type).

deployment architecture

The deployment of architecture artifacts on network nodes.

deserialize

To reconstruct from one data format to its original format (e.g., from a binary stream back to a C# object).

design context

The workspace or domain in which the design policy is to be implemented (e.g., the design context may be an enterprise or a given domain).

design documentation

Refers to identifying how and why design is developed in a given way.

design objective

An abstract statement that expresses the design policy of an enterprise.

design pattern

A methodology that cleverly arranges class interfaces and implementations to overcome a problem that affects the ability of an object to collaborate with other objects.

design policy

A plan that manages the design, integration, and deployment of functionality and data across an enterprise.

destructor

Method declaration to terminate an object e.g., `~aClass()`: used with `Finalize()`.

dictionary

Collection with a key and value association.

DLL

Dynamic Link Library: a code assembly, compiled from a class library, that is encapsulated as a component and commonly used by other assemblies (.dll or .exe files).

DNS

Domain Name Service: translates an IP address (000.000.0.0) to a URL (`http://www.myhome.com/myhomepage.htm`).

do

Loop statement that iterates inside a block until a condition is met; commonly referred to as a "do loop."

documentation policy

A statement that contains a set of rules and controls that manage the way code is documented.

DOM

Document Object Model: a hierarchy of elements that usually models an XML document.

domain application

An application that fulfills the custom or strategic requirements of a given domain (e.g., an organization or department).

double

Double precision floating point: +/--5.0*10 pow -324 to +/-1.7*10 pow 308 with 15 to 16 significant figures.

DTD

Document Type Definition: a methodology to define the elements and attributes of an XML document. A non-XML syntax that does not permit specification of an element or attributes data type.

E

Documentation generation ID string for "Event".

early binding

Methodology whereby binding is determined as design time.

element

Entry in an array or XML document.

else

A statement that is executed only when the head "if" expression is false.

else if

A statement that combines two statements "else" and "if": only when the head "if" expression is false (else), then evaluate this "if" statement.

enterprise application

An application that encapsulates functionality that is common to an industry type, or an industry in general.

enterprise architecture

An architecture that coordinates technology across the enterprise in line with a given business strategy.

enterprise design framework

A blueprint that defines the structures or layers of an enterprise. The structures or layers map conceptually, although not always physically, to a given architecture.

enterprise framework documentation

Documentation of how an application architecture document fits within the enterprise design framework.

enterprise services layer

A common layer through which enterprise functionality is published.

enterprise services layer

A layer that contains the code or functionality considered common across applications or common within a given application.

enterprise-domain dichotomy

The design dilemma that architects and developers grapple with: When is functionality better defined as enterprise or as domain functionality?

enum

A value type that contains an enumerator list (a set of named numeric constants). Enumeration list of named constants: enum keyword or value type that holds a quantity of named numeric constants (byte, sbyte, short, ushort, long, ulong, int, unit).

error

Avoidable occurrence that has not been avoided.

escape sequence

A methodology of substituting a character to escape a sequence of characters (" = \").

event

A methodology by which a class may raise a notification.

exception

Occurrence that is not normal or breaks a rule: it may be caused by an error, but it cannot cause an error.

explicit conversion

Manually coded by a developer when a valid type is assigned to another valid type that is outside of its range of values: it is assisted by a type cast or using the Convert class.

expression

A statement that evaluates to a value: comprises an operand(s) and an operator(s) that evaluate to a value.

expression statement

Evaluates an expression; if any value is merely computed then it is discarded (e.g., y == 7; merely computes a value, unlike y = 7;, which assigns the value "7" to *y* and thus evaluates to "7").

extern

Modifies a method, indicating that unmanaged code is used to implement it.

F

Documentation generation ID string for "Field".

Facade pattern

A type of design pattern that ensures that the complexity of many interfaces is hidden behind a simple, uniform interface.

Factory Method pattern

A type of design pattern that defines an interface for creating objects but delegates the choice of what objects to create to subclasses.

false

Boolean value.

field or member field

A variable that is part of a type or class.

finally

The section of a "try-catch-finally" statement that will always execute once control passes from the try or catch statement.

five-tier architecture

An application architecture that separates functionality over four tiers that reside on two servers—a presentation tier on one server; and UI, Business, and Data tiers on a second server—and in which the data source (fifth tier) resides on a third server.

fixed

A statement that prevents the GC from collecting a reference type during pointer arithmetic operation.

float

Keyword—a primitive type of 32 bits (IEEE754 to IEEE754).

flow control

The process of controlling program flow.

for

An iteration statement that evaluates a set of initialization expressions and then may iterate an iteration block.

foreach

An iterative statement that enumerates each element in a collection and executes the embedded statement for each of the elements.

form

Two contextual meanings: in Windows, a windows form (UI window); in HTML, an HTML tag.

forward compatibility

Compatibility of an ancestor entity with a successor entity.

function

Procedure that returns a value: a method is a function.

function signature

Consists of the return type and parameter list of a function.

GAC

Global Assembly Cache: a directory that holds .NET Framework system and shared assemblies.

generic method

A method that accepts type parameters (C# 2.0 feature).

generics

Methodologies that enable class, delegate, interface, struct types, and methods to be created with type parameters, which are "placeholder" types that can be substituted when the type is known (C# 2.0 feature).

get

An accessor that returns the value of a property of an object.

goto

A statement that redirects the flow of control to another statement, which is marked with a label within the current code block: it transfers the control out of nested scope.

hashtable

Dictionary that is tweaked for speedy retrieval.

hidden—base class

A base class member is said to be "hidden" if it is overridden in a derived class.

hidden—global variable

A global variable is said to be "hidden" if a local variable has the same name.

horizontal design development

Development of functionality within layers or tiers: each layer is seen as a distinct yet coordinated development.

Hungarian notation

A code notation in which a variable is prefixed with a lowercase representation of its type, e.g., iCountan integer type.

identifier

Name given to variables, types, methods, etc.: must start with underscore or letter.

if

A conditional branching statement that redirects the flow of control only if the condition is true.

if-else

A conditional branching statement that redirects the flow of control if the condition is true and offers an option when the condition is false.

immutable

Unchangeable: a string may appear to change, but a method merely returns a modified string object.

implicit conversion

Conversion performed by a compiler when a valid type is assigned to another valid type that is within its range of values.

in

An operator used with looping and iteration statements.

indexer

A special kind of property that enables an object to be indexed. This enables a collection contained within the object to be accessed on the name of the object, using the this keyword.

inheritance

Methodology in which functionality is inherited (class and interface type).

inheritance—implementation

Referred to as implementation inheritance, visual inheritance, class inheritance, or inheritance or subclassing: generally permits a derived class to inherit the implementation of a parent's (base class) state and functionality.

inheritance—interface

Referred to as interface inheritance: generally enables a class to inherit the unimplemented definition of an interface type.

initializer

Act of setting the value of a variable without use of a constructor: public double dValue = 50;.

inner class

A class that is nested inside another (outer) class.

instance members

Fields (variables), methods, properties, and events of a class instance (object).

instantiate

To create an instance of a class, the result of which is an object of that class.

int

A data type: –2,147,483,648 to 2,147,483,647.

integration architecture

A methodology by which artifacts within a domain or across domains are integrated.

interface—default

The nonprivate attributes of a class.

interface inheritance

Offers multiple inheritance of an interface (public members); however, it does not offer implementation, unlike a class. An implementing entity must implement every member of an interface type, unless the inheriting entity is another interface type.

interface type

A complex reference type that may contain properties, methods, events, and indexers.

internal

A modifier that signifies that accessibility is limited to the given assembly.

internal abstract

A modifier that indicates that a class can't be instantiated, it can only be derived from, and has scope within the current project.

IP

Internet Protocol is a unique address by which a website is identified. It has a four-number sequence (e.g., 000.00.00.0); a DNS translates an IP address to a URL.

is

An operator that verifies if two types are compatible: <MyOperand> is <type>.

Iterator

A method used to compute increments of sequential values (C# 2.0 feature).

jagged array

A multidimensional array where the rows are of varying sizes: an array is comprised of elements that are themselves arrays.

JIT

Just In Time compiler: converts source code or intermediate code into machine immediately prior to the running of a program.

JPEG

Joint Photographic Experts Group: a graphics file type.

key

An encryption key created by running sn.exe (strong name). See *symmetric key*.

late binding

A methodology in which binding is determined at runtime.

layer

An abstract or concrete composition of modularity: for example, a business object layer or a network service, also known as a *tier*.

legacy

An entity that has been superseded: a program or control, for example (see *backward compatibility*).

LHS

Left Hand Side: generally refers to a type on the left-hand side of an assignment operator.

line comment

A comment that takes up all or part of a single line.

linked list

A data structure that has a series of connected nodes.

linked list—circular

Linked list: the last node (tail node) in a list, node "Z," has a reference to the first node (head node) in a list, node "A."

linked list—double link

Linked list: node "B" has a reference to node "C," the node that follows it in the list, and a reference to node "A," the node that precedes it in the list.

linked list—head

First node in a linked list.

linked list—single link

Linked list: node "B" has a reference to node "C," the node that follows it in the list.

linked list—tail

Last node in a linked list.

linked list—type of

Three common types of linked list are unsorted, sorted, single link, double link, and circular link.

literal value

A value that is fixed unless changed; differs from a reference. In assigning a value to an integer variable, one assigns a literal value, as distinct from assigning another variable that may have its underlying value change.

local variable

A variable that has scope in the immediate function or method only.

lock

Statement that assists cooperation between multiple threads by placing a "lock" on a reference type.

long

An integer data type: –9,223,372,036,854,775,808 to 9,223,372,036,854,775,808.

looping

The process of repeated code execution: a "do loop" statement is an example of looping.

loosely coupled

The degree of association between two parties, often used in the context of databasesa loosely coupled connection is easier to change than a tightly coupled association between a database and an application.

M

Documentation generation ID string for "Method."

Main()

A function that is the entry of an application program.

manifest

An assembly's contents; it is also referred to as *assembly metadata*.

MDI

Multiple Document Interfaces: a style of GUI development in which several windows or dialogs are housed inside a parent window or dialog.

metadata

Data that is self-describing: describes the data in an assembly.

method

A construct that encapsulates discrete functionality of the class or object. A class may not have two methods with the same signature (method name, the number of parameters, the modifiers of the parameters, and the types of the parameters).

Model–View–Controller

A type of a design pattern that seeks to minimize the impact of fulfilling the requirement of clients to control how they view information of a model.

modularity

The ability to encapsulate functionality into a unit, which exposes an interface, against which other modules may connect.

multidimensional array

An array with multiple dimensions (rows and columns). C# has two: jagged and rectangular.

multicasting

A technique that involves implementing two or more methods through one delegate.

N

Documentation generation ID string for "Namespace."

namespace

A .NET code encapsulation methodology.

nested class

A class that contains another class—an inner class.

nested statement

The nesting of a series of if or if-else statements.

nesting

Code-style technique whereby blocks of code reside within each other.

network architecture

The structure of a network of servers within an enterprise.

new

A keyword that calls a class's constructor.

new-line block

Style of arranging a code block where code commences on a new line after block header.

null

Literal reference type that signifies that no object is currently referenced.

object

A reference type that is an instantiated class.

object browser comment

A type of documentation that Visual Studio automatically publishes in object browser as part of the process of using the XML Documentator tool.

object collaboration

Functionality of an application may be expressed as a set of collaborations between objects.

Observer pattern

A type of design pattern that encapsulates a subscriber-publisher relationship where a subscriber (an observer object) registers with a publisher an interest in being notified when the publisher (a subject object) fires a given event.

obsolete attribute

An attribute that indicates that a type of members are obsolete or flagged to be obsolete.

one-line block

A style of arranging code block where block is on one line.

OOD

Object-Oriented Design.

OOP

Object-Oriented Programming.

open type

A type that leverages type parameters (C# 2.0 feature).

operator

A modifier keyword that is a method that overloads an operator.

operator overloading

A technique whereby an operator is overloaded to give a class the functionality of the operator.

operator precedence

In an expression, operators are evaluated in predetermined sequence.

operators

A methodology used to make an effect: "+" is a mathematical operator that effects the addition of two values. There are three categories: unary, binary, and ternary.

out of scope

Location in which a type is not accessible (not visible).

outer class

A class that contains an inner class.

overloading

The ability to include more than one method in the same class with the same name.

override

A method modifier that prevails over an inherited method.

overriding

When a virtual method in a base class has its functionality superimposed or overridden by a method in a subclass, which has the same name and signature.

P

Documentation generation ID string for "Property."

param

Indicates that the attribute applies to the parameter.

parameter

An argument passed to a method.

parameter array

In a method that has a variable quantity of parameters, the parameter array is the last parameter in a method, so signified by the params modifier, which permits the parameter to be an array.

params

Parameter modifier that identifies that a method's last parameter may hold multiple parameters of the same type.

parent

A class that is the base class of a subclass or a child class.

parenthesis precedence

The order of execution as controlled by parentheses: inner parenthesis first to outer parenthesis.

partial type

A type that is permitted to use the partial modifier, of which there are three permitted types: class, struct, and interface. Note that the partial modifier is not permitted on the delegate class.

Pascal notation

A code notation in which the first letter of each word in a variable name is uppercase: e.g., ThisIsPascal.

passing by reference

Reference types are passed to a calling method by reference—a reference to a memory location ("the heap") is passed rather than a copy of the type (contrast passing by value).

passing by value

Value types are passed to a calling method by way of a copy of the underlying value type—altering the copy does not alter the underlying (original) value type. Passing by value occurs on the stack (contrast with passing by reference).

pattern language

A vocabulary that is composed of design patterns.

peer review

A process in which code and design are reviewed by other professionals.

pel

The smallest element in a coordinate system used by software and hardware to display: an acronym for "picture element," also known as a *pixel*.

pixel

The smallest element in a coordinate system used by software and hardware to display: an acronym for "picture element," also known as a *pel*.

point-to-point integration

A type of integration architecture wherein the client directly integrates with the provider.

pointer

A "point" in memory or an address in memory where a reference type is located.

polymorphism

Object-oriented concept whereby a specialized class may be passed as an instance of a generalized class (class polymorphism): also refers to methods of a class (method polymorphism).

preprocessor directive

A program that runs prior to compilation of code: preprocessor searches precompiled code for preprocessor directives prefixed with "#".

private

Modifier that signifies that accessibility is limited to the containing type (class). A class field, for example, should be modified private and its value accessed through a class property.

private assembly (.NET)

Assembly that is located in the same directory as an application.

private constructor

Prevents a class from being instantiated: used in utility classes that have only static members.

process

Allocation of memory and resources that enable an application to run.

property

A construct that acts as a facade through which client code may access the underlying value or state which is stored in a private member field.

protected

Modifier that signifies that accessibility is limited to the given class and to any class derived from that class.

protected internal

Modifier that signifies accessibility is limited to a member(s) within a given class, a class(es) derived from that class, and to a nonderived class(es) in the same assembly. The protected internal modifier yields protected or internal accessibility.

proxy

An object that provides a local representation of a remote object.

Proxy pattern

A type of design pattern that represents or regulates access to a principal that is scarce or remote.

public

A modifier that signifies that there is no limit to accessibility.

publisher

An object "publishes" an event for other classes to subscribe.

queue

A representation of a set, where the first into the set is the first out of the set.

readonly

Keyword used to declare that a class member variable is read-only and can't be edited at runtime.

rectangular array

A form of multidimensional array with two or more dimensions that has rows of the same length (contrast with *jagged array*).

ref

A pointer to a memory location: a parameter may be passed by reference, in which case a reference to a memory location is passed rather than a value.

reference type

Holds a reference to a memory location on the heap that holds content. Consists of classes, arrays, and delegates.

refactoring

A technique to transform code by altering its internal behavior without affecting its external behavior.

regex

An abbreviation for a regular expression.

regular expression

A language that describes and manipulates string types~~its~~ use results in the return of a modified string version of the original string (string types are immutable).

re-throw exception

An exception once thrown may be re-thrown or consequentially a new exception may be thrown, or the original exception may be wrapped in a new exception and thrown.

return

Statement that returns a type and then exits from a method.

RHS

Right Hand Side: generally refers to a type on the right-hand side of an assignment operator.

RPC

Remote Procedure Call.

RUP (Rational Unified Process)

A process of iterative software design that is built around core best practices, which include the following: develop software in iterations, manage requirements, favor component-based architecture, model software visually, and verify quality.

same-line block

A style of arranging a code block where code commences on the same line as block header.

sbyte

Signed byte: –128 to 127.

scope

Location in which a type is accessible (visible).

SDI

Single Document Interface: a style of GUI development in which there is only one window or dialog.

sealed

A modifier that signifies that a given concrete class cannot be derived from or inherited.

service-oriented architecture

Synonymous with Enterprise Application Integration (EAI): a type of integration architecture that is loosely coupled and through middleware supports asynchronous and synchronous communication between publisher and subscriber.

services application

An application that publishes functionality or services and that is made available to other applications or services.

shallow

A technique that copies an object variable into another variable by value rather than by reference.

short

Signed integer: –32,768 to 32,767.

signature—method

The name, number, and types of parameters.

signed

Used in two contexts: (1) in cryptography it indicates that an assembly is associated with a signature of an cryptographic key, and (2) in data types it indicates that a type is not "unsigned"e.g., int (signed integer) and uint (unsigned integer).

simple types

Elementary data typese.g., numbers and boolean values.

single namespace

Method of arranging a namespace where all functionality is in one namespace in an assembly.

singleton pattern

A type of design pattern that ensures that a given class is instantiated only once.

sizeof

Operator that returns the size of a struct in bytes.

sn.exe

Executable that creates an encryption key (strong name).

SOAP

Single Object Access Protocol: a methodology for invoking objects over the Internet or Intranet.

specialization

The act of deriving a class from a base classthe derived class seeks to specialize (override or extend) attributes of the base class.

stackalloc

Operator that returns a pointer to a specific quantity of value types that are allocated on the stack.

start-from-scratch application

An application development methodology in which functionality is developed as new functionality (green fields) and reuse of existing functionality is nonexistent or trivial.

state

The property values of an object, which represent the underlying values in fields or variables.

statement

A set of program instructions.

static

A modifier that signifies that a given type is member of the class and not a member of an instance of a class (object).

static delegate

A delegate class type that may be called without the need to instantiate it before being called.

static members

Fields (or variables), methods, and properties of a class that are static.

Stop

A method that causes an action to terminateused to stop Web animations or browser navigation, for example.

Strategy pattern

A type of design pattern that presents a family of algorithms or business rules encapsulated in classes that can be swapped polymorphically within a context, which is independent of the client.

stream

An abstraction of a serial device used to read or write data in a linear manner, a byte at a time.

String class

.NET Framework class System.String.

string type

Keyword that is an alias for System.String classnote that it is immutable.

strong name

A unique composite of assembly name, assembly version, and encryption key (uses sn.exe).

struct

A complex value type that may contain constructors, fields, properties, methods, nested types, operators, and indexers. A struct does not support inheritance itself (unlike a class or interface type); however, it may inherit an interface type.

struct function

A function that resides in a struct type.

structural design

Design method concerned with managing the design of a large structure that is a composite of a smaller structures which themselves may be composite structures.

structural pattern

A category of design pattern that encapsulate a design feature where the focus is on the strategic manipulation of classes into a structure.

subscriber

An object subscribes or registers to an event that is published by the publisher object using a delegate class.

switch

A statement that executes code conditionally.

switch-case statement

A switch and a case statement are paired as an elegant alternative to a nested "if" statement, which is easily extensible without adding complexity or degrading readability.

synchronization

Concept whereby one activity is blocked to allow another activity to be active.

syntax

Valid arrangement or composition of code for a compiler (csc.exe).

syntax error

Response from the compiler to an invalid arrangement or composition of code.

T

Documentation generation ID string for "Type."

target architecture

The architecture that an organization wants to have in the future to complement a given business strategy.

technology architecture

Middleware software, which is software that performs as an intermediary between two discrete architectural artifacts.

template method

A type of design pattern that ensures the same structure can be subclassed to house different implementations of an algorithm and defer part of the implementation to the subclass.

ternary operators

Operators that perform on three operands (<test> ? <ifTrue>: <ifFalse>).

text files

File format used to store text data.

this

Keyword that refers to the current object.

thread

A lightweight process that is used for multitasking within one application.

three-tier architecture

An application architecture that separates functionality into two tiers (UI and Business), which reside on separate servers, with access to data via a third tier and server.

throw

A statement used to raise an exception; unconditionally the control flows to the first catch clause in a try-catch block.

tightly coupled

Refers to degree of association between two parties: a tightly coupled association is harder to change than is a loosely coupled association (e.g., use of an abstract class is loose coupling, whereas use of a concrete class is tight coupling).

trees

Refers to a hierarchy (tree) used to describe class inheritance (trees), XML trees (roots and branches), and controls (TreeView), for example.

true

Boolean literal.

try

A block of code that may throw an exception(s).

try-catch

A statement or code block that is a simple exception handler in which executable code may be tried and an exception(s) may be specified and subsequently handled, if applicable.

try-finally

A statement or code block that is a mechanism through which an action may be tried, without a specific catch statement, where code is placed in a finally statement that is guaranteed by the CLR to run, regardless of whether an exception is thrown or not.

two-tier architecture

An application architecture that compacts all of the functionality into a single tier that resides on one server, with access to data (second tier) via a second server.

type

A kind of value or reference.

type conversion

Casting one type to another type.

type member

Methods, properties, fields (variables), events, or other classes are all type members of a class, for example.

typed dataset

Dataset associated with a defined XML schema: faster and more efficient than untyped dataset because the schema is defined and does not require runtime type identification when run.

typeof

Operator that identifies the type of an operand.

ulong

Unsigned long type: 0 to 18,446,744,073,709,551,615.

UML

Unified Modeling Language: used to model software applications—see www.uml.org.

unary operator

Operator that performs on one operand (true, false, +, −, !, ~, ++, --).

unboxing

Process of no longer boxing inside an Object or treating a value type as a reference type.

unchecked

Keyword to unset an expression's overflow checking context.

unhandled exception

An exception that has no handle (catch) statement.

Unicode

Character encoding that uses two bytes per character rather than one byte, as does ASCII; this permits it to handle 65,536 character combinations compared with 256 for ASCII (www.unicode.org).

uint

Unsigned integer type: 0 to 4,294,967,295.

unsafe

Statement or method modifier that allows pointer arithmetic in a given block.

unsigned

Absence of a signature of a cryptographic key.

unsigned type

Indicates that a type can't hold a negative value.

untyped dataset

A dataset that is not associated with an XML schema: slower and less efficient than typed dataset because when run it needs to create a schema and requires runtime type identification.

URI

Uniform Resource Identifier: a Web address e.g., `www.myhome.com`.

URL

Uniform Resource Locator: is a Web page address e.g., `http://www.myhome.com/myhomepage.htm`.

user-defined type

Type defined by a user or developer.

ushort

Unsigned short type: 0 to 65,535.

using

Keyword statement that identifies that references to types in a namespaces may be referred to without a full name qualification.

valid

Indicates whether code is syntactically or conditionally acceptable.

value

Keyword that refers to a "value" passed to a property or the methodology by which a function calls parameters. Passing by value has the same effect as passing a copy of a variable.

value type

Data that is stored in a variable: value types are stored with their contents on the stack. Consists of structures, primitives, and enumerations.

variable

Associated with a procedure. It may be categorized as a local variable in a procedure (e.g., method); an element of an array; an input parameter (as a reference or value type); or an output parameter.

variable scope

Location in which a variable is accessible (visible).

version—AssemblyVersion attribute

An attribute located in an assembly viewable using ildasm.exe.

version number

Version of a .NET assembly that has four parts: Major, Minor, Build No, Revision.

vertical design development

Recognizes that functionality can be developed across layers to fulfill the requirements of a domain application.

virtual

Keyword that indicates that a method may be overridden.

virtual indexer

An indexer that is allowed to be overridden.

void

A modifier that signifies that there is no return type.

volatile

Term used to indicate that a member field may be altered by a thread or by the operating system.

wait state

Term used to describe a thread that is dormant or has nothing to do.

whitespace

Spaces, newlines, and tabs: generally ignored, except when part of a string, for example.

wrapper

Name given to an assembly that wraps around unmanaged code from another era and enables the code to be accessed as if it was from the current era.

xcopy

Process by which an application may be deployed by copying assemblies without requiring registry entries.

XDR schema

XML-Data Reduced schema.

XML attribute

A characteristic of an element: name and ID are attributes of an element, for example.

XML comment

A single line or block of XML comments, visible within or external to a code module—unlike line or block comments, which are not visible outside of the code module.

XML document

File or string in memory that comprises a set of XML data.

XML element

Holds data in an XML document; composed of an opening tag, an element name, data, and a closing tag.

XML file

File format that is extensible, self-describing, and able to store data in a hierarchical and relational representation.

XOR boolean comparison operator

Operand: exclusive OR.

XP (eXtreme Programming)

A programming process built around four core best practices (plan, design, code, and test) that code and test every day.

Index

forums.apress.com

JOIN THE APRESS FORUMS AND BE PART OF OUR COMMUNITY. You'll find discussions that cover topics of interest to IT professionals, programmers, and enthusiasts just like you. If you post a query to one of our forums, you can expect that some of the best minds in the business—especially Apress authors, who all write with *The Expert's Voice*™—will chime in to help you. Why not aim to become one of our most valuable participants (MVPs) and win cool stuff? Here's a sampling of what you'll find:

DATABASES
Data drives everything.

Share information, exchange ideas, and discuss any database programming or administration issues.

PROGRAMMING/BUSINESS
Unfortunately, it is.

Talk about the Apress line of books that cover software methodology, best practices, and how programmers interact with the "suits."

INTERNET TECHNOLOGIES AND NETWORKING
Try living without plumbing (and eventually IPv6).

Talk about networking topics including protocols, design, administration, wireless, wired, storage, backup, certifications, trends, and new technologies.

WEB DEVELOPMENT/DESIGN
Ugly doesn't cut it anymore, and CGI is absurd.

Help is in sight for your site. Find design solutions for your projects and get ideas for building an interactive Web site.

JAVA
We've come a long way from the old Oak tree.

Hang out and discuss Java in whatever flavor you choose: J2SE, J2EE, J2ME, Jakarta, and so on.

SECURITY
Lots of bad guys out there—the good guys need help.

Discuss computer and network security issues here. Just don't let anyone else know the answers!

MAC OS X
All about the Zen of OS X.

OS X is both the present and the future for Mac apps. Make suggestions, offer up ideas, or boast about your new hardware.

TECHNOLOGY IN ACTION
Cool things. Fun things.

It's after hours. It's time to play. Whether you're into LEGO® MINDSTORMS™ or turning an old PC into a DVR, this is where technology turns into fun.

OPEN SOURCE
Source code is good; understanding (open) source is better.

Discuss open source technologies and related topics such as PHP, MySQL, Linux, Perl, Apache, Python, and more.

WINDOWS
No defenestration here.

Ask questions about all aspects of Windows programming, get help on Microsoft technologies covered in Apress books, or provide feedback on any Apress Windows book.

HOW TO PARTICIPATE:
Go to the Apress Forums site at **http://forums.apress.com/**.
Click the New User link.